T0021489

THE DAEMON

THE
DAEMON

A GUIDE TO YOUR EXTRAORDINARY SECRET SELF

ARCTURUS

ARCTURUS

This edition published in 2012 by Arcturus Publishing Limited
26/27 Bickels Yard, 151–153 Bermondsey Street,
London SE1 3HA

Cover image: George Underwood/Portal Gallery/Bridgeman
Cover design: Peter Ridley/Mike Reynolds

ISBN: 978-1-84837-721-9
AD000140EN

Printed in the UK

Contents

INTRODUCTION

Modern physics teaches us that reality at the quantum level is so bizarre and strange that normal causality and logic simply breaks down. Subatomic particles are brought into being by the observation of a conscious observer, and atoms, the basic building blocks of reality, are part of this charade. Put simply, we create reality by observing it – even the reality of objects that existed before mankind had evolved. A majority of the world's leading theoretical physicists believe that the universe splits into identical copies of itself millions of times a second, while many others hold that reality is simply a hologram. The Hindus have a word for this mind-created universe – *Maya*, or illusion. What we see, hear and feel is all a creation of our own mind. We each inhabit one of those trillions of alternative universes. The world is literally what you make it.

In my first book, *Is There Life After Death?: The Extraordinary Science of What Happens When We Die*, I suggest that this strange world of quantum events has a direct and personal relevance to each one of us because within this bizarre view of the universe lie potential clues to our own immortality. In the book I present evidence to suggest that each one of us carries this world-view within our brain, enfolded like a hologram within its structures. There is overpowering scientific evidence that we forget absolutely nothing. All our experiences, thoughts and sensations are held, recorded and waiting to be replayed. This is a literal real-life, virtual-reality holographic experience with you as the star, producer, director and author. So when is this recording screened? The answer is both simple and stunning – because I suggest that this happens at the split second before you die.

Many individuals that have a Near Death Experience, or NDE, report a phenomenon termed the 'past life review'. The endogenous chemicals that are known to stimulate this are exactly the same ones that cause a temporal lobe epileptic seizure. Individuals who suffer TLE say that one regular experience is that time slows down, becoming almost non-existent. An additional experience is vivid *déjà vu* sensations. So what does this all mean?

At the moment before death endorphins and a particular neurotransmitter called glutamate are pumped into the brain, causing a profound slowing of internal time perception. At that point the brain triggers this virtual-reality life re-run in actual real-time. Put simply, the dying person lives their previous life again minute by minute. However, I propose that something even stranger happens at this point. I suggest that consciousness itself splits into two loci of awareness. These I term the Daemon and the Eidolon. The dying person starts their life again, the Eidolon re-living every experience as if it was the first time. However, this is not so for the Daemon. The Daemon remembers exactly who it was in the previous life. In effect this being is a simple continuation of the conscious awareness of the person before the NDE took hold. As this being begins the new life it has, in effect, full precognition of what will take place in this new life – simply because it recalls what happened as a 'future-memory'.

The Daemon finds its home in the non-dominant hemisphere and from here acts as an 'all knowing' passenger. This is because within the dominant hemisphere is a new 'version' of the dying person, the Eidolon. This being has no pre-life memories and begins this life as if it is the first time. Occasionally old memories break through as *déjà vu*. However, the Daemon can, under certain neurological circumstances, guide and assist its ignorant partner when it feels it is needed. Every Daemon-induced change creates a new universe to accommodate the implications of this change.

In the first book I described in detail the mechanism by which this 'Cheating the Ferryman' takes place. In this book it is my intention to focus in more on the evidence for the existence of the Daemon. Can it really be true that you, the being reading these words, consist of not one, but two, personalities? Only you can decide if the evidence I present is convincing or otherwise . . . of course you could always ask your Daemon!

Anthony Peake, March 2008

The universe is built on a plan,
the profound symmetry of which
is somehow present in the
inner structure of our intellect.

Paul Valéry

The Garden of the Forking Paths

So the Platonic year
Whirls out new right and wrong,
Whirls in the old instead;
All men are dancers and their tread
Goes to the barbarous clamour of a gong.

W. B. Yeats

The inner ET

'We are not alone.'

Remember that phrase? It was the tag line for one of the most popular movies of all time: *Close Encounters of the Third Kind*. This film suggested that extraterrestrial life not only exists but that it is intelligent and peaceful. This was a wonderful suggestion at a time when humanity felt very isolated and in danger of nuclear war. The idea that we were being watched over by benevolent and sensitive 'space-brothers' was curiously reassuring and many left the cinema feeling more assured about mankind and its potential future.

This book also suggests that we are not alone. However, it is from Inner, not Outer, Space that this intelligence can be found. Welcome to a secret that has been known for at least 3,000 years. A secret that is a part of all the great esoteric traditions – that the human being is a binary, not a unitary, intelligence.

Let us ponder on this for a few minutes.

I would like to start by asking you a question. What made you pick up this book? What series of events brought about the circumstances whereby you are reading these words? Why this book and not the dozens of others that you could have chosen? Simple answer: you picked up this book because your whole life has been a series of guided coincidences that have placed you here, reading these words, at precisely this time. What is more, by the time you finish the last page of this book you will spot the chance decisions, going back over the years, that made this event take place. This book is your fate. Intrigued?

Up until now your life has been made up of a series of chance events that have coincided to create a history, a memory of what has gone on before. And you, you are the consciousness that has perceived those events as you have travelled through time. From moment to moment your life has consisted of decisions, millions upon millions of them, and each one has changed your future. Every second you decide to do one thing or another – to cross or not cross a road, to speak to somebody or ignore him or her, to watch one television channel rather than another. And within each one of these decisions lie the seeds of a different life, a different course of events. Like snooker balls they bounce and ricochet off in a multiplicity of directions. Every small decision made with no conscious thought changes the future, brings a possible future into an actual event.

Some of those decisions you were very happy with. They were, from your present viewpoint, the 'right' thing to do. But from the moment that you set the train of events into motion you knew that others were wrong. You watched as the cause and effect process rippled out to affect life after life. 'No man is an island', wrote John Donne, and as regards how we interact with others no truer words have ever been written.

This book will present evidence that your decisions, although made by you, have been guided by another being, a higher intelligence that shares your thoughts, your dreams and the good times and the bad. However, it also has knowledge that you do not have. In fact it not only knows everything about you, it also knows everything that you will do. It can do this for one simple reason – it has lived your life before!

And it gives us clues about this knowledge. Indeed, my first book was guided by this intelligence. Let me explain why I believe this to be the case.

Footsteps in the snow

For me it all started with mitochondria.

I had no real idea why – indeed, I had no real idea what I was doing or where I was going. Three months before, circumstances had conspired to allow me a period of free time whereby I could fulfil a life-long ambition: to write a book. This is something that most people would like to do but with me it was different. It was a burning need. I felt that my life would only become complete if I saw my muddled thoughts in print. The idea of what kind of book was clear in my mind. It would consist of pages and be paper-bound. It would be bought by a handful of people and would then languish in obscurity. It would never appear in any libraries and would never be reviewed by any magazine or newspaper. That was clear. However, a much more crucial aspect of my project was in no way clear – the subject matter. That I was going to write a non-fiction book was the only thing that was really clear to me when, in early 2000, I sat myself down in front of a blank computer screen.

Certain subjects had leapt to mind. I had a lifelong interest in the human mind and the nature of consciousness. I had also been fascinated by parapsychology, UFOs, religious belief and quantum physics. All of these seemed totally unrelated, but something inside me drove me on and that something then gave me a clue, not only to its existence but also to the subject matter of my future book.

As I have already stated, it all started with mitochondria. Which is a curious statement in itself in that life as we know it also started with mitochondria. On this tiny planet of ours all living things are divided into two distinct groups: bacteria/archaea and the rest. Human beings and all visible life forms belong to the

> *'If the world may be thought of as a certain definite quantity*
> *of force and as a certain definite number of centres of force –*
> *and every other representation remains indefinite and therefore*
> *useless – it follows that, in the great dice game of existence,*
> *it must pass through a calculable number of combinations. In*
> *infinite time, every possible combination would at some time*
> *or another be realized; more: it would be realized an infinite*
> *number of times. And since between every combination and its*
> *next recurrence all other possible combinations would have to*
> *take place, and each of these combinations conditions the*
> *entire sequence of combinations in the same series, a circular*
> *movement of absolutely identical series is thus demonstrated:*
> *the world as a circular movement that has already repeated*
> *itself infinitely often and plays its dice game in infinitum.'*
>
> FRIEDRICH NIETZSCHE (PHILOSOPHER)

rest, which are collectively known as eukaryotes. What divides these two groups is that the cells of all eukaryotes contain within them smaller structures such as the nucleus, which houses the chromosomes, and curious objects known as mitochondria. On the other hand bacteria and archaea are unicellular. What fascinated me about mitochondria is that they contain their own DNA. This has a totally different code from the more influential DNA contained in the nucleus.

I was interested in this particular fact because I had been reading up about something called the Anthropic Cosmological Principle. This fascinating theory suggests that the universe has developed specifically for the evolution of intelligent and, more crucially, conscious life. A series of hugely unlikely coincidences have fine-tuned the environment in order that you and I can be here to write and read this book. Crucial to this was the split into bacterial, archaeac and eukaryotic-based life forms. This occurred around 2,500 million years ago. By developing the compartmentalization of the cell nucleus and the mitochondria the eukaryotes were freed from the need to have a rigid cell wall, which is used by other organisms to distribute genetic material at cell division. This allowed them to engulf and eat other living structures just as amoeba do today. Evolution had been given a massive kick-start.

I vaguely recalled that mitochondria, and therefore mitochondrial DNA, were only carried down through the female line. At that stage I was in great need of more information on this subject. I took myself over to my library of bookcases, at a loss as to where I would find this particular reference. My eyes then alighted on my collection of Richard Dawkins books. As Dawkins is a zoologist it was possible that I had read about mitochondrial DNA in one of his books. I reached out and pulled off the shelf my copy of Dawkins' *The Blind Watchmaker*. I had read this book only once and that was sitting on Pedi Beach on the Greek Island of Symi 12 years earlier.

Now a little personal note: I adore books. I never throw them away and I try hard to avoid the temptation to loan them out. I also like to keep them as pristine as possible. I try very hard never to break the spine of a book and under no circumstances will I 'dog-ear' a page to keep my place. Indeed, I have dozens of books with bookmarkers in them of various types, designs and sizes.

And that is why I was really surprised to note that of all my books this one seemed to have one page that had been carefully turned over at the top. A much younger version of me had done the unthinkable. He had presumably decided to go for lunch and something in him had decided not to use a bookmark but to 'dog-ear' the page. Even now I find this impossible to do, but on that hot Greek day many years ago I, or somebody, did.

Then a really weird thing happened. A thought that was not my own entered my head.

'That's the page you need,' it said.

I opened the book at the offending fold and read down the

page. I gasped with amazement as my eyes alighted on the following words:

> *Mitochondria and chloroplasts have their own DNA, which*
> *replicates and propagates itself entirely independently of the*
> *main DNA in the chromosome of the nucleus. All the*
> *mitochondria . . . travelled from your mother in her egg.*[1]

I was stunned. How could this be? I opened the back of the book and looked down the index. This was the only page that referenced mitochondria in the whole book. Clearly, this was more than a coincidence. It was a significant coincidence. An earlier version of myself had subconsciously presented me with a clue to something of great significance, but on that morning in March 2000 little was I to know the depth of this significance.

The incident had made me question the nature of time and the possibility of 'future memory'. I was fascinated by the implication that something deep within the subconscious of my younger self knew the future and that I would need the information it had presented to me. Suddenly I realized that this would be the subject of the book. I wanted to find out if there was any hard scientific evidence to support my suspicion that some part of us knows the future. Had anything of significance been written with regard to this fascinating idea?

I began to wonder if time is in some way a construct of our minds; that it does not exist 'out there'. Through secondary sources I realized that two books were essential for me to read: J.B. Priestley's *Man and Time* and John William Dunne's *An Experiment With Time*. As both were not available at my local library I had to order them from the British Library collection.

After a two-week wait I was telephoned by Horsham Library who informed me that my precious copy of the Priestley book had arrived. After collecting it I left it in my study for a few days because I had other books to finish. A few days later I decided to browse through it just before I went to sleep. Flicking through the pages at random I spotted a diagram that looked of interest. It was an attempt by Priestley to explain how Einstein's theory of time caused difficulty with the concept of 'now'.

In order to put this across Priestley had chosen to quote the work of another writer, James Coleman. In his book *Relativity For The Layman*, the source of Priestley's quote, Coleman asks his readers to visualize a 'blowout' on the star Betelgeuse on the night of 17 March 2000.[2] What Coleman was attempting to explain was that by the time the actual light from this event reached Earth the year would be 2350, making it a historical rather than a contemporary occurrence. Although this is, of course, interesting, what was far stranger was the fact that I was lying in bed reading this particular section of Priestley's book on the night of 17 March 2000, exactly the date and time that Coleman had chosen, presumably at random, to have his explosion take place.

This event quite scared me. It seemed to be a coincidence that was aimed directly at me. What was it that had made me pick up that book on that night? Why not any of the other nights on which I had walked past my study? Indeed, why that time of day? I could have picked it up to read at any time. The book itself has 316 pages. Why did I flick through and decide to stop at page 91?

I became convinced that the very same process was taking place that had done so with the Richard Dawkins quote on mitochondria. Something that was part of me and yet not part of me was guiding me along a very specific route. It was as if it wanted

> *'Every soul has existed from the beginning; it has therefore passed through some worlds already, and will pass through others before it reaches the final consummation. It comes into the world strengthened by the victories or weakened by the defeats of its previous life.'*
>
> ORIGEN (EARLY-CHRISTIAN SCHOLAR)

to make sure that I wrote the book in the way that it wanted me to. Over the coming months I found the books I needed when I needed them. This happened over and over again. It became such a commonplace occurrence that I coined the word 'synchrondipity' to define this curious mixture of chance and positive significance. What was even stranger was that each book or article gave me new information that I was not looking for, that pushed me into another line of investigation. Then on 27 October 2000 an event took place that was to give me the final push towards deciding the subject matter.

On that night I had a particularly vivid dream. In that dream I was in a place that I had never been to before. It was a low-lying headland with a town in the distance to my right. I knew that I was looking out at the English Channel. As I looked I could see a storm approaching out at sea. I watched with mounting horror as the storm turned into a twisting tornado. I saw the tornado hit landfall and rip into a town a few miles down the coast and to my left. I then realized that it was heading towards us on this exposed piece of flat land and I looked on in horror as it tore into caravans along the coastline, smashing them into pieces. With this image still in my mind I woke up with a start. The images were so vivid that I can recall them even now, seven years on.

Two days later I heard on the radio that Bognor Regis had been hit by a freak tornado and that a good deal of damage had been done. This was interesting, I thought to myself, in that Bognor was also on the South Coast. I thought I had possibly experienced a precognitive dream.

A few weeks later I visited the town of Selsey with my mother and my future wife. As we got out of the car I had an alarming sensation that I had been to this place before. Everything seemed familiar. It was like a super *déjà vu* sensation. I had experienced these many times in my life but this one was different. I knew what I was about to see next. As we walked towards the seafront I was amazed to find that the view from Selsey Bill was exactly the one I had dreamt about. I looked across the bay to my left

> 'Have you ever had a dream, Neo, that you were so sure was
> real? What if you were unable to wake from that dream?
> How would you know the difference between the dream world
> and the real world?'
>
> MORPHEUS (CHARACTER IN THE FILM *THE MATRIX*)

to see the town that I dreamt had been hit by a tornado. To my surprise and horror I realized that it was, in fact, Bognor Regis. On top of that I could see that between Selsey Bill and Bognor were lines of caravans in exactly the spot I had seen them in my dream. My knowledge of the geography of that part of the South Coast was not good, so I had no idea before arriving at Selsey that it was that close to Bognor.

On my return to Horsham I decided to get some further details about the 30 October tornado. When I referred to the BBC website I was stunned to discover that my dream had been far more accurate than I had at first supposed. The reports on the morning of the 30th had only mentioned Bognor, but the website gave many more details. Apparently the twister had travelled along the coast towards Selsey and on the way had badly damaged over 150 caravans. This is exactly what I had seen in my dream.

I was intrigued. Was this precognition or a form of *déjà vu*? Clearly something had been planted in my brain, just at the right moment, to send me off on yet another intellectual adventure. I came across the work of Dr Vernon Neppe[3] and then the 'Dream Theory of Déjà Vu' as advanced by Dr Arthur Funkhouser of Berne in Switzerland.[4] Dr Funkhouser, in his seminal paper, suggests that a *déjà vu* experience is brought about by the memory of a dream that the subject has experienced in the past. Clearly, this is exactly what happened to me prior to the Selsey tornado of October 2000. However, the implications of Art's theory are staggering: that some as yet unknown mechanism enables us to perceive events that are yet to take place.

> *'When all the souls had chosen their lives, they went before*
> *Lachesis. And she sent with each, as the guardian of his life*
> *and the fulfiller of his choice, the daemon that he had chosen.'*
> *(Republic X)*
>
> PLATO (PHILOSOPHER)

This was the kick-start my book needed. I wanted to understand the mechanism by which *déjà vu* and precognition worked within the brain. I wanted to find a scientifically-based explanation for the seemingly impossible – but an impossible that seemed surprisingly common.

A year later and I had my book – and my theory. I called the theory 'Cheating The Ferryman' and the subsequent book was entitled *Is There Life After Death?: The Extraordinary Science of What Happens When We Die.*

What had started off as an urge to write a book had, with guidance from a source at that time unknown, grown into an all-encompassing theory about life and death. *En route* it explained many mysteries, including precognition, *déjà vu*, intuition, Near-Death Experience, angelic encounters, mediumship, mysticism, spontaneous creativity and possibly even the real nature of such psychological states as temporal lobe epilepsy, migraine, bipolar disorder, multiple personality syndrome and even schizophrenia. But what was particularly interesting was that behind all these seemingly unrelated psychic states lie both the source and the cause of my particular creative surge.

Let me now introduce the being that goes by many names, but which I call the Daemon.

How we cheat the Ferryman

Do you relate from personal experience to my description above of the feeling commonly known as *déjà vu*? If you do then I have got some news that may surprise you. Firstly you are not alone. According to some recent surveys, 70 per cent of people responding to questionnaires have had the feeling that they have lived a particular set of circumstances before. Indeed, I have now presented over 40 lectures across the UK and according to my very unscientific 'show of hands' request I have seen similar figures. Secondly, what would you think if I said that this might show that 70 per cent of British people exist in a world not dissimilar to that of Thomas Anderson in the film *The Matrix*? Not only that but these same people may be caught in a circular life scenario as experienced by Phil Conners in the movie *Groundhog Day*? Sounds incredible, doesn't it? However, there is strong scientifically based evidence to indicate that this may indeed be the case.

The book that eventually came out of my hypergraphic fugue of 2000/2001 offers a totally new theory that presents an intellectually satisfying suggestion as to what happens to human consciousness at the point of death.

My 'Cheating the Ferryman' theory proposes that at the point of death a cocktail of internally generated chemicals floods the brain – specifically a substance called glutamate – and in doing so conscious awareness literally falls out of time. As far as the subject is concerned time slows down to such an extent that the subjective duration of each millisecond takes twice as long as the one previously. As such we have an exponential increase millisecond on millisecond which very quickly has the dying person moving further and further away from the objective moment of their death. As far as an observer is concerned the person is seen to die, but within the consciousness of the dying person (technically termed the 'phaneron' by philosophers) that moment is never reached.

This ever-expanding subjective world is filled by a three-dimensional, all-encompassing, re-creation of the person's previous life that starts again from the moment of birth. This I call the 'Bohmian IMAX'. It is so real that the person cannot tell that it is any different from the real thing. Just like Thomas

Anderson's life experience before he is taken out of the 'matrix', dying people are simply unaware that their senses are deceiving them. This is because in a very concrete sense this inwardly created version of reality is just as real as the one previously experienced. The new science known as consciousness studies has shown that we all perceive the external world through our senses. This perception is buffered and recorded before it is 'presented' to our consciousness. As such, what we believe to be the tangible, solid and consistent world of the senses is, in fact, an illusion. Whatever 'out there' is, it is not what our brains tell us it is.

Over the last 100 years or so quantum physics has shown us that the universe of solid, material objects that we take so much for granted is made up of mostly empty space. What we think of as solid and secure objects such as tables, chairs, planets, stars and galaxies are in fact constructed out of tiny ripples of energy that flit in and out of existence. Even the brain that does the perceiving is constructed out of these ephemeral phantoms. It is all just a grand illusion or, as the Hindus call it, *Maya*.

So 30 per cent of human beings and, who knows, maybe all conscious beings, are experiencing their life for the first time. Laying down memories and experiences within the brain. These are the people who do not experience *déjà vu*. For the other 70 per cent this is not the first time they have lived their lives. It could be the second or the seventy-second time. A *déjà vu* experience is simply a breakdown in the memory inhibitors that denies the dying person the knowledge that they have experienced all this before. A *déjà vu* is exactly what it seems to be – a recollection that this is not the first time that particular circumstances or events have taken place.

However, only a part of the person lives this life as an unknowing observer. This part I call the 'Eidolon'. This is the everyday self that calls itself 'I' or 'me'. It lives its life, all of its lives, in a linear fashion. It sits within the Bohmian IMAX and watches the events take place around it. The term 'Eidolon' is from the ancient Greek and it is the source word from which modern words like heathen and idol come. It is an image of a god, a representation of something non-physical. For the ancient Greeks the Eidolon was exactly as I use it in my first book – the lower, everyday 'self'. By implication this means that there is a Higher Self that is a reflection of the gods. This being was called the 'Daemon' and I have continued to use this term to describe the part of us that knows that we have lived this life before.

I suggest that just before the objective death of a person consciousness splits into two independent points of being. The Eidolon starts its life again as a fully unaware newborn whereas from that moment onwards the now fully aware Daemon carries within its neuronal network all the memories of the previous life. In other words it knows exactly who it was before and what will happen next. This is analogous to two people watching a movie. One has seen it before and knows all the twists and turns of the plot, but the other does not because as far as they are concerned they are seeing the film for the first time.

Under normal circumstances the Daemon and the Eidolon sit watching the film in total darkness. They sit next to each other but only the Daemon knows what is going to happen. On top of that the Eidolon is totally unaware that its silent neighbour is even there. However, under certain circumstances the Daemon can communicate with its lower partner. The neural pathways have to be open sufficiently for a message to get through. When it does the message may be received by the Eidolon as a hunch, a dream or even a voice. Whichever method takes place the Eidolon is taken by surprise, particularly when the message clearly implies a future event.

Now this is where it gets interesting. If my theory is correct then a Daemonic message may, if heeded, bring about a change in the direction that will be taken by that life. For example a warning that saves the life of an Eidolon means that from that moment onwards a new life-path is followed by both Daemon and Eidolon.

The idea of following different life-paths is not as strange as it first appears. Indeed, the idea that there are multiple realities has long been accepted by many of the world's leading quantum physicists, including Stephen Hawking, David Deutsch, Michio Kaku and Max Tegmark. In July 1999 at a conference on quantum computation held at the Isaac Newton Institute in Cambridge, England, Tegmark carried out an informal poll of the quantum physicists in attendance. The overwhelming majority considered that this weird, and totally counterintuitive theory was not only viable but the only real explanation for certain observed effects that take place inside the atom.

What this means in practical terms is that there is an infinite number of versions of every living human being, each one living a different life. Some will be subtly different and some will be totally different. Indeed, it is argued that a version of you will experience every possible outcome of every minute decision that you make in your life. You are the version of you that has read this far in this book. It is entirely possible that there as many versions of you as there are words in this book. By this I mean that after reading each word you have the option of putting the book down and giving up. You may stop at the end of this paragraph, but another version of you will go on and finish the chapter today, or tomorrow, or the day after. Each one of you is a conscious, self-aware being that will continue to make decisions and continue splitting into ever-increasing versions of yourself. Mindblowing, isn't it?

Is this what happened to me in 2000? Could it be that my Daemon was keen to ensure that this time round I followed through and wrote my first book? Could it be that all the daemonic assists were there to push me along the new road it had forced me along, and was the precognitive dream about the Selsey tornado just a metaphoric nudge in the ribs to let me know that this is not my first time here?

In my first book I reviewed all the evidence for 'Cheating The

Ferryman'. However, for me the most intriguing element was that of the Daemon. I wanted to follow up on the evidence for this most fascinating of possibilities. In this book I will attempt to show how such a proposition is not as crazy as it first seems. As with my first book I have tried to make the exposition as interesting and as challenging as possible. If by the end of this work you remain unconvinced so be it. But I certainly hope you enjoy the journey.

The journey inside

In this book I will present the evidence for what I term the 'Daemon-Eidolon Dyad'. I will focus on specific elements of this theory in turn. Each chapter can be read in isolation but I suggest that you follow the normal start to finish approach. This is because each chapter is iterative in that it will contain certain references to information that has been presented earlier. In this way the full power of the argument can be appreciated.

In the first chapter I will present the scientific evidence for the Daemon. It will review some of the fascinating discoveries with regard to split-brain research and deep hypnosis. The second chapter will continue on this theme by suggesting a scale of transcendence by which everyday consciousness relates to the external world. This will introduce some interesting, and not uncommon, psychological states such as migraine, temporal lobe epilepsy and schizophrenia.

The third chapter will discuss certain elements of the mystic-religious experience, particularly the hearing of voices. It will take the life of Joan of Arc as an example of this phenomenon and will present evidence to show that Joan's voices were precognitive and that they really came from one source, the Daemon.

Within Chapter 4 I will move on to present the theological and metaphysical support for human duality. I will review the esoteric belief systems of the three great Western religions: Christianity

> 'The quantum theory of parallel universes is not some
> troublesome, optional interpretation emerging from arcane
> theoretical considerations. It is the explanation – the only one
> that is tenable – of a remarkable and counter-intuitive reality.'
>
> DAVID DEUTSCH (QUANTUM PHYSICIST)

(Gnosticism), Judaism (Kabbalah) and Islam (Sufism). I will then suggest that similar beliefs can be found within the great Eastern philosophies of Buddhism and Vedanta and the traditional belief systems of Africa and the Americas. I will finish the chapter with a discussion of the most relevant belief system of all, the Kahuna of the Hawaiian Islands.

The Kahuna and most shamanistic traditions use dreams as a way of communicating with the daemonic. In Chapter 5 I will discuss some fascinating examples of how, even in Western society, dreams seem to give the dreamer access to higher levels of perception. Chapter 6 will continue this theme with particular reference to precognition.

In dream-states some strange experiences take place. One of these is the meeting with one's own double, or *doppelgänger*. Chapter 7 will present evidence that affirms that this 'double walker' is, in fact, the most powerful manifestation of the Daemon and will present testimonies from neurology and psychiatry that will show this phenomenon to be a very real experience.

Chapter 8 will continue along this theme by suggesting that the Being of Light, encountered in many Near-Death Experiences, is, in fact, another aspect of the Daemon. In Chapter 9 the theme of the Daemon as a life-long protector will be discussed, together with many examples from the lives of the famous and the not so famous.

The final chapter can be read as a stand-alone essay. It reviews the evidence for the Daemon-Eidolon Dyad within the life-experiences of one man, the science-fiction writer Philip K. Dick.

This series of intensely personal real-life experiences will, I hope, pull together all the strands of my argument.

I would now like to end this introduction with a fascinating piece of evidence for 'Cheating the Ferryman' that did not make it into the first book. I feel that it encapsulates so well the reason why I am sure that the Ferryman is more than mere supposition.

A passage to India

Bhagawhandi was dying. That was obvious to all who knew her. The doctors had diagnosed a malignant brain tumour, an astrocytoma, which was impossible to remove. She was only 19 years old. What surprised everybody was how remarkably cheerful she was, accepting totally that she had but a short time to live. The tumour was growing larger day by day and was inching forward towards her temporal lobe. Up until this stage she had suffered occasional seizures but nothing particularly debilitating. However, as soon as pressure was placed upon her temporal lobe, her seizures became more frequent – and stranger.

In the early stages of her illness the seizures had been *grand mal* convulsions, but her new ones were altogether of a different nature. She would not lose consciousness, but would drift into an epileptic-like dream-state. However, this dream-state soon developed into something far stronger. Bhagawhandi began to have very realistic hallucinations about being back in India and not just India but the India of her childhood. In these semi-waking states she actually found herself back on the dusty streets of her old village, interacting with people and circumstances that had long disappeared into the mists of time. She would find herself listening to a speech being made in the village square. On one occasion she was in a church, on another in a graveyard. She claimed that she was actually reliving these memories as actual events.

As Bhagawhandi's present life began to ebb away she began to live more and more in her new world created from her own past. The visions ceased being occasional and began to take up most of her waking hours. She lay with her young face rapt in attention to a world inside her own mind, a faint, mysterious smile on her face. What was happening had a profound effect upon the nursing staff around her. All accepted that something very strange, but very wonderful, was taking place. Nobody disturbed her, allowing her her dreams.

The psychiatrist responsible for her was also fascinated. He felt awkward but was keen to know exactly what was taking place. He asked her quietly.

'Bhagawhandi, what is happening?'

'I am dying,' she answered. 'I am going home. I am going back where I came from – you might call it my return.'

During the next week she disappeared totally into the world of her memories. She ceased responding to all external stimuli but lay with the same faint smile on her face. Three days later she quietly slipped away, returning permanently to her own past. And in this way she died, as the psychiatrist poetically described it 'or should we say, arrived, having completed her passage to India.'[5]

In this sad, but ultimately uplifting true story I hope you can see why I find these strange mental states so fascinating. Could it be that Bhagawhandi's mind was going through a series of trial runs of the Bohmian IMAX, to test it out before it was run properly? Is this yet again evidence for how we may all 'Cheat The Ferryman'?

[1] Dawkins, Richard, *The Blind Watchmaker*, Penguin, p.176 (1988)

[2] Priestley, J.B., *Man And Time*, Aldus, p.91 (1964)

[3] Neppe, V.M., 'The Concept of Déjà Vu', *Parapsychology Journal of South Africa* 4:1 (1983)

[4] Funkhouser, A.T., 'The Dream Theory of Déjà Vu', *Parapsychology Journal of South Africa* 4:2 (1983)

[5] Sacks, O., *The Man Who Mistook His Wife For A Hat*, Duckworth (1985)

CHAPTER 1

Neurology

'Like two golden birds perched on the selfsame tree:
Intimate friends, the ego and the Self
Dwell in the same body. The former eats
The sweet and sour fruits of the tree of life
While the latter looks on in detachment.'

Mundaka Upanishad

Sleeping partner

This was not the reaction that was expected. It had started as a straightforward process to assess the level of epilepsy in the young male patient. A few minutes before, the Wada test had been started.[1] This procedure, also termed the intracarotid amobarbital procedure (IAP), involved the patient having sodium amytal, a short-acting anaesthetic agent, injected into his left carotid artery. There are two carotid arteries, each one supplying its respective cerebral hemisphere, so the intention was to bring about unconsciousness in only one side of the brain – the left hemisphere. It was hoped that this would allow the team to elicit information about how the normally non-dominant hemisphere functioned.

As the anaesthetic took effect the normally dour and taciturn young man began to smile – something that the team had never seen before. They realized that the young man's right brain was suddenly in control of his body. The dominant personality was fast asleep. This was a new person surfacing. The new personality looked round the room and gave a hearty laugh. This being was very aware of who he was and pointed out that he was always aware, but could never communicate directly with the outside world. After ten minutes or so it became clear that the left brain was slowly regaining consciousness. The anaesthesia was beginning to wear off. Suddenly the happy inhabitant of the right brain was pushed aside.

'I think we just got done with this niceness', the dominant hemisphere stated as it announced its return to awareness. In a fascinating act of resignation the left hand made a slow chopping movement. The significance of this gesture was not lost on any of those present. The left hand is controlled by the right hemisphere. It was a goodbye gesture pointing out that the drug was losing its control. In a flash the young man's face changed from a relaxed visage to a scowling snarl. The left brain was back in control.

This compelling incident took place in the early 1990s and it contributed to the ongoing debate about the nature of personality and its relationship to the physical duality of the brain.[2]

Is this an isolated case or is there strong proof from science that my theory on human duality may be more than just supposition? In this chapter it is my intention to show that my Daemon-Eidolon Dyad may be an explanation for some very strange discoveries made by modern neuroscience and psychiatry.

Mind's a double

It was once said that religion explains in terms of agents what science explains in terms of processes. To me this is a very effective description of the approach I am now going to take with regard to my 'Daemon-Eidolon Dyad'. In a later chapter I will show how religion explains the mysteries of the personality, but for now I wish to review the science.

First I have to explain exactly what I mean by the term Daemon-Eidolon Dyad. According to the dictionary a dyad is a combination of two vectors. For the Pythagoreans it was two points connecting a line. For me it is simply a way of describing a relationship between the two elements of the conscious mind.

For those of you of a scientific inclination the idea that we are all dual beings seems, at first, to be a totally ridiculous statement. You are sure that you are yourself and that inside your head is only one person – you. However, a moment's reflection will show that you cannot, with any absolute assurance, believe this to be the case. How would you know? How could you really tell if another being was looking through your eyes and hearing all the things that you hear? After all, light waves processed by the optic nerve and sound waves causing the ear-drum to vibrate are external to you, as indeed are the nerves that carry these messages to your brain.

And this is where the conundrum starts. You consider yourself to be a 'something' located a few inches behind your eyes – a 'something' that perceives 'reality' and reacts to it. A moment's reflection will show that this is an illusion. If your eyes and ears were located on your knee where then would you think you were located? Clearly, you feel you are in your head simply because of an accident of evolution. Indeed, does watching a television programme mean that you are located in the television studio? Clearly not, but to think this was the case would be the same sort of error.

There is an interesting debate to be had as to whether the brain is the location of consciousness or simply some form of transmitter that sends the perceptions of the senses to another location where 'you' actually reside. Unfortunately, however attractive this idea may be, there is simply no scientific evidence for such a belief. In order for this to be the case there would need to be some evidence of transmission, which there is not. Certain thought processes can clearly be seen on an encephalograph. Of course there could be a form of transmission that modern science is unaware of, but in accepting such a possibility we lead ourselves down an infinite regress. How does this consciousness-at-a-distance process the information it is being sent? Presumably, it must have organs of vision, hearing, etc., and these must feed a brain-like object that processes the incoming data. If this is the case then this locates consciousness within a structure similar to the brain so why bother with the first leap of logic?

I cannot possibly say which of these two alternatives is true. My heart would like to believe that 'I' exist outside the meat that is my brain, but my head tells me that this is simply not scientific.

So if I am inside my head my Daemon must also coexist with me. Using evidence both from history and the modern scientific method by which I dismissed consciousness outside the brain I will attempt to review the evidence for duality with the same rigour. So here we go.

Split brains

In the 1950s a series of fascinating experiments took place at the California Institute of Technology. A team of neurologists and neurosurgeons lead by Dr Roger Sperry embarked upon an intensive study on the splitting of the brain into its two component hemispheres. This pioneering work was to lead to Sperry receiving the Nobel Prize in 1981. The cortices of all advanced animals consist of two symmetrical halves, linked by a massive web of nerve fibres known as the great cerebral commissure, or *corpus callosum*, and by several smaller links. Science has no real clue as to why this double brain is needed – particularly as each half is absolutely identical in structure. As well as the cerebral cortex (the part that most laymen would identify as 'the brain' when shown a photograph) there is a series of smaller structures called the limbic system. With only one exception a mirror image of each structure is found on either side of the brain. We all have a right and left hippocampus, a right and left amygdala and a right and left thalamus. The exception is the pineal gland that sits in splendid and mysterious isolation.

One of Sperry's graduate students, Ronald Myers, invented a complex operation that involved the cutting of what is known as

> 'All the evidence indicates that separation of the hemispheres
> creates two independent spheres of consciousness within a
> single cranium, that is to say, within a single organism.
> This conclusion is disturbing to some people who view
> consciousness as an indivisible property of the human brain . . .
> it is entirely possible that if a human brain were divided in a
> very young person, both hemispheres could as a result
> separately and independently develop mental functions of
> a high order at the level attained only in the left hemisphere
> of normal individuals.'
>
> MICHAEL GAZZANIGA (COGNITIVE PSYCHOLOGIST)

the 'optic chiasm'. This is the crossover point where signals from the eyes go to both hemispheres. The cutting of this group of nerves ensures that the visual signal from the eyes ends up in only one of the hemispheres. In 1953 Sperry and Myers reported that when they performed this procedure on cats they found that the visual images were still received by both hemispheres. It was clear to them that the information crossed over from one hemisphere to another along the *corpus callosum*. This was then confirmed when it was shown that cats that had had this latter structure cut had visual stimulation in only one hemisphere. The term 'split-brain' was soon used to describe this operation and from then on Sperry and his associates would be seen as the pioneers of this fascinating area of neurological research.

Within a comparatively short time techniques were developed by which the operation could be repeated in higher animals such as monkeys. It was then that the first surprising result was observed. One of Sperry's co-workers, Colwyn Trevarthen, showed that split-brain monkeys could learn two conflicting visual discriminations simultaneously: in other words, they became two consciousnesses!

By the early 1960s it had been shown that although the split-brain animals showed double consciousness, in all other respects they showed no other ill-effects. It was at that time that Los Angeles neurosurgeon Joseph Bogen suggested that maybe the procedure could be used to relieve the symptoms of epilepsy. He proposed that the cutting of the *corpus callosum* of severe epileptics would isolate the seizure into one hemisphere and therefore stop the whole brain from being affected by the electrical storm reverberating backwards and forwards across the commissure. In 1962 Bogen and another surgeon, Philip Vogel, performed an operation that totally cut the *corpus callosum* of a man who suffered frequent and debilitating epileptic attacks. The man fully recovered from the operation and Sperry had his first conscious and verbally adept split-brain human being. As the operation was so successful, many other double-conscious individuals were soon available to Sperry.

However, Sperry had one real problem. In order to reproduce the full experiment that had been done with the cats he would need to cut the optic chiasm of the split-brain patients also. Clearly, this was not an option so he needed another solution. Fortunately, a little-known fact about the nature of vision was suddenly to become of great help to Sperry and his team. Most people assume that the visual signal from the right eye feeds into the left hemisphere of the brain and vice versa. However, this is not true and a moment's reflection will show this to be the case. We have two eyes in order for us to have binocular vision – stereo imaging. In this way we are presented with a three-dimensional visual image of the world. If the signals of each eye fed into each hemisphere then each hemisphere would lose a sense of visual depth. As we always have a dominant and non-dominant hemisphere then the dominant hemisphere would always 'see' a flat image, one that would only be of limited use – particularly for a predator.

Nature's solution to this is that each eye has two visual fields – right and left. The right visual field of the left eye feeds one hemisphere and the left field feeds the other. This is then reversed for the right eye. In this way both hemispheres receive stereo vision. Sperry realized that by showing patients an object in the left or right visual field of one or the other of their eyes he could, in effect, reproduce the cutting of the optic chiasm without the surgery.

The experiment was tried. When the split-brain subject is presented with a picture of an object, say a pencil, to his right brain, the subject says that he sees nothing, yet with his left hand he can pick up the corresponding object. This happens because of a really weird situation. As I explained earlier we all have two hemispheres to the brain. However, experimentation has shown that the being that calls itself 'me' receives all its information about the world through one hemisphere. This hemisphere, usually the left, is where 'me' – the Eidolon – 'lives'. This is called the 'dominant' hemisphere. The right hemisphere is non-dominant and, as we shall see, it has a totally different inhabitant – the Daemon.

The Daemon sees the pencil and when asked happily identifies the pencil as being what it saw by picking it up. For reasons that will become clear later, in most circumstances – but not all as we shall discover later – the Daemon cannot speak and so it shows its choice by moving the arm and hand it can control, the left. However, the Eidolon of the subject is blissfully unaware of what is happening. It fails to see the pencil because it is not in its visual field and when asked if it has seen anything it truthfully answers in the negative.

Sperry was quite categorical about what he thought these experiments proved. In 1966 he wrote:

> *Each hemisphere appears to have its own separate and private sensations, its own concepts and its own impulses to act. The evidence suggests that consciousness runs in parallel in both the hemispheres of the split-brain person.*

These words need to be pondered on for a few seconds. Here is a world-renowned neurosurgeon, 'the expert' on split-brain research, stating in unequivocal terms that 'we' consist of not one but two independent sources of consciousness. What was needed was an alternative way of communicating with the Daemon and this was discovered by Michael Gazzaniga of the University of California and Joseph LeDoux of New York University, when they worked with a split-brain patient identified simply by the initials 'P.S.'.

The problem that Sperry found was that it seemed impossible to communicate verbally with the right hemisphere. Using images worked, but words simply could not be conveyed. Unfortunately, the wiring of ear-to-brain communications works differently to eye-to-brain transmissions. There is no equivalent of the optic chiasm that can be manipulated to open up a direct aural channel of communication. If a verbal question is asked the dominant hemisphere will always respond first, in effect 'shouting down' its non-dominant partner as one researcher so evocatively described it.

Of all the split-brain patients that had been studied, P.S. was unique in that both of his detached brain hemispheres had a reasonably good command of language. It was believed that he had suffered damage to the left side of his brain when very young. This had forced his right hemisphere to compensate by becoming more language-proficient than usual. At sixteen he underwent a full commissurotomy operation that fully cut communication between his two hemispheres. The problem was that although his non-dominant mind knew how to talk it

'If we accept that P.S. does have two independent minds then we are presented with a remarkable situation. Presumably, before the operation each split-brain subject possessed but a single consciousness; but afterwards there are two! In some way, the original single consciousness has bifurcated.'

ROGER PENROSE (MATHEMATICAL PHYSICIST)

couldn't do so because the brain's speech centres are all located in the left hemisphere.

Gazzaniga and LeDoux devised an elaborate experiment to get round this problem. One of their associates, Eran Zaidel, had designed a special contact lens that refracted light in such a way that any light entering it would only hit one side of the retina of each eye. In this way Sperry's pioneering work could be extended for longer periods of time. Gazzaniga and LeDoux had P.S. wear the contact lenses and then presented him with spoken phrases with one crucial word missing. This word would be the one that made the question answerable. This missing word would then be presented to the non-dominant hemisphere.

For example, a question could be 'do you like . . .' and then a card showing the word 'ice cream' would be presented to the right, daemonic, hemisphere. The overbearing left, eidolonic, hemisphere is left puzzling over the question whereas the right has all it needs to answer the question. P.S. had a set of scrabble letters in front of him so his Daemon had, for the first time, an opportunity to show its personal preference instead of having to listen to its Eidolon speaking for both of them.

The results of these experiments are of profound importance to our knowledge of how the brain works. Consistently, it was shown that P.S. had two independent areas of consciousness. They shared some likes and dislikes but, like two separate people, there were areas of total difference. For example on one occasion P.S. was asked what he would like to do when he graduated. The Eidolon was looking forward to being a surveyor whereas the Daemon was far more ambitious. When its turn came it spelt out the words A-U-T-O-M-O-B-I-L-E R-A-C-E-(R).[3]

P.S. was also asked about things he liked and disliked. He was presented with a range of responses from one to five with one being 'like very much' and five being 'dislike very much'. The Daemon regularly responded with a higher figure than the Eidolon but these differences varied from day to day. When P.S. was happy and relaxed his two parts gave similar answers, but when he was unhappy or tense the responses were sharply at odds. Could this be evidence that when our Daemon and Eidolon are in agreement we are happier?

In a fascinating echo of Sperry's quote, cited above, Gazzaniga and LeDoux concluded that:

> Each hemisphere in P.S. has a sense of self and each
> possesses its own system for subjectively evaluating current
> events, planning for further events, setting response priorities,
> and generating personal responses. Consequently, it becomes
> useful to consider the practical and theoretical implications of
> the fact that double consciousness mechanisms can exist.

In his book *The Bisected Brain*, Gazzaniga was later to write:

> Just as conjoined [Siamese] twins are two people sharing a
> common body, the callosum-sectioned human has two
> separate conscious spheres sharing a common brain stem, head
> and body . . . A slice of the surgeon's knife through the midline
> commissures produces two separate, but equal, cognitive systems
> each with its own abilities to learn, emote, think, and act.

The million dollar question is whether a commissurotomy brings about the bifurcation of personality or whether this state of affairs is the natural state and the split-brain operation just brings this to the fore. If my Daemon-Eidolon Dyad is correct then the latter is the only conclusion. What evidence is there that this is the case?

The Hidden Observer

Over the years there has been strong evidence that a communication channel that does not involve drastic brain surgery can be opened up with the Daemon. This channel is the controversial area of psychology called hypnotism.

Hypnotism is one of the great mysteries of the mind. Even today, psychologists and neurologists are at a loss to explain how it actually works. The whole mystery began with the work of Franz Mesmer, the son of a gamekeeper, who was educated at a Jesuit college in Bavaria and attended the University of Ingolstadt, where he was awarded a doctorate in philosophy. In 1759 Mesmer moved to Vienna to study for his MD degree, completing this with a dissertation entitled 'A Physical-Medical Treatise on the Influence of the Planets'. This title reflects the fact that even in the mid-18th century astrology and occultism still found a home at the great seats of learning. Mesmer was quick to ingratiate himself with the world of cultured Viennese life. He made a good, and financially advantageous, marriage and was soon a friend of the rich and powerful. It was during this period that he developed the process that was to become known as 'mesmerism'. Mesmer believed that the universe is full of 'magnetism'. His magnetic force was similar to that of electrical magnetism, the effects and potentials of which were being discovered at the time. He considered his magnetism to be an invisible fluid that influenced all living things. To differentiate his version from ferromagnetism he termed his force 'animal magnetism'. Mesmer believed that the body itself was a magnet and ailments were caused by an imbalance of vital 'currents' in the body. As such the physician could use his own body to affect the magnetic balances of his patient and thereby cure certain ailments. This new form of medicine was to become very popular. Paris, in 1781, was to see him open the first of his schools for teaching the new 'science'. For a substantial fee students could attend Mesmer's Society of Harmony establishment, and there learn the secrets of animal magnetism.

In 1784 a student of the Parisian Society of Harmony was attempting to cure a peasant of some minor illness by using Mesmer's techniques. The Marquis de Puységur was applying this process to a 23-year-old by the name of Victor Race. The method involved passing a large magnet over the head and body of the subject. For a reason that is not entirely clear, Race had been tied to a lime tree. As the Marquis was making the passes the young shepherd fell asleep. This was not unusual, but when de Puységur tried to awaken Race he discovered that he could not do so. De Puységur demanded that Race wake up and untie himself. Race acted on the instruction but did so without coming out of his sleep state. The Marquis realized that he had somehow induced a trance state in the young man, a trance state that allowed him to command the shepherd to do things without him being awake. By simply telling him to do so, de Puységur could get Victor to stand, sing or follow any other instruction. However, what particularly fascinated the Marquis was that he could suggest to Race that he was in some social situation such as a dance or a hunt. Victor would then go through all the gestures involved in that pursuit. It was as if Race was, in his mind, really doing those things. De Puységur termed this newly discovered state 'magnetic sleep'.

What intrigued de Puységur was that magnetic sleep seemed to separate a person into two totally independent states of consciousness. Victor had no memory of what had occurred whilst he was in his trance state. In turn the consciousness that came to the fore whilst he was 'asleep' had a continuity of memory from the last trance period. Each consciousness had its own memories. It was as if de Puységur was dealing with two different people. This was the first recorded case of what was to become termed 'Double Consciousness'. As we shall discover later, this was the first time that the communication channel with a Daemon had been reversed. 'We' were talking to 'them'!

This phenomenon, which was to become known as 'artificial somnambulism' because of its similarities with sleepwalking, was soon to become an area of serious scientific research. William Gregory, a professor of chemistry at the University of Edinburgh, was particularly interested and applied the technique to many subjects. He described the effect in this way:

> *The first (phenomenon) is a twitching of the eyelids, which*
> *begin to droop, while, even when the eyelids remain open,*
> *there is in many cases a veil, as it were, drawn before the*
> *eyes, concealing the operator's face and other objects. Now*
> *also comes on a drowsiness, and, after a time, consciousness*
> *is suddenly lost, and on awaking the patient has no idea*
> *whatever how long it is since he fell asleep, nor what has*
> *occurred during his sleep. The whole is a blank, but he*
> *generally wakes, with a deep sigh, rather suddenly, and says*
> *he has had a very pleasant sleep, without the least idea*
> *whether for five minutes or five hours. He has been, more or*
> *less deeply in the mesmeric sleep.*[4]

During a hypnotic trance the conscious ego, the part of your brain that calls itself 'I', falls asleep. This must be the case because on awakening the subject recalls nothing of the events that take place during the hypnosis session. However, somebody reacts to the words of the hypnotist in that the suggestions made are responded to and carried out. It is reasonable to conclude, and many psychologists do conclude, that the 'person' who is speaking during a hypnotic session is in fact the non-dominant hemisphere of the brain. Thus by hypnotising a person we can communicate directly with their hidden self.

And this is exactly what Professor Ernest Hilgard discovered when he was performing a classroom demonstration at Stanford University. Hilgard and his students were exploring the phenomenon known as 'hypnotic deafness'. This involves a blind subject being placed in a light trance and being told that they are deaf. What is interesting about this state is that even when a loud unexpected noise is created the subject shows no reaction. Hilgard's intention was to demonstrate how hypnotism can override sensory experience. As expected the subject showed no reaction even when two blocks of wood were banged together close to his ear. However, as the experiment was taking place, one of the students asked a simple, but fascinating question – whether 'some part' of the subject might be aware of what was going on. After all, there was nothing wrong with the subject's ears. Hilgard agreed to this and he had the instructor whisper into the ear of the subject. The instructor said the following in a very quiet voice:

> *As you know, there are parts of our nervous system that carry on activities that occur out of awareness, of which control of the circulation of the blood, or the digestive processes, are the most familiar. However, there may be intellectual processes also of which we are unaware, such as those that find expression in nightdreams. Although you are hypnotically deaf, perhaps there is some part of you that is hearing my voice and processing the information. If there is, I should like the index finger of your right hand to rise as a sign that this is the case.*[5]

To everybody's surprise the subject's index finger raised itself as requested. What was even more surprising was that the blind-deaf subject suddenly spoke.

> *Please restore my hearing so you can tell me what you did. I felt my finger rise in a way that was not a spontaneous twitch, so you must have done something to make it rise, and I want to know what you did.*

The instructor then asked the subject what he remembered. Because the trance was light the student never actually lost consciousness. All that occurred was that his hearing ceased. In order to deal with the boredom of being deprived of both sight and sound he decided to work on some statistical problems in his head. It was while he was doing this that he suddenly felt his finger lift. This was obviously strange to him because under normal circumstances he was, like all of us, the 'person' who decides on how the body moves. In this case he was not. Not only that but somebody else in his head was responding to an external request that he had not heard. As far as Hilgard was concerned the person who responded was the 'Hidden Observer'.

Hilgard then re-hypnotized his subject and spoke directly to this Hidden Observer that had made the man's finger rise. This is what it said:

> *After you counted to make me deaf you made noises with*
> *some blocks behind my head. Members of the class asked me*
> *questions to which I responded. Then one of them asked if I*
> *might not really be hearing, and you told me to raise my*
> *finger, so it is all clear now.*

Here we have a direct communication with the being that I call the Daemon. It shows a far more chatty and garrulous individual than that implied by the split-brain experiments. Of course it must be stressed that Hilgard never suggested that he was communicating with the non-dominant hemisphere of the brain. Indeed, I have the impression that this possibility was never pondered upon.

Hilgard went on to do many other experiments in this area, all of which added weight to his belief. Indeed, there is evidence that this other being is aware of all sensory input to the brain. A classic example of this was when a hypnotized woman had her hand immersed in iced water. Her hypnotized self steadily reported that she felt no pain. What the experimenters had asked her to do was to grade the pain from zero to ten but the hypnotized 'self' continued to report a level of zero. However, her other hand, with access to a pencil, reported an increase in pain using the numbers '0 . . . 1 . . . 2 . . . 4 . . . 7 . . . '. Thus the Hidden Observer was not only feeling the pain, but was evidently becoming concerned that the hand was about to be ice-burned. Later, Hilgard asked the subject to explain what she was sensing at this time. She said:

It's as though two things were happening simultaneously.
I have two separate memories as if two things could have
happened to two different people. Both parts (of me) were
concentrating on what you said – not to feel pain. The water
bothered the hidden part a little because it felt a little but the
hypnotized part was not thinking of my arm at all.
The hidden part knew that my hand was in the water and it
hurt just as much as it did the other day (in the waking
control session). The hypnotized part would vaguely be aware of
feeling pain – that's why I would have to concentrate really
hard. The hidden part knows the pain is there but I'm not
sure it feels it. The hypnotized part doesn't feel it but I'm not
sure that the hypnotized part may have known it was there
but didn't say it. The hypnotized part really makes an effort.[6]

This suggests to me that this being was another locus of consciousness. The subject was subsequently to make the following observations regarding this being:

The hidden observer is cognisant of everything that is going on
. . . the hidden observer sees more, he questions more, he is
aware of what is going on all of the time but getting in touch
is totally unnecessary . . . He is like a guardian angel that guards
you from doing anything that will mess you up . . . the hidden
observer is looking through the tunnel, and sees everything in
the tunnel . . . Unless someone tells me to get in touch with
the hidden observer I'm not in contact. It's just there.

She calls her hidden observer a 'guardian angel'. This is a very interesting comment and together with her very curious description of the entity looking down 'a tunnel' evokes imagery reminiscent of a phenomenon that I will be discussing later: Near-Death Experience.

This analysis was strongly reinforced by the work of the English psychologist Roland Puccetti. In 1973 Puccetti had an article published in *The British Journal for the Philosophy of Science.*[7] In this article Puccetti came to the conclusion that even without commissurotomy there are always two independent centres of consciousness in the human brain. He appeals to the cases where a complete hemisphere is removed. In this event, and whichever hemisphere is left, there remains a person. He argues that if people were unitary then these operations or circumstances would leave only half a person. Puccetti says that the only way he can explain the completeness of the remaining person is by supposing that before the operation there was not a unitary person. He says:

He or she was a compound of two persons who functioned in concert by transcommissural exchange. What has survived is one of two very similar persons.

If the Daemon does exist in the non-dominant hemisphere it is likely that during normal life it is non-verbal or, more accurately, non-communicative. However, there is indirect evidence that under certain conditions of very deep trance state communication it is possible, giving rise to the implication that, rather than being unable to communicate, this entity chooses not to communicate. Under normal circumstances the Daemon exists in isolation within the non-dominant hemisphere (usually the right). As the major speech centres of the brain are located in the dominant (usually left) hemisphere the Daemon simply cannot access the mechanisms that will allow it any form of verbal communication with the outside world. Clearly, communication with the Eidolon can take place across the *corpus callosum* because this does not involve actual physical verbalization, but to speak is beyond the Daemon's abilities. I say 'under normal circumstances' because deep trance states and other psychic 'abnormalities' may allow the Daemon to access the mechanisms of the dominant hemisphere. Indeed, it may be the case that under these circumstances – and others that we shall encounter later – the subject may become a unitary being with open access to all brain functions available to both the Daemon and the Eidolon. As we shall see this state is one that mystics have tried to achieve for centuries.

Evidence of this can be seen in the work of psychologist Charles Tart. In the 1960s and 1970s Tart was keen to see just how deep a trance state could be brought about by hypnotism. Depth cannot be described solely by responsiveness to suggestion. Indeed, at greater depths responsiveness can actually disappear. In experiments the subject is required to assign self-consistent numerical values to the depth they subjectively feel: the higher the number, the greater the depth.

Tart had a particularly good subject called 'William' who was in the highest one or two per cent of hypnotic responsiveness. He had been hypnotized 18 times previously for various reasons, often with an emphasis on depth. William usually reported depths with a numerical value of 40 or 50, with amnesia experienced at 30. He had never gone beyond 60. It was agreed that an attempt would be made to take him much deeper than he had gone before. He was instructed that at each 10-point interval on a depth continuum he should remain at that depth while the experimenter had him describe what he was experiencing.

As William went through the levels he experienced the normal effects: early relaxation followed by a sensation of distance, an increase in peacefulness and a gradual withdrawal from the environment. Beginning at a level of about 50 on this scale he began to have distortions of consciousness. As we shall see later, these distortions are similar to those reported in mystical experiences. At this stage the passage of time becomes meaningless and the body seems to be left behind and a new sense of infinite potentiality emerges. However, at a level of 50 another consciousness was experienced. William described this consciousness as being both him and not him. This 'other' William showed that he was fully aware of the experiment and what was going on. What is strange was that this other being was amused by the attempts of the psychologists to understand the human mind. This event is described as an 'intrusion' by Tart. The other entity accompanied William from level 50 to level 90 where it totally disappeared. It was at its strongest at level 70.[8]

What is of great interest is that the 'intrusion', at the early stages of the now deeper hypnosis of the subject, is amused by William's participation in these experiments. As was clearly evidenced from the example at the start of this chapter, amusement is not something one would expect of the non-dominant hemisphere of the brain. This seems to be a being that knows exactly what is going on and is observing from a position of superiority not inferiority.

This superiority sometimes shows itself in the most interesting of circumstances. In the 1957 Grand Prix race in Monaco the legendary Argentinean driver Juan Fangio found his leg flexing and his foot crashing down on his brake pedal as he approached a blind bend. In an automatic response reminiscent of Hilgard's subjects, this movement was actioned by something other than Fangio's everyday consciousness.

This change of direction and speed was so marked that when Fangio came round the bend his car was perfectly positioned for him to steer his car through the pile-up that had just taken place. The Argentinean went on to win the race, but for months afterwards he was puzzled as to who, or what, had forced his foot down on to the brake pedal.

The automatic flexing of the leg muscles as experienced by Fangio is fascinating when reviewed in the light of what has now become known as the Kornhuber Experiment.[9]

A number of human volunteers agreed to have an EEG (electro-encephalograph) record the electrical signals at a certain position on their skull. While this was picking up any electrical activity in the brain the subjects were asked to flex the index finger of their right hand. The decision as to when this movement was to occur was left totally to the subject. Hans Helmut Kornhuber and his associates were trying to isolate what sort of mental activity was generated when a decision to make a movement was made. What was discovered was another facet of the curious way in which the human mind functions. It seems that there was a delay of between a second and a second and a half from when the decision to move was made and the actual movement took place. Yet the subjects perceived that the decision to move and the actual movement were simultaneous. This in itself was interesting, but it was then discovered that a response to an external signal to engender a particular movement was much faster than the body's ability to cause the physical action. As mathematician Roger Penrose comments:

> For example, instead of it being 'freely willed', the finger
> flexing might be in response to the flash of a light signal.
> In that case a reaction time of about one-fifth of a second is
> normal, which is about five times faster than the 'willed'
> action that is tested in Kornhuber's data.[10]

A graph of the results of the experiment shows the point at which the decision to flex was made. Penrose says that this suggests a 'foreknowledge of the intention to flex'. Is this what happened to Fangio? If so, two questions have to be asked: who actioned the flex reaction that brought Fangio's foot down on the brake and how did it know about something before it happened?

Early one morning, a few months after the incident, Fangio found himself in that strange half-asleep, half-awake state known as hypnopompia. He suddenly found himself being presented with a vivid flashback of the incident. He was back on the Monte Carlo track reliving the approach to the blind bend. However, this time he saw the incident from the viewpoint of another conscious awareness – his Daemon. What the Daemon saw (and then presented to its Eidolon) was a very unusual sight. It was looking up at the stands and was surprised to see that the members of the crowd were not looking in the direction of the 'Great' Fangio, but that all the faces were turned sideways to view an incident taking place round the bend. The Daemon, realizing the danger, took action and pressed down hard on the brake pedal and in so doing saved its Eidolon's life. Of course there is also another possibility: that Fangio's Daemon was acting upon foreknowledge of what was about to happen and acted upon that precognition – a possibility that I will turn to later.

If I am correct, Fangio's Daemon, like that of most other human beings, is 'located' in the right, non-verbal hemisphere. As such it is mute. It could not tell its Eidolon of the danger (and it is reasonable to conclude that insufficient time was available anyway), so it had to take over and have the foot it controlled press the brake. Here we have a real life-saving example of Kornhuber's 'intention to flex'.

Clearly, life must be very frustrating for the Daemon. It is given the gift of hyperacuity, or precognition if you prefer, and yet because of its location in the non-verbal hemisphere it cannot verbally communicate this useful information to its Eidolon. It is left with sending images across the *corpus callosum* or 'grabbing the reins' as Fangio's Daemon had to do. Indeed, I believe that the hypnopompic images that Fangio experienced that morning were placed into his Eidolonic consciousness when the channels of communication were open because of his peculiar semi-conscious state. For most people the Daemon can only communicate via images or hunches. The images are shown in dreams and the hunches are those ill-defined sensations that suggest that one course of action is a good or a bad thing. Later in this book I will give example after example of this subliminal guidance. However, for a small group of Daemons the channel of direct verbal communication is available. A classic example of this is described in the following quote:

In Boston, I had for about a week been studying and
autistically pondering some of the problems in this book,
particularly the problem of what knowledge is and how we

can know anything at all. My convictions and misgivings had been circling about through the sometimes precious fogs of epistemologies, finding nowhere to land. One afternoon I lay down in intellectual despair on a couch. Suddenly, out of an absolutely quiet room, there came a firm, distinct loud voice from my upper right which said, 'Include the knower and the known.' It lugged me to my feet absurdly exclaiming, 'Hello?', looking for whoever was in the room. The voice had an exact location.

The writer is the psychologist Julian Jaynes and it was from this strange event that he was stimulated to write his most famous work, *The Origin of Consciousness in the Breakdown of the Bicameral Mind.*

Bicameralism and schizophrenia

In this rather mystifyingly-titled book the late Julian Jaynes argued that his experience, although strange, was not unusual. Spurred on by such an obscure instruction Jaynes was stimulated to research the phenomenon of aural hallucinations. He was surprised to discover that among the Anglo-Saxon race one man in twelve experiences this form of discarnate advice. For women it is even more common – one in eight. Indeed, this was quite low in relation to other groups. In Russia and Brazil the figure was twice as high. These are normal people, not those under mental or psychological stress. From this Jaynes concluded that under certain circumstances many, if not all, individuals might experience auditory hallucinations, the differences being purely cultural.

For Jaynes this particularly vivid form of auditory hallucination explained the universal religious experience of communicating with the gods. It is quite understandable how an individual, living in a particular culture or historical period where the existence of gods is unquestioned, could naturally assume the voice to be the words of a god. The curiously portentous and somewhat obscure meaning of what the voice says then reinforces this belief.

However, for Jaynes, there was more to it than that. He pointed out that for 99 per cent of human evolution men and women grouped together in tightly bonded, mutually dependent groups. Within these groups each individual had no sense of individuality, no sharp sense of 'ego-self'. The concept of selfhood came about, according to Jaynes, around the first millennium BCE. Jaynes bases his theory upon studies that he made on early writings such as *The Iliad* (*c.*1000BCE). He notes that this book has no reference to concepts such as thought and mind, human actions being the results of the gods willing men to do things. From this he concluded that at some time in the recent past human consciousness has split into two entities. Not only that, but it was this very process of splitting that brought about self-consciousness.

For Jaynes most modern human beings exist as bicameral – literally, two-roomed – beings with two self-conscious elements within their brains. However, for a small group of people, this bicameralism is not fully developed. Instead of two separate rooms they have an access door between the two. This door usually opens only one way and only the Daemon has the key. These people, as we shall see later, are migraine-sufferers and temporal lobe epileptics. However, for one group, the rooms do not just have a door, they have a full-length French window as well. As such they can experience what is happening in the next room. These people are schizophrenics.

Sufferers from this potentially inherited illness show some very curious side-effects that fail to fit in with any easy explanation. An example is the result of a survey of profoundly deaf schizophrenics. In this it was discovered that 16 out of the 22 individuals questioned 'heard' the voice of the Hidden Observer.[11] The issue here is how can a person who has never heard another human voice somehow hear the voice inside their head? Indeed, how does a congenitally deaf person understand language without ever hearing it? One 32-year-old woman that had been born deaf was continually being told off by her voice for having had a therapeutic abortion a few years previously.

If we are to accept the evidence presented thus far then it is logical to conclude that the human brain hosts not one but two self-conscious states. These two entities share all of the sensory inputs, but the seemingly more advanced but elusive being processes the inputs over a far broader area of the sensory spectrum. As such it is not unreasonable to consider that schizophrenia seems to expose the lower, everyday consciousness to the sensory environment of the hidden observer. This allows direct communication between the two on a regular, if not continual basis. It is as if the two consciousnesses overlap in some way.

What is the significance of this curious illness? In my opinion it is clear that schizophrenia, together with a collection of related 'illnesses', offers some fascinating insights into the nature of consciousness itself. Can it be that certain human beings can access a different version of reality than that which is made available to the majority? I would like to examine this possibility in the next chapter.

Summary

Supporting the theological belief of dual consciousness is a whole raft of information gleaned from neurology. Studies of split-brain subjects have clearly implied that each hemisphere is home to its own unique personality – one that has different motivations, likes and dislikes from its cranial partner. Under normal circumstances the non-dominant (usually right) hemisphere has no means of communication with the outside world. However, by the application of certain experimental tools, the non-dominant hemisphere of split-brain subjects can communicate in a limited, non-verbal way. I consider that this split is identical to my Daemon-Eidolon Dyad. The Daemon is usually trapped in the non-verbal world of the non-dominant hemisphere.

In the non-split-brain population it has been shown that certain hypnotic states can open up these communication channels to the Daemon. When this takes place this being is seen to be far more sophisticated and aware than was originally believed. It has a strong conception of self and even a sense of humour. In addition it seems to have a super-awareness that implies precognition.

According to the bicameral theory of Julian Jaynes this split came about around 3,000 years ago when *homo sapiens* acquired self-awareness. However, sometimes there is 'leakage' across the *corpus callosum* and we again 'hear' the voice of the gods. This communication occasionally happens to 'normal' people, but it is far more common with schizophrenics.

[1] Wada, J.A., & Ramussen, T., 'Intracarotid injection of sodium amytal for the lateralisation of cerebral speech dominance: Experimental and clinical observations', *Journal of Neurosurgery*, 17:266–82 (1960)

[2] Ahern, G.L. et al., 'The association of multiple personality and temporolimbic epilepsy: Intracarotid amobarbital test observations', *Arch. Neurol.*, 50: 1020–25 (1993)

[3] LeDoux, Joseph, Wilson, D.H. & Gazzaniga, Michael, 'A Divided Mind', *Annals of Neurology* 2, pp.417–21 (1977)

[4] Gregory, W., *Letters to a Candid Inquirer on Animal Magnetism*, Taylor, Walton (1851)

[5] Hilgard, Ernest & Hilgard, Josephine R., *Hypnosis in the Relief of Pain*, William Kaufmann, California, pp.166–7 (1975)

[6] Ibid.

[7] Puccetti, R., 'Brain Bisection and Personal Identity', *Br. Jour. Phil. of Science* (1973)

[8] Hilgard, Ernest, 'The Hypnotic State' in *Consciousness, Brain, States of Awareness and Mysticism*, D. Goleman & R.J. Davidson (eds), Harper Row, New York (1979)

[9] Deeke, L., Grotzinger, B. & Kornhuber, H.H., 'Voluntary finger movements in man: cerebral potentials and theory', *Biol. Cybernetics*, 23, 99 (1976)

[10] Penrose, Roger, *The Emperor's New Mind*, Vintage, p.569 (1991)

[11] Raines et al., 'Phenomenology of Hallucinations in the Deaf' in W. Keup (ed.) *Origins and Mechanisms of Hallucinations*, Plenum, New York (1970)

CHAPTER 2

Opening the Doors of Perception

If the doors of perception were cleansed
Then everything would appear to man
As it is, infinite, for man has closed
Himself up, till he sees all things
Through narrow chinks of his cavern

William Blake

Break on through (to the other side)

In our day-to-day lives we take for granted that the reality we perceive through our senses is real and 'out there' in space – the space that exists outside the confines of our heads. This is a perfectly reasonable assumption. When we close our eyes and open them again everything remains the same. Objects remain in the same positions and do not change shape or colour. A second supporting fact is that other people seem to perceive the same things in the same way. If I watch a television programme with a friend we can both prove that we watched the same programme by discussing it afterwards. However, for some people reality is not consistent at all: one small event can bring about a lifelong questioning of the nature of the cosy construct we call reality.

Take, for example, what happened to the Swedish playwright August Strindberg. He was in a wine shop having a sensitive discussion with an old friend who was planning to give up a promising military career. As the discussion progressed, Strindberg decided to describe a moment in their mutual past where they had had a similar discussion in a tavern many years before. As he described the scene he felt that he was losing consciousness. He then found himself back in the tavern he had been describing only moments before. He had, in his opinion, fallen out of time and had entered a three-dimensional reconstruction of a moment in his own past. He describes the sensation:

> 'Wait a minute. I am now in the Augustiner tavern, but I
> know very well that I am in some other place, don't say
> anything . . . I don't know you anymore, yet I know that I
> do. Where am I? Don't say anything. This is interesting.'
> I made an effort to raise my eyes – I don't know if they were
> closed – and I saw a cloud, a background of indistinct colour,
> and from the ceiling descended something like a theatre
> curtain; it was the dividing wall with shelves and bottles.

The sensation only lasted a few seconds but it had a profound effect on Strindberg and led to him questioning the nature of reality itself.

What had happened to Strindberg that evening? It seems that he suddenly perceived that reality was some form of illusion and that the past sat behind the veneer of the present like a palimpsest. His mind seemed to access another level of reality that is ordinarily denied to everyday consciousness. There is strong evidence that given certain neurological conditions strongly creative individuals can receive a glimpse of an alternative reality where the world of normality is left far behind. The great Russian writer Dostoevsky described this sensation in the following way:

> The forces of life gathered convulsively all at once to the
> highest attainable consciousness. The sensation of life, of
> being, multiplied ten-fold at that moment; all passion, all
> doubts, all unrests were resolved as in a higher peace; then a
> peace full of dear, harmonious joy and hope. And then a
> scene suddenly as if something were opening up in the soul;
> an indescribable, an unknown light radiated, by which the
> ultimate essence of things was made visible and recognizable
> . . . this feeling is so strong and so sweet that for a few

seconds of this enjoyment one would readily exchange ten
years of one's life, perhaps even one's whole life . . . When
the attack has passed I have a feeling of a tremendous weight
bearing down on me. I believe I have committed an offence,
a gruesome crime . . . for two or three days I was unable
to work, write or even read, because I am a wreck,
body and soul.

Just like Strindberg, Dostoevsky finds himself experiencing the indescribable. And these two are not alone. As we shall see later there is example after example of painters, writers, poets and authors all of whom experience a glimpse of the real world behind the façade of reality.

Information about the external world comes to us via the senses, be they photons of light (vision), sound waves (hearing) or molecules (smell). However, if you think hard about this it is one of the strangest things imaginable. Photons hit your eye and form an image on your retina. So far so good, we can understand the idea of an image, after all this is exactly how a camera works. However, and this is where the magic takes place, that image is then transferred into electronic impulses which are sent to your visual cortex. Here 'something' converts them back into an image and 'something else' 'sees' the image. What takes over is that mysterious entity human consciousness.

This same process occurs with all the senses. 'We', in the sense of the observer in our head, receive not photons, sound waves or molecules, but electrical impulses. We do not interface with reality. It is similar to watching a television programme. We see the television studio on the television screen, but we are not in the studio. There is a process in our mind that converts these nerve impulses into subjective experience.

The massive question is whether what is presented to our consciousness is an accurate representation of what is 'out there', or is there some form of 'fine tuning' that presents only what we need in order to survive? Could it be that what Strindberg and Dostoevsky perceived was a glimpse of the 'reality behind the reality'?

The implication here is that the human brain actively filters external sensory stimulation and presents to consciousness a watered-down version of reality. The French psychologist Henri Bergson was convinced that the brain's function was eliminative and not productive. This idea was carried forward by the British philosopher C.D. Broad who wrote:

> *The function of the brain and the nervous system is to protect*
> *us from being overwhelmed and confused by this mass of*
> *largely useless and otherwise irrelevant knowledge, by shutting*
> *out most of what we should otherwise perceive.*

In his fascinating work on the nature of human consciousness, *The Doors of Perception,* the writer Aldous Huxley refined Broad's idea by commenting that reality 'has to be funnelled through the reducing valve of the brain and nervous system'. Huxley called this expanded conscious awareness 'The Mind At Large'.

He argued that a drug such as mescaline inhibits enzymes that regulate the glucose supply to the brain cells. This brings about a decrease in the amount of sugar available to the brain, which in turn inhibits the effectiveness of the reducing valve. Suddenly more of 'reality' comes through. In his book *Heaven and Hell,* Huxley suggested that this is why fasting leads to mystic experiences. Furthermore, he considered that yogic breathing techniques and the use of chanting and singing lower the efficiency of the reducing valve by increasing the carbon dioxide content of the brain.[1] This would certainly explain why these techniques are used to raise conscious awareness without the use of drugs.

To understand the power of Huxley's argument we need to review the structure of the brain. If one takes a section of brain material and views it through a powerful microscope, what is seen is a dense network of cells. Most of these will be what are called 'glial' cells. It seems that the role of these is simply to 'glue' the brain structure together and ensure it keeps its shape. However, dotted among these glial cells at a ratio of approximately one to ten are 'neurons'. These are cells that are adapted to send, receive and carry electrical impulses. Each neuron has a central, usually star-shaped, section where the cell nucleus is located. Spreading out from this central body are long, thin tendrils that can vary from one millimetre to one metre in length. These tendrils reach out and can receive or send electrochemical signals to and from as many as 10,000 other neurons.

These cells are designed to exchange electrochemical messages with their fellow neurons, sending or receiving as required. When a nerve cell is activated, or fired, an electrical current runs along the nerve fibre and releases a chemical substance called a 'neurotransmitter'.

These neurotransmitters are the chemical agents that are released by the neurons to stimulate other neurons and in the process transmit impulses from one cell to another. In turn this facilitates the transfer of messages throughout the whole nervous system. The site where the neurons meet is called the 'synapse', which consists of the 'axon terminal' (transmitting end) of one cell and the 'dendrite' (receiving end) of the next. A microscopic gap called a 'synaptic cleft' exists between the two neurons. When a nerve impulse arrives at the axon terminal of one cell a chemical substance is released through the membrane close to the synapse. This substance then travels across the gap in a matter of milliseconds to arrive at the post-synaptic membrane of the adjoining neuron. This chemical release is stimulated by the electrical activity of the cell. Across the other side of the cleft, at the end of the receiving dendrite, are specialized receptors that act as docking areas for particular neurotransmitters. The newly activated neurotransmitters then 'instruct' the dendrite to send a particular signal along to its

> *'In the implicate order the totality of existence is enfolded within each region of space (and time). So, whatever part, element, or aspect we may abstract in thought, this still enfolds the whole and is therefore intrinsically related to the totality from which it has been abstracted. Thus, wholeness permeates all that is being discussed, from the very outset.'*
>
> DAVID BOHM (THEORETICAL PHYSICIST)

nucleus then out to its own axons. When it does this it is said to be 'excitatory'. Sometimes the effect of the neurotransmitter(s) released by the pre-synaptic axon is to inhibit rather than excite the post-synaptic dendrite. In this case it is said to be 'inhibitory'.

The existence of neurotransmitters, although long suspected, was confirmed in the 1930s, but it was only in the 1960s that their role was fully understood. To date 50 or so have been isolated, the most important being 'serotonin', 'noradrenaline', 'glutamate' and a group of painkilling opiates called 'endorphins'. These chemicals can have a marked effect upon mood and temperament. By stimulating the internal creation of these neurotransmitters an individual's whole personality can be changed. For example the much discussed 'feel good' drug Prozac works its magic by enhancing the production of serotonin within the axons. As such it comes as no surprise to discover that anything that stimulates or suppresses these chemicals can have a profound effect upon the subject.

In recent years a good deal of research has taken place with regard to the similarities in chemical structure between psychedelics and internally generated neurotransmitters such as dopamine, serotonin, norepinephrine and, most significantly, glutamate. The implication is that psychedelics can disrupt the transmission of messages between brain cells. It is therefore not unreasonable to conclude that Bergson and Huxley were certainly on the right track. However, another question remains. What room lies at the other side of the open 'Doors of Perception'?

I disagree with Bergson and Huxley in their belief that the reducing valve allows direct access to the 'outside world' as it really is. I argue that the 'Doors' open up to allow access to the everyday awareness of the Daemon. Put simply, the Eidolon perceives the world as the Daemon does and the Daemon perceives the actual nature of 'reality' – a very sophisticated, internally-generated illusion – a recording of a life that was once lived, a recording generated by a process similar to holography.

Not to touch the Earth

Sounds crazy? Well, not according to Professor David Bohm. Bohm was professor of physics at Birkbeck College in London and died in 1992. He had studied under Einstein and Oppenheimer, and had received his B.Sc. degree from Pennsylvania State College in 1939 and his Ph.D. in physics at the University of California, Berkeley, in 1943. He was the last graduate student to study with Oppenheimer at UC in the 1940s, where he remained as a research physicist after Oppenheimer left for Los Alamos to work on the atomic bomb. He worked at Berkeley on the Theory of Plasma and the Theory of Synchrotron and Synchrocyclotrons until 1947. From 1947 to 1951 he taught at Princeton University as an assistant professor and worked on plasmas, theory of metals, quantum mechanics and elementary particles.

He was blacklisted during Senator Joe McCarthy's witch-hunt trials while teaching at Princeton. Rather than testify against his colleagues, he left the United States. Bohm subsequently became a professor at the University of São Paulo, Brazil, the Technion of Haifa, Israel and Birkbeck College, University of London, as well as a research fellow at Bristol University and a Fellow of the Royal Society in 1990.

Clearly such a technically capable individual as Bohm would ground his theories in 'hard science' and would not be given to flights of fancy. However, in the early 1980s he became fascinated by the implications of a little-known but potentially world-changing experiment that took place at the University of Paris. A small team led by Professor Alain Aspect proved beyond any doubt that Einstein's long-held principle that nothing can travel faster than the speed of light was incorrect.

Although the implication was that this was the case, the result implied something far stranger about the nature of reality itself. Aspect was able to show that two subatomic particles could communicate information from one to the other absolutely instantaneously irrespective of the distance between them. The particles could be five metres or five million light years apart but the message would be received in no time at all. It is still accepted that for solid objects such as spaceships and planets Einstein's speed rule still applies – in order to travel faster than the speed of light an object must have infinite mass. So by what method of communication was the 'information' sent from one particle to another?

Bohm's solution was simple and logical. We have been wrongly interpreting the nature of matter and the universe itself. The message never travelled across space and time at all because both these constructs are an illusion brought about by the brain. In fact the two particles were really one particle all the time and as such they both 'knew' what was happening to each of them.

He postulated that the ultimate nature of physical reality is not a collection of separate objects (as it appears to us), but rather it is an undivided whole that is in perpetual dynamic flux. For Bohm, the insights of quantum mechanics and relativity theory point to a universe that is undivided and in which all parts merge and unite in one totality – a counterintuitive scenario that had already been observed in certain little-known observed characteristics of holograms.

In 1947 a British physicist, Dennis Gabor, was trying to find a way to improve the resolution of electron microscopes so that scientists could see individual atoms. He came across the notion that by splitting a beam of light objects could be photographed so that the whole image could be viewed. Gabor called these images 'holograms'. However, at the time the technology did not exist to build a device that could split the light in the way Gabor envisaged. In 1960 his dream came true. The invention of the laser gave him the exact source of light he needed to make his holograms a reality. What was strange was that central to Gabor's model of the hologram was a factor he termed 'interference waves'.

What was soon discovered was that not only could holographic light be used to generate three-dimensional images, but also when a holographic image is cut up each fragment amazingly contains a degraded version of the whole image not, as one would logically expect, just a segment.

This was exactly how Bohm considered that the universe works. He argued that each part of the universe contains information about the whole. Reality is a vast hologram in which everything is part of everything else. This is how the two particles in the Aspect experiment 'communicated' with each other. They are, in a very real sense, the same particle because within each of them can be found the other.

As such Bohm believed that 'out there' is also 'in here' in the sense that our brains contain the universe within them. In other words, we all have a personal universe inside our heads. We use our brain to access information about the outside world, but in reality that world is already available without any need to interface. Amazing, isn't it? But it becomes more fascinating when we add the theories and the work of another great scientist, Karl Pribram. Are you ready for this? Pribram suggests that the brain, and therefore conscious awareness, is also holographic in nature. His quest started when he became interested in the way in which the brain stores memories. But in order to follow his logic we have to go back to the 1930s and the pioneering work of the great Soviet psychiatrist Alexander Luria.

Over a period of years Luria had conducted many experiments to isolate the location of memories. He concluded that memories were localized to the neurons found in the small brain structure called the hippocampus and the reticular formation. However, he failed to find actual physical evidence of memory recording, called an 'engram' by psychologists.

The search for the engram was to become the lifetime quest of psychologist Karl Lashley. For 30 years he probed rats' brains to find the location in which memories were stored. He would take a rat and teach it how to negotiate a maze. Then he cut out a small section of the rat's brain and checked to see if it still remembered the route. It did. By the late 1930s he had sacrificed many rats, but even though he had cut away up to 80 per cent of the brain matter of individual rats they still found their way round the maze. In his frustration he semi-jokingly concluded that there was either no location of memory in the brain or memory was located right across the brain. In his frustration he suggested that these spread memories were formed by the action of a magical something he termed 'interference waves'.

At that time the idea of a component part of a larger object being located at every location within that object was logically impossible. It was this mystery that stimulated Stanford neurophysiologist Karl Pribram to take up Lashley's idea and suggest a revolutionary theory not only about memory but also human consciousness itself. In 1966 Pribram proposed that the brain might interpret information in a similar way to the process by which a hologram records an image. He suggested that the fine fibres in the nerve cells digitize incoming information and store the data in this format. The brain then decodes these stored memory traces in the way a hologram decodes, or more accurately de-blurs, its original image.

But Pribram went further. He suggested that the brain itself is a form of hologram. In this way he felt that he could explain how the brain can store so much information. For example, it has recently been shown that holograms have an absolutely astonishing capacity for information storage. Simply by changing the angle at which two lasers strike a piece of photographic film would make it possible for one cubic centimetre to hold as much as 10 billion bits of information. This is why scientists can never find the engram because it is stored right across the brain and exists in a far more complex version of the universe: one that we are only just starting to understand.

Just as Pribram was applying holographic principles to the brain, so Bohm was applying the same principles to the universe as a whole. The implications of this Bohm–Pribram holographic theory of reality are simply staggering; the universe is a vast hologram that is processed by an observer's brain which is, in itself, a hologram that contains the whole universe! Is this what the non-scientific, but profoundly perceptive, philosopher Broad was trying to explain when he made the following observation with regard to the reductive nature of perception?

> *Each person is at each moment capable of remembering all that has ever happened to him and of perceiving everything that is happening everywhere in the universe. The function of the brain and nervous system is to protect us from being overwhelmed and confused by this mass of largely useless and irrelevant knowledge, by shutting out most of what we should otherwise perceive or remember at any moment, and leaving only that very small and special selection which is likely to be practical and useful.*[2]

And many years before, the mystic British poet William Blake made a similar observation when he suggested that we should all be able to see 'the universe in a wild flower'.

In honour of David Bohm I term this inwardly generated universe the 'Bohmian IMAX'. It is to this I will now turn.

You make me real

In his fascinating book *Consciousness Explained*, Professor Daniel Dennett suggested a concept he called the 'Cartesian Theatre'. By this he meant the location in the brain whereby the internally generated facsimile of the external world is presented to consciousness. He likened this to a stage whereby a performance is observed by the 'little man in our head' – termed the homunculus. This is the place where it 'all comes together'. Dennett was using this analogy to show that such a concept is impossible. It has long been known that different parts of the brain process different sensory stimuli. For example, sight is processed in one part of the brain and sound in another. As such, they will arrive at different times. This goes for all stimuli. So how is it that our perception shows us everything happening at the same time? Surely the delays would bring about a sensation rather similar to watching a movie where the soundtrack and the film are out of synchronization with each other? This is why historically there has been a belief that there is one point in the brain where everything arrives at the same time. However, if this is the case then some form of buffering must take place – a process whereby the brain waits until it has got all the information before it presents it. We shall see later, in the chapter on precognition (Chapter 6), that Dennett has strong empirical reasons for suggesting such an idea.

So if external information is buffered then there must be a mechanism whereby it is stored until all the required information is received. This implies a process of recording. The completed recording is then presented in the Cartesian Theatre. Clearly this is not what Dennett suggests really happens. Dennett considers that the brain and the consciousness are the same thing. He reasonably argues that to accept the Cartesian Theatre will bring about an infinite regress. If the homunculus is viewing the show in the theatre then it must have eyes and ears to perceive the production and a brain to process the sensory inputs. Is there then another Cartesian Theatre in the mind of the homunculus with another homunculus sitting in it? Clearly Dennett has a point. However, I really like the concept and I use it in the same way as Dennett does: as an example of the common-sense, if not entirely logical, model of how the brain acts as a medium connecting conscious awareness with the external world.

My theory suggests that Dennett is right. The idea of the Cartesian Theatre is beguiling but incorrect. I suggest that we really process 'reality' in a far more complex, dynamic and ultimately fascinating way. This I call the 'Bohmian IMAX'.

In a theatre the audience sits in front of a stage and a performance is presented to them. They have no control over the performance. It takes place in a linear fashion, progressing from past to future – from 'already perceived' to 'to be perceived' with 'now' moving ever forward from past to future. The future cannot be known and the past can never be re-experienced because the performance is 'live'.

Now let's compare a theatre performance with a digital, holographically-generated super DVD 'SenSurround' experience, presented in a wraparound super IMAX theatre. In this situation the audience is experiencing something that is totally immersive, similar to a virtual reality computer game.

Imagine now that what is being projected in this super theatre is a version of Second Life, the popular website. The observer simply cannot tell this performance from reality itself. In fact it is so effective in its emulation of reality that it might as well be real. This is my Bohmian IMAX.

I argue that 'reality' is exactly how Bohm and Pribram suggest that it is. It is a huge hologram. However, where I differ from them is I that I believe that the hologram is internally generated by the brain itself. It is not 'out there' at all. Reality is, in a very real sense, an illusion. My Bohmian IMAX is a technological *Maya* – the Advaita

Vedanta (Hindu) belief that reality does not exist outside the mind of the observer. It also has elements of quantum physics – specifically the Copenhagen Interpretation whereby reality is brought into existence by the act of observation.

So how does this work?

I suggest that the real world outside is not at all what our senses tell us it is. It consists of buzzes and swirls of pure energy. The laws of physics tell us that the very building blocks of what we see as solid matter are, in fact, insubstantial points of energy. These are aggregated together by the act of observation into an indistinct holographic image – analogous to a three-dimensional holographic picture before it is illuminated by laser light. In this case, the illumination is the act of observation. This weird and wonderful blur of colour and sounds is then processed by the holographic brain. The brain modulates the signal and presents to consciousness an interpretation that has little, if any, resemblance to the actuality. This is the inhibitory mechanism or reducing valve suggested by Bergson and Huxley. They were not aware of Pribram and Bohm. Had they been so, I am sure that they would have come to a similar conclusion. I would like to term this holographic universe the 'Pleorama'. This is a Gnostic term describing the real universe behind the illusory one that we all take for reality. I have chosen this word very carefully. The significance of that will become clear later.

As such the Pleorama is re-configured before it is presented to consciousness within the Bohmian IMAX. This is recorded using the wonderful dual processing of the mutually entangled brain-universe hologram. Each of us have experienced our 'life performance' as a never-before-seen first performance. However, many of us are being shown the recording for the second or even the seventy-second time. We simply cannot tell. Well, that is not exactly true. We have clues that we are experiencing a rerun – we call them *déjà vu* experiences. However, we never see these for what they really are. I will return to the significance of *déjà vu* later.

This is the world as seen by the Daemon. Unlike its Eidolon it does not need the protection of the Bohmian IMAX because it is neurologically and psychologically prepared. The Pleorama is its natural environment.

Can there ever be a circumstance whereby an Eidolon, under certain neurological circumstances, can see past the Bohmian IMAX and perceive the Pleorama as the Daemon does – the real, holographic, nature of the external world? I believe so and I also contend that there is a continuum of intensity as regards this perception. I further contend that an Eidolon's position on this continuum relates directly to its level of creativity. At one end we have what is generally termed as 'normal', which then carries on through three defined levels. These are migraine, temporal lobe epilepsy and schizophrenia. Each one allows greater Eidolonic exposure to the world as it is perceived by the Daemon.

Take it as it comes

Migraine is a French word taken from the Greek for 'half skull'. This is because the headache is usually focused on one side or the other of the head. For those that experience the classic variety the pain is just one element of the overall migraine attack. Preceding the headache is a whole series of sensations, mostly visual in nature. These can involve some or all of the following: flashing lights, zigzag patterns and temporary blindness. For a minority, there are also tingling sensations and numbness on one side of the body, usually in the arm. In rare forms, various neurologically-based symptoms may be experienced including vertigo, slurred speech and mental confusion. As a person who experiences all of these sensations before an attack I can vouch for just how frightening they can be.

All of these curious pre-headache sensations are termed the 'migraine aura' and they usually act as a form of early warning system. In my experience I know that in around 20 minutes the headache will hit me.

In his book *Migraine*, Dr Oliver Sacks allots more than a whole chapter to the mysteries of this peculiar psychological state but considers it deserves a whole book. I acknowledge that most of the neurological and quotation material I use for the next few pages is taken from this fascinating and, as far as I am aware, unique book.[3] Sacks feels that the aura of the classic migraine attack has been curiously ignored by most researchers and writers. He finds this very surprising. Indeed, he notes that the very terminology used, that of 'classic' and 'common', implies that migraine without aura is common and that the classic with aura type is rare. In fact the opposite is true. Sacks states that in his experience the migraine aura is the most common symptom.

He is particularly fascinated by the fact that many individuals experience aura without the subsequent headache. As he rightly points out, this implies that the aura sensation, although linked to the headache, may be a phenomenon in its own right. Again I can personally vouch for this because in recent years I have experienced strong aura sensations without a full migraine headache developing.

For me it usually starts with a disruption in my visual field. For years I have struggled to explain this in words – a problem, it seems, that many other classic migraine-sufferers have. However, in my research I came across this particularly apposite quote:

It may be likened to the effect produced by the rapid gyration of small water-beetles as they are seen swarming in a cluster on the surface of the water in sunshine . . .

The technical term for these visual disturbances is a 'scotoma'. In my case the scotoma advances across my visual field for about 20 minutes or so. When it crosses the midpoint of my sight I become effectively blind and I have to stop what I am doing. I am particularly concerned if the aura starts when I am driving.

One of the most interesting facts about these visual 'hallucinations' is that they can seem part of the objective, external world, rather than be immediately recognized as a subjective and internally generated neurological state that is projected into the visual field. Sacks gives an example that I can fully associate with – that of taking off one's glasses to clean them in the belief that the visual disturbance is actually a smear on the lens. This shows just how 'real' the aura seems to the subject.

However, the aura can bring about hallucinations that involve the other senses. For example small sounds may become amplified and reverberate or smells will appear that will be so real that the subject will search out the source of the odour. Indeed, this is when things can become very strange. At this level of aura-hallucination, external reality and subjective experience start to merge and, in extreme circumstances, can be so involving that the hallucination takes on dream-like properties. By this I mean that the subject believes that what they are experiencing is totally real.

For Sacks this state of awareness is very peculiar. He says:

> *This state is thus one of an excruciating overall sensitivity,*
> *patients being assaulted by sensory stimuli from their*
> *environment, or by internal images and hallucinations if they*
> *insulate themselves from their environment. Such states*
> *are often succeeded by a relative, and on occasion,*
> *absolute extinction of sensation, especially in severe auras*
> *where syncope occurs.*[4]

This feeling of being assaulted by sensory stimuli is interesting. It is as if the aura allows the subject to perceive a level of reality that lies behind everyday perception. It has been argued by some neurologists that the brain acts as an attenuator rather than an amplifier of sensual experience. If this is the case then maybe what is taking place with a migraine aura is that whatever brings about the aura does so by opening Aldous Huxley's 'Doors of Perception'.

By its very definition a hallucination is a creation of the mind and in no way involves the external world. However, there is one symptom of the migraine aura that implies that it manipulates 'reality' in a very strange way. This symptom is called 'macropsia', or 'Brobdingnagian vision'. The subject perceives that distant or small objects become enlarged as if viewed through a telescope or a microscope. What is fascinating about this experience is that the detail is perceived as if the object was actually enlarged. It would be fascinating to know if any research has been done to support my suspicion that the subject really does see the object in greater detail. If this is shown to be the case, then macropsia is not an illusion but an actual objective increase in visual acuity.

A similarly strange visual effect is termed 'cinematographic vision', whereby the migraine sufferer loses all perception of motion. The subject does not see a moving object but a series of rapidly flickering 'stills', similar to what would be seen when a film is run too slowly. Sacks describes one woman in a hospital ward who had started to run water into a tub for a bath. She stepped up to the tub when the water had risen to an inch deep and then stood there, transfixed by the spigot, while the tub filled to overflowing with water running on to the floor. Sacks came upon her and touched her and she suddenly saw the overflow. She told him later that the image in her mind was of the water running from the tap into the inch of water and that no further visual change had occurred until he had touched her.

In his later book, *The Island of the Colorblind*, Sacks himself experienced cinematographic vision following the drinking of *sakau*, a popular intoxicant in Micronesia:

> Ghost petals ray out from a flower on our table, like a halo
> around it; when it is moved, I observe, it leaves a slight
> train, a visual smear, reddish, in its wake. Watching a palm
> waving, I see a succession of stills, like a film run too slow,
> its continuity no longer maintained.[5]

In my last book, *Is There Life After Death?: The Extraordinary Science of What Happens When We Die*, I suggest that reality as perceived by a conscious being may be an inwardly-generated illusion, a three-dimensional projection of past-life memories running past conscious awareness like a Super SenSurround motion picture. I call this projection 'The Bohmian IMAX'. The nature of this recording is holographic but the principle of motion pictures still applies. As with all recordings it can be slowed down, fast-forwarded, focused in and out and stopped altogether. In my opinion this is why migraine-sufferers (and as we shall see later, individuals who experience temporal lobe epilepsy and schizophrenia) perceive 'reality' as they do.

In a particularly revealing section Sacks describes how a migraine can lead the subject to question the solidity of reality itself. He writes:

> *Finally, the perceptual world, in such states, seems to run completely amok, everything moving and alive, in a state of gross distortion and perturbation. There may be a sense of winds and waves and eddies and swirls, of space itself – normally neutral, grainless, immobile and invisible – becoming a violent, intrusive, distortive field.*[6]

What is clear is that the migraine aura is related in some way to the structure of the brain, particularly to the role in brain functions of chemicals known as neurotransmitters. I suggest that these chemicals facilitate a widening of sensory perception which gives the experiencer a glimpse of the real nature of reality as suggested by David Bohm and Karl Pribram. A classic migraine aura gives a glimpse of the holographic nature of reality.

Migraine, and as we shall soon see, epilepsy and schizophrenia are the price that some of us have to pay for having the most amazing object in the universe sitting a few inches behind our eyes. Like all complex systems the more elaborate they are the more chances there are for small things to go wrong. In the case of the brain the potentially problematic process is that of the transfer of messages across its vast network of cells.

If the Bohmian IMAX is a recording then the cocktail of neurotransmitters that allows the migraine-sufferer the upgraded ticket should also allow access to other facilities denied to the rest of humanity. As I said earlier, the analogy of a digital recording can be applied to my Bohmian IMAX and as such the recording can be manipulated in many ways. It can be put into fast-forward or fast-reverse; it can be freeze-framed or skipped. For example, an observer could 'zoom out' and see a few frames into the 'future' – a future that already exists in the recording but is yet to be experienced by the observer.

In his novel *Minority Report*, Philip K. Dick (lots more about him later) describes a group of individuals called 'precogs'. These mutated human beings have the ability to see the short-term future. It is as if they can focus out of reality and look down at it from a vantage point where they can see further. In one section of the book, used to great effect in the film version starring Tom Cruise, a precog protects the hero by advising him exactly where to stand so as to be always out of his pursuer's line of vision. This is very short-term precognition – a knowledge of what is just about to happen. Clearly, if I could show that this happens to migraine sufferers then the evidence for my Bohmian IMAX would be strengthened. Well, I consider that there is strong evidence that this is indeed the case. The proof is popularly called *déjà vu*.

In 1907 the neurologist Sir W.R. Gowers wrote the following:

The subject . . . was a man, an officer in the army, aged 20. The seizures were not frequent; they had occurred about once in six months for twelve years, ever since he was 8 years old. Earlier in the day he had been in especially good mood – an antecedent often noted. Quite suddenly, a dreamy state came on, a reminiscent state, the well-known feeling that whatever

was happening had happened before. It was not momentary,
as in epilepsy, but continued . . . His own sensation was that
he was dying, passing out of physical existence.[7]

Déjà vu is the most common anomalous psychological state and is experienced across the world. In recent years the Seattle-based psychiatrist Vernon Neppe has attempted a series of definitions of the phenomenon in an attempt to isolate exactly what we mean when we describe a *déjà vu* sensation:

Any subjectively inappropriate impression of familiarity of the
present with an undefined past.

This has now become the accepted definition as used by specialists in the fields of neurology and psychiatry. Many of the *déjà vu* experiences reported by Sacks' patients fit into this definition. An example is the following:

It was a late summer afternoon, and I was winding along a
country road on my motorbike. An extraordinary sense of
stillness came upon me, a feeling that I had lived this
moment before in the same place – although I had never
travelled on this road before. I felt that this summer
afternoon had always existed, and that I was arrested in
an endless moment.[8]

This is a classic *déjà vu* experience and it includes one of the most interesting elements of the phenomenon; a sensation that seems to imply that a curtain has been drawn back – or a door opened – to present a glimpse of the world beyond the five senses. This is usually accompanied by a feeling of the ineffable. It is a sensation I can very much relate to and one that I have experienced many times, not only as a forewarning of a migraine attack but also as a stand-alone experience.

However, Sacks reports other experiences that imply an even more expanded level of awareness. Here is one example:

> *There is a greater depth and speed and acuity of thought. I keep recalling things long forgotten; visions of early years will spring to my mind.*[9]

This is clearly more than just a simple *déjà vu* sensation. Here we have the patient reporting that unbidden memories are spontaneously appearing within everyday conscious awareness. Indeed, one of Sacks' classic migraine patients reported a very peculiar event that implies that access was been given to records, memories, or engrams buried deep in the subconscious – or superconscious.

And then there are the experiences that challenge our long-held beliefs that reality is both solid and somehow a permanent feature of 'out there'.

> *A very strange thing happened. Shortly after my vision came back. First I couldn't think where I was, and then suddenly realized that I was back in California . . . it was a hot summer day. I saw my wife on the veranda, and I called her to bring me a coke. She turned to me with an odd look on her face and said, 'Are you sick or something?' I suddenly seemed to wake up, and realized it was a winter's day in New York, that there was no veranda, and that it was not my wife but my secretary who was standing in the office looking strangely at me.*

It is reasonable to conclude that migraine is an illness that can be very mild in its effects or very debilitating. I suggest that 'common' migraine without an aura is at one end of a continuum with 'classic' migraine sitting somewhere in the middle. However, the last two quotations from Sacks imply that there is yet another level of intensity that sits at the far end. At its furthest extreme I would place the case of Arthur Crew Inman.

Inman was an eccentric and very rich Bostonian who suffered some form of breakdown when he was 21. He found that he suddenly became hyper-aware of all his sensory inputs. In 1916 the sensory overload become so overpowering that he retired to a darkened, soundproof suite of apartments. He never ventured out of these rooms for the rest of his life. During his self-imposed exile of 47 years he completed a 17-million-word diary.[10] In 1949 he attempted an analogy of how he perceived the world. He wrote:

> *I live in a box where the camera shutter is out of order and*
> *the filter doesn't work and the film is oversensitive,*
> *and whatever that is beautiful or lovely registers painfully*
> *or askew.*[11]

And:

> *The simplest factors of existence, sunlight and sound, uneven*
> *surfaces, moderate distances, transgress my ineffective barriers*
> *and raid the very inner keep of my broken fortifications so*
> *that there exists no sanctuary or fastness to which I can*
> *withdraw my sensitivity, neither awake or asleep.*

It is interesting to note that at the time it was thought that Inman suffered from a severe form of migraine. Only in recent years has it been thought that the culprit was the next section of my continuum, temporal lobe epilepsy or TLE. In a sad coda to a sad life Inman committed suicide in 1963 when the soundproofing of his rooms could not protect him from the noise of the building of Boston's first skyscraper.

Migraine leaves Blake's 'door' slightly ajar. However, in order to glimpse a sight of the Pleorama in all its dreadful glory the door through the Bohmian IMAX needs to be opened halfway, as the unfortunate Arthur Crew Inman did, by entering the world of the temporal lobe epileptic.

Riders on the storm

The young man was keen to explain to the neurologist exactly what had been happening to him. He described how his first seizure had made everything clear to him and that he had received a rapturous sensation of oneness with the Supreme Being, God or the Creator. His frustration on failing to explain the feelings that welled up inside him was clear. He said:

> Well, it's not easy doctor. It's like trying to explain the
> rapture of sex to a child who has not yet reached puberty.
> Does that make any sense to you?

The next day Paul returned to the laboratory office carrying a huge bound manuscript. He explained to a startled neurologist that this was a project that he had been working on for several months. He explained that within its green bindings the document contained his views on philosophy, mysticism and religion. During this meeting Paul was to add a few comments about his strange memory flashbacks. He explained:

> The other day, during a seizure, I could remember every little
> detail from a book I read many years ago. Line after line,
> page after page, word for word.

The above example is taken from a fascinating book called *Phantoms in the Brain*. Written by Anglo-Indian neuroscientist Dr V.S. Ramachandran, it describes his encounter with a 35-year-old temporal lobe epileptic by the name of Paul. Paul was of particular interest to Ramachandran because he had been diagnosed with the next stage of my scale of transcendentalism: temporal lobe epilepsy.

> 'Consciousness is much more of the implicate order than is
> matter . . . Yet at a deeper level [matter and consciousness]
> are actually inseparable and interwoven, just as in the
> computer game the player and the screen are united by
> participation in common loops. In this view, mind and matter
> are two aspects of one whole and no more separable than
> are form and content.'
>
> DAVID BOHM (THEORETICAL PHYSICIST)

The word 'epilepsy' is Greek in origin and has its root in the verb *epilambanein*, which means 'to seize' or 'to attack'. This is of great interest because even at this stage it was recognized that epilepsy in some way involved another entity in the mind of the sufferer. A 'seizure' in its literal sense involves an attack by, or being taken over by, another. In this way captives are 'seized' by an enemy or a city is seized when it falls into the hands of hostile forces. In the same way, epilepsy involves the body and mind being seized by another. This other was readily identified as a disincarnate spirit or demon. The person became 'possessed'.

So what exactly are the physiological causes of epilepsy? Earlier I discussed the structure of the brain with specific reference to brain cells, or neurons. Most of the time these cells communicate easily with each other, but on occasion the brain can become over-excited. This can be caused by damage to the brain or an inherited genetic tendency to excitability. Whatever the cause it can lead to certain areas of the brain going out of control and all the neurons firing together. This can then spread to the surrounding areas causing an electrical storm in the brain. This usually lasts only a short time, but during this period the person may lose consciousness.

Epileptic seizures can be divided into two types: 'generalized' and 'partial'. It is the partial seizures that we are particularly interested in, but it is useful to explain briefly what occurs during a generalized seizure. As the name implies these arise over wide areas of the brain and affect both sides of the body. The effect is immediate and total.

The most common form of generalized seizure is termed 'tonic-clonic'. This used to be termed *grand mal* and is the classic seizure that most people associate with epilepsy. This involves the person losing consciousness and falling to the ground. In this first or 'tonic' phase the muscles of the body contract, the mouth clenches tight and the whole body goes stiff. The seizure may end at this point or it may move on to a second or 'clonic' phase. Here, all the muscles of the body jerk in unison, starting at the rate of one a second and slowing down to one every four to six seconds.

A second form of generalized seizure was termed *petit mal*, but this term has been replaced by the more descriptive term of 'absence' seizure. During an absence the person, usually a child, seems to become blank and will stare vacantly into space. These periods can last from a few seconds to half a minute. There may be slight jerking of the limbs, but because this is a generalized seizure affecting the whole brain these will be seen on both sides of the body. The curious thing to an observer is that when the attack is over the child will continue doing whatever had their attention before the attack. The child will not recollect anything that occurred during the 'absence'. This form of seizure usually ceases by adulthood.

However, there is a form of epilepsy that involves not an absence of consciousness but a total change of consciousness. The electrical storm in this type is highly localized to a specific area of the brain. For this reason the neurologists term it 'focal'. These in turn can be classified as 'simple' or 'complex'.

It is important to recall that the brain is highly compartment-alized. Different areas are responsible for different physical or mental processes. When the abnormal firing occurs in one particular area, the right or left frontal lobe for example, specific physical effects can be observed. In this example, spasmodic jerking will start from one area of the body, for example the right thumb, and then spread across the whole of the right side of the body (if the focus of the attack is the left frontal lobe). These effects will be different depending upon the location. When a seizure starts in the area responsible for vision, the occipital lobe at the back of the brain, a person will experience abnormal vision, which can be in the form of flashing lights, balls of light or complicated colour patterns. Again, the area of the visual field that is affected will depend upon whether the source is the right or the left occipital lobe.

Seizures emanating from the occipital, frontal and parietal lobes of the brain have purely physical symptoms: twitching of the limbs, disruption in the visual field or sensations of tingling or warmth in specific areas of the body. However, there is an area of the brain in which partial seizures have a much more profound effect upon the subject. These areas are the limbic system and the mysterious temporal lobes.

As I described earlier, each hemisphere of the brain has its own series of small structures that sit underneath the respective cortex. These organs – the hippocampus, amygdala, septum, thalamus, fornix, cingulate gyrus and reticular formation – are believed to be the location of man's basic instincts. It is this part of the brain that governs automatic responses such as fear, anger, parenting behaviour and aggression. It is also the seat of deep-rooted emotional reactions such as tears and laughter. This does not mean that it is 'primitive' in the accepted sense of the term because some of man's most noble attributes such as love and the creative process may also be rooted here. It is important to recognize that this area is unconscious and acts without the will and control of the conscious mind.

However, the reticular formation, found within the limbic system, is also believed to be the part of the brain that is responsible for the general state of awareness and is involved in the brain as a whole or within some specific areas of the brain. Some neurophysiologists have, in an apparent contradiction, argued that this could be the seat of consciousness. It is reasonably argued that if this area is damaged then unconsciousness will result. When the brain is awake the reticular formation is active. However, a major point is that during sleep the RF ceases its activity and remains so during dreaming and as such cannot be involved in this crucial activity. Whatever else, this shows that neurologists have still got a great deal to learn about these curious and little-known areas of the brain.

We now turn our attention to the most interesting area of the cortex, the temporal lobes. These sit just behind each ear and seem to be a very common source of focal epileptic seizures. Unlike the frontal, parietal and occipital lobes, which have single clearly-defined functions in terms of moving, feeling or seeing, the temporal lobe has many functions. Therefore, when seizures arise in this part of the brain, the experience is varied and powerful.

What makes temporal lobe epilepsy so interesting is that many neurologists consider that this area of the brain is involved with the storage of memories in some basic way. This is not to say that memories are actually located within the temporal lobes but simply that they act as a librarian does in a library. They do not have the books with them but they know exactly where to find them when asked to. We have seen that researchers such as Lashley and Pribram have evidence that memory is stored within the brain as a hologram stores an image. That is to say, that memories are everywhere and nowhere. As such it is believed that the temporal lobes work closely with a particular structure within the nearby limbic system, the amygdala.

The amygdala is a strange and interesting structure. In 1969 the Yale University neurosurgeon José Delgado reported that he had stimulated the exposed amygdala of conscious subjects and discovered that he could engender an immediate *déjà vu* sensation. From this he concluded that the amygdala was somehow directly responsible for the processing of short-term memory. It is therefore no surprise to discover that when a partial seizure moves from one part of the brain to another – and becomes what is termed a 'complex partial seizure' – the most dramatic effects are seen when the storm moves from the temporal lobes into the limbic system, specifically the amygdala.

This transfer is used to explain the frequency of *déjà vu* sensations in those individuals who suffer from temporal lobe epilepsy. It is also reasonable to conclude that the electrical disturbance can also stimulate long-dormant instincts within the limbic system. These sensations are nearly identical to those reported by migraine-sufferers. Indeed, the term 'aura' is again used to describe this neurological early warning system.

However, in most cases the level of intensity of the aura seems to be greater in relation to epilepsy than migraine. One major difference seems to be the psychological impact of the sensation. In many cases the epileptic feels an intense feeling of ecstasy.

The word 'ecstatic' is from the Greek *ekstasis* and means 'standing outside oneself'. What is taking place to these prophets is a sensation and an experience that is so out of the ordinary that the feelings cannot be conveyed. This is clearly described by the Russian epileptic Fyodor Dostoevsky in the following extract from his novel, *The Idiot*.

> *That in his epileptic condition there was one phase before the attack itself (provided the attack came in waking hours) when suddenly in the midst of sadness, mental darkness, oppression, his brain momentarily was as if set on fire, and all his vital forces strained themselves at once, in an unusual outburst. His consciousness and feeling of being alive became almost tenfold during these moments, which repeated themselves like lightning.*

This is Dostoevsky struggling to explain a glimpse of the Pleorama. Those who suffer from temporal lobe epilepsy report that they perceive reality in a totally different way to the non-epileptic population. Indeed, so unusual are these perceptions that epileptics are continually frustrated at the inadequacy of language. Some report transcendence and a perceiving of the infinite. Others say that within the aura they find God. Evidently, something very peculiar is taking place. Could it be that like schizophrenics epileptics can also access the world of the Daemon? Let us review the evidence.

If you accept my 'Daemon Hypothesis' you will accept that we all have two aspects to our 'self'. The everyday self, or Eidolon, lives within time and perceives a limited amount of what we term 'reality'. The other aspect of the self, the Daemon, exists outside time and knows not only what has happened but also what will happen. As such any accidental access to this being's perceptions will involve heightened sensory awareness and an ability to foresee the future.

Since records began it has been believed that epileptics have the gift of second sight. An example of this is found in the works of the Arab author Ali b'Rabban at-Tabari. Writing in the 9th century CE he discusses the illness known as *sar'un* or 'the falling sickness'.

> *The people call it the diviner's disease because some of them prophesy and have visions of wondrous things.*[12]

Indeed, those that could foretell the future, the *kāhan*, were thought to be possessed by the *djinn*, demons that caused madness and epilepsy. As such it was believed that another entity took them over during the epileptic attack and that entity was the one responsible for the prognostications. Here we have evidence of all our suspicions regarding the duality of human consciousness. In the first place we see the link between possession and epilepsy. We then have the belief that the victim is taken over by another entity, a *djinn* or demon, and then we have a perceived link between madness (schizophrenia?) and epilepsy. In addition at-Tabari writes that these *kāhani* also had 'visions of wondrous things'. In our modern terminology we would describe this as expanded or higher consciousness.

However, there is another factor that is known by neurologists to be inextricably tied to epilepsy and that factor has profound echoes of the falling out of time experienced by schizophrenics. As we have already seen the factor in question is *déjà vu*.

As we have seen, *déjà vu* is the most common psychic phenomenon on record.[13] However, it is so common among epileptics, particularly as part of the pre-seizure aura, that it is considered to be one of the classic symptoms. There have been various attempts to explain this experience but none have really succeeded. The reason for this failure is obvious in that *déjà vu* is exactly what those that experience it claim it to be: a reliving of an event brought about by a hiccup in temporal perception. But why do epileptics, particularly temporal lobe epileptics, experience *déjà vu* with such regularity? Again the solution lies in brain chemistry. In the same way that the perceptions of schizophrenics are heightened by the release of dopamine into the brain so it is that a similar neurotransmitter produces the identical effect in TLE sufferers: it gives accidental access to the perceptions of the Daemon.

A seizure in either of the temporal lobes is caused by a neurotransmitter known as glutamate. Under normal circumstances glutamate is the main neurotransmitter within the temporal lobes, in particular the hippocampus. When a message is transferred from synapse to synapse it is this chemical that brings about the transfer. Usually this is a harmless process. However, in large amounts, glutamate can over-excite the synapses and cause a massive increase in electrical activity. Once started this rapidly gets out of control and a seizure takes place. However, there is a short period of time when the excess glutamate stimulates neuronal activity without loss of consciousness. This period is perceived as the pre-seizure aura by the affected person. It is this

> *'It gradually unfolds and develops itself; you feel a slight*
> *electric shock strike your head and at the same time seize you*
> *at the heart; that is the moment of genius.'*
>
> GEORGE LOUIS DE BUFFON (MATHEMATICIAN AND EPILEPTIC)

increased activity, while still allowing consciousness, which brings about the Eidolon's access to the world of the Daemon. Thus in the same way that dopamine allows the schizophrenic to open the door so it is with glutamate.

During this flood there can be an immediate loss of temporal awareness. For a few seconds the Eidolon glimpses reality as it really is and that time is an illusion. For that period the Eidolon's 'specious present', as the psychologist William James termed it, becomes longer. In its confusion, the everyday consciousness thinks that it is seeing a re-run of the previous few seconds of perception. This is not the case. What has happened is that the glutamate flood has temporarily nullified the usually effective censorship of real perception. This is perceived as a *déjà vu* experience. Within a few seconds the processes of censorship regain control and either the seizure begins or normal perceptions are regained. During this 'time' epileptics sense that they are not alone.

But there is one massive question that is yet to be addressed. Every human being has two temporal lobes and as such all of us should, under the right circumstances, feel the presence of the Daemon. In order for my case to have any credibility I have to present evidence that this is the case. And evidence there is and it is known as the Visitor Experience.

Persinger's 'visitor experience'

In my first book I discuss in some detail the work of Wilder Penfield. Like Penfield, Dr Michael Persinger is an American citizen working at a Canadian university and, like Penfield, Persinger has made some amazing discoveries about the transcendental nature of the temporal lobes. It was in the early 1990s that neuro-psychologist Persinger became interested in the origin of UFO sightings, alien abductions and demonic possession. In his laboratory in the Laurentian University in Sudbury, Ontario Persinger designed a way of unlocking the secrets of the temporal lobes without the invasive surgery employed by Penfield. He rigged up a motorcycle helmet with electromagnets!

The helmet directed electromagnetic energy to specific parts of the brain. The subject was blindfolded and the helmet was placed on his head. The solenoids were activated and the energy stimulated specific areas of the brain. Persinger was pleased to discover that he could reproduce many of the psychic states experienced by Penfield's patients of 50 years earlier. These included out-of-body experiences, mood swings and the evocation of long-dormant memories. However, there was something new. Dr Persinger's subjects often have spiritual and religious reactions triggered by the energy fields. In addition, the subjects also encountered a presence that Persinger was subsequently to call 'The Visitor'. By increasing the energy levels Persinger found that he could increase the intensity of the experience. For subjects of a religious nature this 'presence' was God. To others it was a being of great power and awareness.

Interestingly neurologists think that these experiences are correlated with the mesiobasal portions of the temporal lobes – the amygdala and the hippocampus. It is believed that these curious structures are responsible for our sense of self and its relationship to space-time. This can bring about a sensation of spinning, floating and, interestingly, non-invoked memory recall. A clue that these sensations come from the temporal lobes is the perception of flickering in the edges of the visual field. This is because the temporal lobes receive visual information from exactly this location.

As an aside, this peculiarity of the visual field has led to some fascinating work by Dr Fredric Schiffer of the Harvard Medical School. Schiffer had noted that Marcel Kinsbourne at Tufts University had found that when asked to perform a verbal memory task (considered to be a left-brain task) the subjects returned better scores if they gazed to the right. Kinsbourne came to the conclusion that looking to the right fed visual data into the left hemisphere. This little-known experiment has been repeated many times since it was first designed in 1973 and its results have been confirmed time and time again.[14] For example, it has been shown that you have more chance of convincing somebody of your argument if you stand to their left (thus activating the right brain) than vice versa.[15] Schiffer noted this and designed a pair of safety glasses with tape covering both lenses with the exception of the extreme right-hand section of the right lens. He then began using these glasses during his therapy sessions. As he had hoped, he was able to stimulate the non-dominant hemisphere. In his fascinating book, *Of Two Minds*, he describes his results in detail. Suffice it to say that his work very much supports the overall proposition of this book.

As regards Persinger's work, there is strong evidence of a continuum of susceptibility (the technical term is 'lability'). People who display complex partial epilepsy (without convulsions) occupy the extreme portion of this continuum.[16] In other words the sensation is more likely to be evoked in those who experience temporal lobe epilepsy without any subsequent tonic-clonic incident. What is very exciting is that various studies have now shown that 'normal' people who show greater temporal lobe alpha activity than the average also experience similar effects to those with TLE.[17,18] As an aside the term 'normal' is here defined by the Minnesota Multiphasic Personality Inventory psychometric profile and, as such, has no pejorative connotations.

Persinger considers that such phenomena as alien abductions, kundalini experiences and channelling may all be brought about by this psychological state, a state he now terms 'the visitor experience'. He specifically references Whitley Strieber's *Communion*, a classic UFO abduction report; *Agartha*, by Meredith Young, a biography of a channeller, which tells of an 'other-dimensional' presence; and Gopi Krishna's *Kundalini*, a description of the emergence of a mystical energy. In all of these accounts, the experiences were associated with the predominant metaphor of the sense of a presence, swirling or vortical sensations, internal vibrations, floating sensations, alterations in perception (seeing auras and glowing outlines around the edges of objects), psi (parapsychological) phenomena and a profound sense of meaningfulness.

Clearly, this feeling is so strong that it could be interpreted as a religious experience. Indeed, many temporal lobe epilepsy patients describe very strong sensations of feeling that they are in the presence of God or the gods. In many cases this sensation of the presence of another intelligence within the brain has led the subject to believe that they are in some way a dual being.

It has been long recognized that epileptics seem to see the world in a totally different way from the rest of the population. In 1875 the German psychologist Samt reported that some of his epileptic patients not only believed that they were already in heaven but that they were surrounded by divine beings. In some cases the patients even confused these divine beings with the physicians that were treating them. Samt termed this curious psychological state 'god nomenclature'.[19]

An allied phenomenon was noted by Harvard-based neurologist Norman Geschwind. For over 20 years, from the early 1950s onwards, Geschwind had been treating people with a variety of neurological problems. During this period he had noted that sufferers of TLE share a tendency to write or draw vast amounts of material of a religious or philosophical nature. He termed this tendency 'hypergraphia' and he postulated that this was brought about by the abnormal stimulation of the temporal lobes by epileptic scar tissue. He believed that the normal functions of emotion and memory in the temporal lobes were being heightened by this stimulation. He found that some patients wrote huge amounts in journals, diaries and general notes. They seemed preoccupied with spiritual matters and had a compulsive desire to record the minutiae of their lives.

However, what he, together with his associate Stephen Waxman, discovered was that a good deal of this religious and mystical interest was generated by the belief of the TLE patients that they were being controlled 'from outside'. They felt that one or more beings were responsible for their thoughts and actions. Some thought that the beings were God, others saw them as creatures from outer space. For Geschwind the problem that these patients had was that they had 'hyperconnectivity' or too many and too rapid connections in the emotional parts of the brain. In this way they saw emotional significance in everything they perceived and experienced. In many subjects this was manifested in hyper-religiosity. On Geschwind's death in 1984 these personality traits were termed 'Geschwind's Syndrome' in his honour.

This feeling of a god-like presence is technically termed 'numinousity'. Again I refer to how Dostoevsky described this sensation:

> I felt that heaven descended to earth and swallowed me.
> I really attained God and was imbued with him. All of you
> healthy people don't even suspect what happiness is,
> that happiness that we epileptics experience for a second
> before an attack.

These words are very similar to those of Ramachandran's patient Paul, discussed at the start of this chapter. Indeed, it is fair to assume from this that Dostoevsky, like Paul, also had Geschwind's Syndrome.

Another potential Geschwind subject was the Welsh author

Margiad Evans. She was diagnosed with epilepsy in her late thirties. As a writer she described in great detail how her epilepsy affected her awareness of both internal and external reality. Her book *A Ray of Darkness* is a harrowing but essential read for those who wish to appreciate exactly what happens to consciousness when Huxley's 'Doors' are half opened by 'the Falling Sickness'. She describes one particular experience in this way:

> *I had experiences like 'yogiism' . . . Once I saw an aura of*
> *a dog . . . I had visions of unity. Time has come to mean*
> *nothing to me. I slip out of its meshes like a sardine*
> *through a herring net. I had the feeling that I was split*
> *into two or more entities.*

Here we have all the classic signs of an epileptic aura: hyper-awareness, a falling out of time and the sensation of being two people in one body.

This perception of the splitting of personality becomes even more pronounced when the doors are fully opened. When this happens the subject becomes aware of the real nature of reality in all its horrific glory. They see past the façade and perceive reality as it really is. This state, where the 'Doors of Perception' are flung open, is not the wonderful state of awareness suggested by William Blake but the dark and terrifying world of the schizophrenic.

Shaman's blues

Schizophrenia as an illness is a symptom rather than a cause. Schizophrenics themselves tell of an overload of sensory detail that brings about the insanity. It is being aware of too much and not having the psychological strength to deal with what is being presented that causes madness. In my opinion this is because these individuals, through the chemical release in the brain, accidentally access the sensory inputs of their Daemon. In most cases migraine and TLE bring about perceptions of the Bohmian IMAX. As such the subject is probably emotionally capable of accepting, if not understanding, the nature of what they perceive. A slowing down of time perception, a glimpse of the future or a feeling of a sensed presence, are disturbing of course but they are as nothing to that sometimes experienced by the schizophrenic. The cocktail of neurotransmitters dissolves the Bohmian IMAX altogether and presents to the unprepared schizophrenic Eidolon the Pleorama in all its terrifying intensity.

For example Australian physicist Raynor Johnson discovered that his awareness of the world around him was changing. He found that he was becoming hypersensitive to all his sensory inputs. He wrote this wonderfully evocative image of how his mind was changing.

> We are each rather like a prisoner in a round tower
> permitted to look out through five slits in the wall at the
> landscape outside. It is presumptuous to suppose that we can
> perceive the whole of the landscape through these slits –
> although I think there is good evidence that the prisoner can
> sometimes have a glimpse out the top![20]

The 'glimpse out the top' is brought about – forgive the laboured analogy – by the opening wide of one of Blake's 'Doors of Perception'. This time it is the trapdoor in the roof of the round tower. The subject can climb out and stand on the roof and see, for the first time, the swirls and eddies of the Pleorama. The key that fits the lock is called schizophrenia.

This phenomenon of heightened awareness can, in certain cases, drive the person involved to insanity and worse. Indeed, some neurologists are of the opinion that many schizophrenics are really TLE sufferers who simply cannot handle the way in which their senses become overpowering. Psychiatrist John Kuehnle argues that in many cases TLE is misdiagnosed as schizophrenia. He writes:

Fifteen to twenty per cent of so-called schizophrenics, including
many of the 'chronic residual schizophrenics' on the back
wards of state hospitals who don't respond to traditional
treatments for psychoses, are actually temporal lobe epileptics.[21]

The similarities are so great that psychiatrist David Bear suggests that certain forms of extreme TLE should be termed 'schizophreniform'. Bear is of the opinion that many artists and writers that show signs of insanity are in reality suffering an extreme version of TLE.

Earlier I introduced the hyperreligiosity and mystical nature of Geschwind's Syndrome. If schizophrenia is but another step along a continuum of transcendental experience from TLE then there should be strong supportive evidence that schizophrenics experience an even more extreme form of religiosity. The research does seem to support this position.

In 1981 R. W. Hood and R. J. Morris designed the Mystical Experience Questionnaire. In 1987 researcher Michael Siglag administered the Hood and Morris questionnaire to 75 schizophrenic adult inpatients. He found that 52 per cent of the schizophrenic respondents reported having a mystical experience.[22] This is a far higher figure than the results of a series of surveys conducted by Raymond Prince on a general population. His results had between 20 and 40 per cent answering 'Yes' to having experienced a mystical event.[23] Of course it is highly possible that many of those positive respondees could have been TLE patients, schizophrenics or migraine-sufferers.

The symptoms of schizophrenia are quite specific. The patient feels that he is no longer in control of his thoughts. In many cases he will hear voices that tell him what to do and, in the acute stage, he will have massively detailed and subjectively consistent hallucinations and delusions.

What is curious about schizophrenia is that unlike other forms of mental illness its symptoms are the same throughout the world and across cultures. It remains consistent across social class and remains unchanged during periods of high sociological stress, such as in times of war or natural catastrophe.

So what is the history of this strange 'illness'?

In the last years of the 19th century German psychiatrist Emil Kraepelin attempted to classify the various forms of 'insanity' into two major disorders of the mind. He termed one group manic-depressive insanity and the other 'dementia praecox'. The major difference between these two varieties was that whereas the former was episodic in that it manifested itself at various times during the patient's lifetime, with each episode resulting in complete recovery, the latter followed an inexorable downward course with no real recovery. This variation usually started in adolescence or early adulthood, hence Kraepelin's choice of terminology. In 1911, the Swiss psychiatrist Eugen Bleuler expanded Kraepelin's definition and termed this new typology 'schizophrenia' – literally 'split mind'. By this, Bleuler meant that the patient experienced a 'splitting' or loss of co-ordination between different psychic functions, particularly the intellectual and the emotional aspects of the personality.

So is it any wonder that schizophrenics behave so strangely? They are adrift in a sensory world that is beyond understanding. Within this world they can also sense the presence of another within their mind. They know that the Daemon exists and this adds to their seeming insanity. However, within this confusion lies another clue to the real reason for our existence in this world: the inescapable fact that schizophrenics, in accessing the world of this other entity, also slip out of time. Bleuler made the following comment in his book *Dementia Praecox*:

> *Perceptions can also be transposed into voices without the*
> *patient being at all aware of it. In that event the voices*
> *become prophetic; a patient hears, 'Now someone is coming*
> *down the hall with a bucket of water'; then the door opens*
> *and the prophecy is fulfilled.*[24]

Here we have not only a direct verbal communication from a Daemon to a schizophrenic Eidolon but also evidence that for the Daemon temporal flow has no meaning. It knows with certainty what is about to happen next.

This 'slipping out of time', of knowing what is about to happen next, of perceiving the future as a memory of the past, is clearly related to *déjà vu*. The following episode is an example of this:

> *A chronic schizophrenic woman who had an exacerbation of her illness seemed to have lengthy episodes of* déjà vu, *which she used in a psychotic way to indicate she knew everything that was going to happen next. For example, she began an interview by stating, 'I know all about this. I've been through this same thing many times before. I know what is going to happen.' She continued by describing the situation in minute detail to prove her foreknowledge.*[25]

Could this be an alternative explanation for the Fangio incident I discussed earlier? Could it be that for the Daemon the future has in some way already been experienced? This would certainly explain how it seems that the Daemon can advise its Eidolon as to what is the correct course of action in a particular circumstance.

What is even more curious, and this comes as a surprise to many laymen, is that even now, nearly 100 years after Bleuler came up with the term, we have no real idea of what schizophrenia is, let alone what causes it.

However, one clue is that post-mortem examinations show that the number of dopamine receptors in parts of the basal ganglia of the brain is increased in chronic schizophrenia. Some recent developments in pharmaceutical research have shown that drugs such as phetamine and levodopa may worsen the symptoms of schizophrenia. This is because these drugs increase the release in the brain of 'dopamine' and this neurotransmitter has been found in abnormal quantities in the amygdala of schizophrenics. What is of direct relevance to my overall theory is that the amygdala is a small structure found buried deep in the temporal lobes and as such supports the conclusion that temporal lobe epilepsy and schizophrenia are related.

I would like to suggest that dopamine somehow facilitates access to areas of consciousness not normally available to everyday consciousness. An Eidolon perceiving this 'broadband' of information will simply not have the psychic framework to process such an assault on the senses. This assumption seems to be confirmed by the ways in which schizophrenics describe their perception of the outer world. For example the schizophrenic writer Norma McDonald describes it in this way:

> Each of us is capable of coping with a large number of
> stimuli, invading our being through any one of the senses.
> We could hear every sound within earshot and see every
> object, line and colour within the field of vision, and so on.
> It's obvious that we would be incapable of carrying on any of
> our daily activities if even one-hundredth of all the available
> stimuli invaded us at once. So the mind must have a filter
> which functions without our conscious thought, sorting stimuli
> and allowing only those which are relevant to the situation in
> hand to disturb consciousness.[26]

As I have already said this could be what the Daemon sees, hears and senses as regards its environment – the Pleorama in all its glory. Reality – whatever it is that is 'out there' – is not the ordered sensible world that is presented to consciousness via our sensory inputs. It is a holographic miasma of colours, sounds and smells that swirl and buzz. For the Daemon, the holographic swirl and buzz of reality is interpreted in a different way to its Eidolon. The Daemon perceives the universe as it really is. It seems reasonable to conclude that this cocktail of neurotransmitters allows the schizophrenic Eidolon accidental access to the sensory inputs of its Daemon. But for an Eidolon to perceive such a world is to invite insanity, paranoia and hallucinogen-induced psychosis. Indeed, in a curious philological coincidence the word 'paranoia' – *para nous* in the original Greek – means 'other mind'. Could this be a semantic clue to the existence of the Daemon?

No wonder schizophrenics behave so strangely. They are adrift in a sensory world that is beyond understanding. Within this world they can also sense the presence of another within their mind. They know that the Daemon exists and this adds to their insanity. However, within this confusion lies another clue to the real reason for our existence in this world; the inescapable fact that schizophrenics, in accessing the world of this other entity, also slip out of time. As we saw earlier, the inventor of the term schizophrenia, Bleuler, described how one of his patients seemed to acquire short-term precognitive abilities. In another version of the description cited above Bleuler wrote:

> *A janitor is coming down the hall and makes a slight noise*
> *of which the patient is not conscious. But the patient hears*
> *his hallucinated voice cry out, 'Now someone is coming down*
> *the hall with a bucket of water.' The door opens and the*
> *prophecy is fulfilled.*

If we take what Bleuler reported at face value what we have is evidence, albeit extremely subjective, that schizophrenics sometimes exist in a temporal world very different from our own. Bleuler is not alone in reporting this. A loss of time perception is a recognized symptom of schizophrenia. Sufferers claim that time slows down for them, freezes and, very occasionally, speeds up. Psychiatrists assume that these reports are describing hallucinations, but to those who experience these sensations the feeling is very real. Who is to say that within the sense-universe of the schizophrenic Eidolon time really does slow down? After all, we have seen that reality itself is a very subjective thing. Just because I do not share your experience that does not mean that either viewpoint is incorrect. The American science writer Gay Gaer Luce cited experiments proving that people demonstrably change their sense of time when they are under the influence of hallucinogenic and excitatory drugs such as LSD or psilocybin. If they are asked to tap on a Morse code keyboard at a self-chosen rate and are then instructed to tap as evenly as possible, they will tap fastest at the peak of the drug state. At the time of increased tapping, they experience a 'flood of inner sensations' or time contraction. She says that under the influence of psychedelic drugs many people have felt as if months of experience were compressed into a few hours.[27]

This inner time, termed *durée* by the French philosopher Henri Bergson, may be the only real time that a human being experiences. Bergson considered that the major obstacle to realizing this simple fact is that we cannot differentiate real time from that measured by clocks. He remarks, for example:

> When I follow with my eyes on the dial of a clock the
> movement of the hands . . . I do not measure duration
> (durée) . . . Outside of me, in space, there is never more
> than a single position of the hand . . . Within myself a
> process of organization or interpenetration of conscious states
> is going on, which constitutes true duration . . .[28]

With some notable exceptions we all experience the subjective fluctuation of time perception. However, these minor fluctuations are different both in type and quality from those experienced by schizophrenics. However strange these sensations seem to us we still remain *in* time. Schizophrenics fall *out* of time. The reason for this is quite simple, if somewhat profound, in that we are describing two totally different phenomena. Psychological time is experienced by all human beings and will be seen to be of great relevance later in this pages. However, it is a normal psychological state. Schizophrenic time is not normal. As I stated above, this comes about because endogenous (internally created) chemicals such as dopamine stimulate abnormal neuronal activity in schizophrenics. These neurotransmitters allow 'illegal' access to the sensory perceptions of the entity we know as The Daemon.

Summary

The hallucinations experienced by schizophrenics, temporal lobe epileptics and classic migraine sufferers are not illusions in the general way in which that word is understood. They are very real perceptions of a reality that is usually inaccessible to the lower partner of my Daemon-Eidolon Dyad. The only difference between these three brain states is the level of exposure to the Bohmian IMAX and the Pleorama as facilitated by the neurotransmitter cocktail. Indeed, there are not three isolated states, but there is a continuum of intensity by which more and more of the Daemonic Reality is presented to Eidolonic consciousness. Because of the fairly minor and infrequent exposure experienced by migraine-sufferers and temporal lobe epileptics these individuals usually remain sane. However, for those at the schizophrenic end of the continuum the ongoing assault literally drives them to actions that seem insane to the unaware Eidolonic consciousnesses that they encounter.

However, society has always had a place for individuals that are to be found further along my scale of transcendence. Indeed, in some societies, both historical and modern, these people are recognized as being special, conduits to another reality. They hear a voice in their head, a voice that is both part of them and yet not, and they receive direct communication from beyond the Bohmian IMAX and the Cartesian Theatre. It is to those individuals I now turn my attention because within the Bohmian IMAX these individuals have a guide who knows its way round the highways and byways of this strange reality. That guide is, of course, the Daemon.

1 Huxley, Aldous, *The Doors of Perception & Heaven & Hell*, Flamingo Harper Collins (1994)

2 Broad, D.C., *Religion, Philosophy & Psychic Research*, Routledge, pp.22–3 (2000)

3 Sacks, Oliver, *Migraine*, Picador (1992)

4 Ibid., p.67

5 Sacks, Oliver, *The Island of the Colorblind*, Alfred A. Knopf, New York, p.90 (1997)

6 Sacks, O. & Siegel, R.M., 'Migraine Aura and Hallucinatory Constants' in *Migraine*, op. cit., p.278 (1992)

7 Gowers, W.R., *The Borderland of Epilepsy*, P. Blackiston (1907)

8 Sacks, Oliver, *Migraine*, Picador, p.86 (1992)

9 Ibid., p.84

10 Inman, A.C., *The Inman Dairy – A Public and Private Confession*, ed. D. Aaron, Harvard (1985)

11 LaPlante, E, *Seized*, Harper Collins, p.235 (1993)

12 Rabban at-Tabari, A., *Paradise of Wisdom*, Berlin, p.138 (1928)

13 Neppe, V., 'The incidence of déjà vu', *Parapsychological Journal of South Africa*, 4, 94–106 (1983)

    "   'The concept of déjà vu', *Parapsychological Journal of South Africa*, 4, 1–10 (1983)

    "   'The causes of déjà vu', *Parapsychological Journal of South Africa*, 4, 25–35 (1983)

14 Kinsbourne, M., 'The mechanism of hemisphere asymmetry in man' in *Hemispheric Disconnection & Cerebral Function*, Charles C. Thomas (1974)

15 Schiffer, Fredric, *Of Two Minds*, Free Press, New York, p.53 (1998)

16 Persinger, M.A. & Makarec, K., 'Temporal Lobe Signs and Correlative Behaviors Displayed by Normal Populations', *The Journal of General Psychology*, 114: 179–95 (1987)

17 Persinger, M.A. & Valliant, P.M., 'Temporal Lobe Signs and Reports of Subjective Paranormal Experiences in a Normal Population: A Replication', *PMS* 60: 903–9 (1985)

18 Persinger, M.A., 'People Who Report Religious Experiences May Also Display Enhanced Temporal-Lobe Signs', *PMS* 58: 963–75 (1984) *See also* Persinger, M.A., 'Propensity to Report Paranormal Experiences Is Correlated with Temporal Lobe Signs', *PMS* 59: 583–6 (1984)

19 Samt, P., 'Epileptische Irreseinsforman', *Archiv für Psychiatrie und Nervenkrankheiten* 5, pp.344–93 (1876)

20 Ferguson, M., *The Brain Revolution*, Taplinger, New York, p.226 (1973)

21 LaPlante, E., *Seized*, Harper Collins, p.111 (1993)

22 Siglag, Michael A., *Schizophrenic and Mystical Experiences: Similarities and Differences*, New York, NY, p.4 (1987)

23 Prince, Raymond, 'Religious Experience and Psychosis', *Journal of Altered States of Consciousness*, 5: 167–81 (1979)

24 Bleuler, Eugin, *Dementia Praecox or the group of schizophrenias*, trans. J. Zinkin, International Universities Press, New York, p.98 (1950)

25 Kirshner, L.A., 'The mechanism of déjà vu' in *Diseases Of The Nervous System*, pp.246–9, Hamilton Ford (1973)

26 McDonald, N., 'Living With Schizophrenia' in *Consciousness, Brain, States of Awareness and Mysticism*, D. Goleman & R.J. Davidson (eds), Harper Row (1979)

27 Luce, Gay Gaer, *Bodytime*, p.25, Maurice Temple Smith (1972)

28 Bergson, H., 'Time and Free Will' from *Modernist Fiction*, R. Stevenson, Prentice Hall,

CHAPTER 3

The Voices

If only I could still hear the wind in the trees, the larks in the sunshine,
The young lambs crying through the healthy frost,
And the blessed, blessed church bells that send
My angel voices floating to me on the wind.

George Bernard Shaw (from: Saint Joan)

The Counsel of Domrémy

The summer of 1425 had been typical. The weather was warm and the pastures were green and verdant. However, this was northern France and the fear of war was continually in the air. The English army was not that far away and the countryside was alive with rumour and fear. Walking across the fields was a young girl, no more than 13 years of age. But she was unusual, both for her time and her age. To her friends and family she was known for her extreme piety and her complete lack of a wish to marry. At that point the church bells of Domrémy rang out across the rolling hills of Bar. They were ringing out the noonday time. As they ended the young woman fell to her knees with a look of ecstasy flashing across her face.

The young girl in question was Jeanne d'Arc, known to the English-speaking world as Joan of Arc. What she was about to achieve in her short life was to be nothing short of astounding, but what is even more interesting is that she claimed that what she did was at the behest of a voice that spoke to her, a voice that seemed to know exactly what was going to happen in her life. This voice, known to her as her 'Counsel', shows all the aspects of the entity we know as The Daemon.

The sound of the church bells seemed to stimulate something in Joan's brain. She saw this as a flash of blinding light. As her eyes recovered she heard a voice in her right ear. Thinking it was somebody calling to her she turned towards the direction of the church. To her surprise there was nobody there. The voice was inside her. It spoke with a commanding tone and told her that it was of great importance that she behaved well and went to church. For a religious girl such as Joan this was an instruction she would be happy to follow.

Over the next few years the voice continued to talk to her. If I am correct then this being was, in fact, Joan's Daemon communicating directly with its Eidolon in the form of Joan's everyday personality. Sometimes the Daemon's voice manifested itself as male and sometimes female, but it was always consistent in its insistence that Joan kept herself chaste and prepared herself for a great calling. She followed these instructions to the letter. The idea of a dissolute life was anathema to her. Indeed, she had for many years feared that she might be whisked away because her father Jacques had once had a dream. Later Joan was to describe this dream. She said:

> My mother had told me that my father often dreamed that I
> would run away with a band of soldiers. That was more than
> two years after I first heard the voices. She told me that he
> had said to my brothers, 'If I believed that the thing I have
> dreamed about her would come to pass, I would want you to
> drown her; and if you would not, I would drown her myself.'

Clearly, she was concerned about the 'running away with soldiers' part of her father's strange dreams. As such, one can only imagine her worry when, in late 1427, Counsel implored her to go to Chinon and seek out the Dauphin, Charles. It explained that she was to liberate the kingdom of France from the invading English and drive them out of the country.

For Joan this was impossible. She spoke back to the Daemon saying that she was but a poor girl with no knowledge of war.

She could not ride and had no leadership skills of any sort. It is also reasonable to conclude that Joan might have seen this as the fulfilment of her father's dream. The voice continued to insist that this was what she had to do. At that time the Hundred Years War between France and England was at a crucial phase. The English had laid siege to the French city of Orléans and it seemed only a matter of time before this crucial strategic location fell into the hands of the invaders.

However, Counsel was so forceful that she eventually gave in. In May 1428 she left Domrémy for Vauculeurs, the nearest strong-hold still loyal to the Dauphin. Already the voices had changed the personality of this simple country girl. But despite her protest-ations the captain in charge of Vauculeurs could not take a 16-year-old girl and her visions seriously. However, in January 1429 she tried again and her piety and strength of character gained the respect of all who encountered her. She was allowed to travel on to see the Dauphin in Chinon. On 24 February she arrived at Chinon and on the 26th she was granted an audience with the young king-to-be.

Acting in a way that was typical of his subsequent dealings with the Maid, Charles lost his nerve and before she entered the room he disguised himself and hid among the many courtiers and advisers. In an act of stunning perceptual ability, aided by her hidden adviser, Joan was able to immediately identify Charles and engage him in conversation. This act convinced many in the room that this young woman had to be taken seriously, particularly when she told Charles that she intended to make war against the English and have him crowned king in Reims. That it was her voices that assisted in the identification is clearly stated by Joan herself when she said:

> And when I entered the King's chamber, I knew him among
> the rest, for the voice counselled me and revealed it to me. And
> I told the King that I would go to make war on the English.

But Counsel told her more. When she had Charles out of earshot of his courtiers she whispered to him some information that history has termed 'The Secret of the King'. What she said to him has never been disclosed, but it is suspected that she put him at rest regarding a question of his legitimacy. Whatever the disclosure the Dauphin was clearly in awe of this young woman's powers and he decided to allow her to assist him. In an amazingly accurate comment, Joan told Charles to make good use of her because her services would be available for little more than one year.

After a short return to Domrémy, Joan was soon back in Chinon and preparing for her campaign against the English. The Dauphin supplied her with a standard and a military household which she readily accepted. However, when it came to the question of a sword she insisted that she should have a special one, one that would be found hidden in the church of Sainte-Catherine-de-Fierbois. She claimed that on her way to Chinon she had called in to the church to pray and while there her voices had told her that an ancient sword lay buried behind the altar. Unknown to her a man was sent from Tours to check this out and, yet again, her voices were proved right when he returned, sword in hand. It had been found in exactly the place her voices had predicted.

Her Daemon became more and more vocal as her mission began to build up momentum. It was keen to let Joan know that she would be victorious at Orléans and that although she would sustain an arrow wound to the shoulder this would not be life-threatening. She would survive to see the Dauphin crowned as Charles VII in a ceremony in Reims Cathedral that summer.

These predictions were of such import that an officer at the court of the Dauphin quoted them to a Lyons-based Flemish diplomat called De Rotselaer. Similarly impressed, De Rotselaer jotted them down and sent them off in a letter dated 22 April 1429. This letter was subsequently delivered and its contents recorded in Brussels.

On 27 April 1429 several hundred men set out from Blois with this incredible young woman at their head. Although she claimed she could not ride a horse it was as if she had been born to the saddle. Like all the other skills needed for war, her voices had supplied the skills required. On 29 April the small force camped close to the besieged city of Orléans. The Maid had been told by her advisers that she should wait for reinforcements before considering an attack on the well-entrenched English forces.

On the evening of 4 May Joan was woken up by her Daemon. Inspired by this she decided that now was the time to attack. Something had told her exactly where to go and, sure enough, she arrived at exactly the location where a small skirmish had just started. On seeing her approach, resplendent in her unique white armour, the French forces rallied and a fort was taken from the English. She arrived just at the right moment and in doing so gave the French something they had not tasted for a long time – victory. Over the next few days Joan showed an astonishing knowledge of tactics as well as stunning bravery. The Maid fought as if she were possessed which, in a very real sense she was – possessed by an entity that knew exactly what was going to happen to its lower self.

On 7 May the French forces advanced against the fort at Les Tourelles. During this attack Joan sustained a wound to her shoulder – exactly as predicted by Counsel. Also as predicted, not only did she survive but she quickly returned to the fight and under her leadership the English capitulated.

The decisive battle was to take place on 18 June when the French and English forces faced each other at Patay. Again Joan predicted outright victory. Obviously, all military leaders make such claims before a battle, but with her previous precognitive accuracies it is reasonable to conclude that this prediction was again inspired by Counsel.

It is, therefore, not surprising that Joan's prediction that Charles would be crowned king in Reims also came to pass on 17 June 1429. However, only part of France had been liberated and Joan

> 'Philemon and other figures of my fantasies brought home to
> me the crucial insight that there are things in the psyche
> which I do not produce, but which produce themselves and
> have their own life. Philemon represented a force which was
> not myself. In my fantasies I held conversations with him, and
> he said things which I had not consciously thought. For
> I observed clearly that it was he who spoke, not I. He said I
> treated thoughts as if I generated them myself, but in his view
> thoughts were like animals in a forest, or people in a room, or
> birds in the air . . . It was he who taught me psychic
> objectivity, the reality of the psyche.'
>
> KARL GUSTAV JUNG (PSYCHIATRIST)

knew that she had much more to do. She felt that until Paris was taken victory could never be fully claimed by the French.

It is interesting that although Joan clearly had clairvoyant powers she did not respect this in others. In September 1429 she was staying with the king at Bourges when she was introduced to a local seer. This woman informed Joan that she must bring about reconciliation between the king and his major rival and supporter of the English, the Duke of Burgundy. Joan was clear in her opinion of the advice and the skills of the prophet who gave it. She said that no peace could be found except at the point of a lance and that the woman was misguided and foolish. Clearly, in her mind it was Counsel who knew best, not some misguided charlatan. Indeed, as Counsel continually reminded her, she had little more than a year to live and complete victory had to be achieved in that short time. Any delay brought about by pointless negotiations would ensure that she would not be around to see the final outcome of her work.

The Daemon regularly reminded Joan that she had only a little time left to fulfil her destiny. In April 1430 the voice made it clear that she would be captured by the enemy before Midsummer Day.

By this time war had again started between the French forces and those of the Duke of Burgundy. In late May the town of Compiègne was under siege by the Burgundians, under the leadership of John of Luxembourg. At sunrise on the 24th Joan appeared at the town in her now well-recognized white armour. By evening she had decided that her small force of 500 men should attempt a sortie against the vastly greater number of Burgundians. Her group left the safety of the town and rode out across the drawbridge to assault the enemy. Even Joan could not deal with such a mismatch in numbers and the survivors of the attack found themselves pushed back towards the walls of Compiègne. Unfortunately, by mistake – or perhaps panic on the part of her lieutenant Guillaume de Flavy, who had remained within the walls of Compiègne – the drawbridge was raised, leaving Joan and many of her surviving band trapped between the Burgundians and the town wall. They were quickly captured and taken to Margny where she was visited by the Duke of Burgundy himself.

Joan did not take well to captivity. With Counsel reminding her of time running out she tried to escape from John of Luxembourg's castle at Vermandois. John was not willing to allow his prize to escape that easily so he had her moved further away from Compiègne to another fortress tower at Beaurevoir. This was the one and only time that Joan ignored Counsel. She made another attempt at escape by jumping from the tower. Counsel was adamant that she should not do this as it would gain her nothing. She went ahead and leapt, falling straight into the moat where she was knocked unconscious. This vain attempt at escape made her captors decide that she should be taken to Arras where escape would be impossible.

This turned out to be her crucial error. Had she listened to Counsel it is possible that a more opportune moment might have subsequently presented itself and she might have escaped. Escape from Arras was, as it turned out, impossible.

It seems that her Daemon was quite upset about this

disobedience. She never questioned the advice again and the voice forgave her and told her that she should not worry about Compiègne. It said that it would be relieved 'before Martinmas' (11 November). Again this was accurate because the siege was lifted on 26 October. However, this one disobedience may have thwarted the plan of Joan's guiding entity. Henceforth, things turned out for the worst.

On 25 May the news that Joan had been captured reached Paris. Within a day the pro-English university had realized that it now had a golden opportunity to silence Joan. The university requested that the Duke of Burgundy hand her over to the Inquisition for trial on the grounds of heresy. Subsequently 10,000 francs was given to John of Luxembourg in exchange for Joan. On 3 January 1431 the deal was done and Joan was handed over to the Bishop of Beauvais.

Joan was subjected to a series of interrogations on 13 January 1431. These were to clarify exactly the terms upon which she would be subsequently tried. During this time there were some startling examples of precognition. One that stands out is that on 1 March she was asked whether her voices predicted her liberation. She answered, 'Ask me in three months and I will tell you.' Three months later, on 30 May, Joan was burned at the stake in the Place du Vieux Marché in Rouen.

As would be expected, her Daemon was fully aware of the exact date that its Eidolon was to die. It knew that no other outcome was possible at this stage. It is possible that it had known this since Joan ignored its advice at Beaurevoir.

After the interrogations the trial proper started on 25 March. There were 70 charges made against her which principally related to her pronouncements on divine revelation and prophesying the future. Clearly Joan could have denied the charges by claiming that her 'voices' did not foresee the future. Indeed, she could have simply denied their existence. This she did not do. When asked whether she had prophesied her wound by an arrow at Les

Tourelles, and her subsequent recovery, she simply answered, 'Yes'. I would argue that the Daemon knew that whatever it advised its Eidolon to do they were both doomed this time around. And that it might as well get it over with.

However, during the trial it was in regular communication with Joan. In a quote from the trial notes Joan was recorded as saying:

I heard my voice yesterday and today. Yesterday I heard it three times – once in the morning, once at vespers, and the third time when the bells were ringing for 'Hail Mary' in the evening. I was sleeping and the voice waked me. And I thanked it, sitting up in my bed, and joining my hands.

The trial continued until 24 May when the sentence was read out. She was told that she was guilty and that she would be handed over to the secular authorities for execution. In real terms this meant being burned at the stake. At this news, and for the first time, the young woman that up to this stage had been a model of courage lost her nerve. She said that she would do whatever the Church wished her to do. She was given a form of abjuration to sign which, after a slight hesitation, she signed. With this she was informed that she would be imprisoned for life.

However, by 29 May she had again found her courage. The voice had returned and told her that by agreeing to abjure and revoke her former confession in order to save her life, she had damned herself. It was as if the Daemon needed the execution to take place. It then informed her exactly what would take place on the day of her execution.

The next day, on 30 May, Joan of Arc was burned at the stake and her ashes scattered to the winds. And so died the most fascinating woman of the medieval period. What drove her to such actions and the accuracy of her predictions have remained a mystery for both theologians and psychologists. In the next chapter I will discuss in some detail the nature of mysticism and Joan will be seen to fit clearly within this typology. However, her experiences were much more intense and focused around one particular element of the mystic experience – aural hallucinations.

Could it be that Joan has presented us with yet more proof of the Daemon-Eidolon Dyad?

Voice from the D'Arc?
Possibly, but in order for this to be the case certain elements of proof have to be presented . . . Firstly, there has to be evidence that Joan was at least a sufferer of migraine, if not temporal lobe epilepsy. Secondly, it needs to be shown that the 'voices' that she experienced were, in fact, a single voice, that of her Daemon, and thirdly that this voice showed all the classic abilities of this 'hidden observer'.

As we have seen, temporal lobe epilepsy has certain symptoms that categorize this form of psychic confusion. Looking back to the chapter on mystics, a classic symptom of TLE is hyperreligiosity.

That Joan was strongly religious there is absolutely no doubt. It is also fair to conclude that her religious beliefs were excessive even for Late Medieval France. She carried her religious convictions through to a very traumatic and painful execution. But can this belief be linked to TLE? You will recall that American neurologist Norman Geschwind, together with his colleague Stephen Waxman, isolated a whole galaxy of symptoms and behaviours that implied temporal lobe epilepsy. These included a general sense of 'illumination', 'mission' and fate.

As you will also recall, Dr Michael Persinger has shown that by stimulating the temporal lobes of non-epileptic volunteers he has been able to reproduce mystical experiences in non-religious individuals. Not only that but some subjects report what Persinger terms the 'sensed presence'. Could this be what Joan perceived?

Neurologist Dr Lydia Bayne is convinced that Joan was a temporal lobe epileptic. Bayne argues that she even knows what may have triggered Joan's epilepsy. It will be recalled that the 13-year-old Joan first heard her voices after she had heard the church bells ringing out the noonday time. On hearing these sounds Joan experienced a 'flash of light' and then the voices started. For Bayne this is reasonable evidence that Joan experienced a particular form of temporal lobe focus epilepsy termed 'musicogenic'. This is a form of reflex epilepsy which manifests itself with an ecstatic aura. Sounds, particularly those that hold emotional significance for the experiencer, can trigger a tremendously powerful state of altered perception. Usually the sound is music, but to a strongly religious child like Joan the association could be church bells. Could this have been the trigger that brought about the glutamate-induced communication pathways that opened up young Joan's Eidolon to its daemonic alter-ego?[1]

Indeed, it is possible that Joan had inherited her TLE from her father. It will be recalled that he had predicted that his young daughter's life would be in danger if she 'left with the soldiers'. Clearly, he had misinterpreted this as being some form of abduction of a potentially sexual nature. What took place was far more subtle but still ended in the premature death of his child.

If TLE is the culprit then it would also explain another of the experiences Joan described – that of the flash of blinding white light immediately after she heard the church bells. In 1847 it was reported by a Chinese epileptic called Kung Tsu Chen that the sound of a street vendor's flute was enough to trigger a seizure in him. It is therefore not unreasonable to suggest that a similar trigger opened up the neural communication channels for Joan.

The 'voices' then began a regular communication with the young woman. Who then were these voices? Joan was to eventually identify them as being Michael the Archangel (mentioned in the Bible in Daniel, Jude and Revelation), Catherine of Alexandria and Margaret of Antioch. Although of great popularity in France at that time, it is generally accepted that these individuals never actually existed. As such it is reasonable to conclude that something was communicating to Joan in a way that a person of her time and religious beliefs would accept. It is recorded that on occasion Joan actually saw these saints, but she was always very vague in her descriptions. Could it be that Joan's TLE was reproducing Persinger's 'sensed presence'?

In his laboratory in Sudbury, Ontario, Persinger has been able to reproduce a physical manifestation of the 'sensed presence'. Persinger and his team have monitored their subject's brain activity while the experience is taking place. It seems that the activity starts in the temporal lobes. This brings about the feeling that something is present. However, when the activity flows across into the occipital lobes, a visual image is seen. What the subject reports is seeing a cowled figure with its face and hands visible. Is this what Joan may have seen?

That Joan heard three separate voices is well attested. However, one of the few independent sources regarding Joan's visitations is the testimony of d'Aulon, her maître d'hôtel and companion throughout her short career. He reported that the Maid said to him that she had three counsellors, but only one was with her at all times. A second occasionally came to her and the third she never spoke with directly but only indirectly through the other two. Clearly this implies that there was only really one regular 'voice'. As the one that the other two deliberated with was male, it is clear that the 'companion' was female.

Research by Karen Sullivan, the Associate Professor of literature at Bard College, suggests that Joan only began describing the 'voice' as such during the later stages of her trial.[2] In 1996, Sullivan reread the trial transcripts and all the historical material referring to Joan's voices and came to a startling conclusion: no saints were ever named prior to the trial! Sources outside the trial referring to these saints by name are all either anti-Joan and cite the trial, or they come at least 14 years after the trial when the notion of specific saints as the source of Joan's voices has become commonplace mythology. Joan, apparently, never mentioned these saints by name even to her closest relations, friends or companions in arms who testified she heard the voice of God.

> *The clerics ask Joan repeatedly for further identification of her voice. On the second day of the trial, though the transcripts do not convey the interrogator's question, they relate that 'Joan added that her interrogator would not obtain from her, at this time, under what form this voice appeared to her.' On the third day of the trial, the transcripts report that Joan is 'interrogated if the voice that she says to appear to her is an angel or if it comes from God immediately or if it is the voice of a saint.' Joan responds, 'The voice comes on the part of God, and I believe that I do not tell you perfectly all that I know, and I have greater fear of failing these voices by saying something that displeases them than I have in responding to you. And, as for this question, I ask for a delay.' For two days, therefore, the clerics press Joan for further specification of her voice, whether for the form under which the voice appeared to her or for the identity of the voice as an angel, a saint, or God Himself. For two days, Joan refuses to satisfy these demands for a greater specification, deferring her response to a later date.*
>
> *It is only on the fourth day of the trial that Joan performs the identification of her voice which the clerics have repeatedly sought. On this day, the transcripts record, '. . . interrogated if it was the voice of an angel that spoke to her, or if it was the voice of a saint or of God without intermediary, she responded that it was the voice of St Catherine and St Margaret, and their faces are crowned with beautiful crowns, very opulent and very precious.*[3]

The transcripts continue:

> *Interrogated which appeared to her first, she responded, 'I did not recognize them so quickly, and I knew well once, but have forgotten, and if I had permission I would say willingly, and it is in the register at Poitiers.' Item she also said that*

she had comfort from St Michael. Interrogated which of the aforesaid apparitions came to her first, she responded that St Michael came first. Interrogated if much time elapsed after she first had the voice of St Michael, she responded, 'I do not name to you the voice of St Michael, but I speak of a great comfort.' Interrogated which was the first voice coming to her, when she was thirteen years old or around that age, she responded that it was St Michael whom she saw before her eyes . . . 'and he was not alone.'

It is as if once Joan has been obliged to identify her voices as St Catherine, St Margaret and St Michael, the voices begin to reveal themselves to her to be these three saints and she began to perceive them as such.

If, as I have attempted to show here, Joan not only begins to name her voices as the Saints Catherine, Margaret, and Michael in the course of her interrogations but begins to experience her voices as these saints, the consequences of this development are apparent. While the clerics and the subsequent readers of these transcripts have presupposed that truth exists prior to the representation of this truth, these trial transcripts demonstrate the contrary possibility. They show the potential of an interrogation to create the very truth that it is purporting to represent. This power of interrogation to end not in the revelation of the suspect's understanding but in the transformation of the suspect's understanding so that it reflects that which the interrogators seek to reveal, can help explain the prevalence of false confessions today even in societies where the traditional causes of such confessions, such as torture, lengthy incommunicado detentions, and the deprivation of legal counsel, have been eradicated.

In other words, Joan did not know who these voices were and had assumed the messages were to be taken simply as God counselling her. Accepting the repeated suggestion that they could be angels, saints, or – less likely, perhaps? – God, she began to see them as saints living in paradise, and from that time forth, as her voices continued, began to experience them and seek out details allowing her to embellish their appearance and characteristics. Sullivan concludes:

> It is this capacity of interrogation to introduce a possibility, in
> the form of a question and to transform this possibility into
> a probability and then into a certainty, to lead a respondent
> to believe that her voices are those of three saints,
> which Joan's case demonstrates.

If Sullivan is correct, then it was only with scholastic prodding that Joan began to question what heretofore she had just accepted as simply being the voice and counsel of God. She then sought to identify her source(s) of revelation more precisely, and as she did so her voices adapted themselves, becoming in her continuing experience of revelatory voices the characters that she now expected.

If it is agreed that in actual fact Joan was guided by a single entity then could this not again be seen as evidence of the Daemon? This would certainly explain many of the mysteries surrounding the Maid. For example it is clear that the voice had very effective precognitive abilities. In addition it seemed to guide Joan along a very specific path that led to her execution. Or did it? The Daemon tried hard to talk her out of the attempted escape from the tower at Vermandois. Was this because it knew that such an action would lead to its Eidolon's early death? As I said earlier, is it possible that this act was premature and that a better opportunity to escape may have offered itself later? Clearly this is pure conjecture on my part. Indeed, a counterargument could be that Joan's ultimate purpose was to become a martyr and so be immortalized. Whatever the answer, this tragic, heroic and utterly fascinating young woman offers strong evidence for the Daemon.

Joan's case is interesting but not at all unique. There are many cases from history where a person has been driven to effective 'suicide-by-proxy' by a guiding voice. Probably the classic case of this was Socrates.

The Socratic dialogue

Socrates, together with Plato and Aristotle, is considered to be one of the founding fathers of Western philosophic thought. Unfortunately, we have no direct writings of this influential philosopher. In order to understand his life and personality, we have to use the dialogues of Plato and the *Memorabilia* of Xenophon. However, what becomes immediately evident when reading Plato's accounts is that Socrates experienced one of the earliest recorded relationships with our friend the Daemon. From his childhood onwards, he received recurrent visits from a voice that he variously called his 'divine sign', his 'spiritual sign', his 'prophetic power' and, interestingly enough, his 'daimonion'.

As his student, Plato recorded many of Socrates' teachings and beliefs in two great works. The first is known as the *Dialogues*. This consists of a series of discussions between two characters, one called Socrates and another person whose name is the title of that particular dialogue, for example *Euthydemus* or *Phaedrus*. The second is known as the *Apology*. Now, although the English word 'apology' is the direct descendant of the Greek word *apología*, the meaning has changed. Socrates was not *apologizing* or making excuses. The Greek word *apología* simply and precisely meant a *defence*, or a *defence speech*. This meaning has been preserved in some related English words: an 'apologist' is still someone who argues a *defence* of someone or something, and 'apologetics' is still a discipline or system of argued *defence* of something, usually a doctrine, cause, or institution. Socrates' speech thus might be translated as *The Defence of Socrates,* thereby avoiding any possible confusion over the modern meaning. But after long usage, it is hard to imagine calling the *Apology* anything else.

It is clear from the works of his student, Plato, that Socrates' Daemon was an extremely active element in his life.

> *At all previous times, my familiar prophetic power, my*
> *spiritual manifestation, frequently opposed me, even in small*
> *matters, when I was about to do something wrong, but now*
> *that, as you can see for yourselves, I was faced with what one*
> *might think, and what is generally thought to be, the worst of*
> *evils, my divine sign has not opposed me, either when I left*
> *home at dawn, or when I came into court, or at any time*
> *that I was about to say something during my speech. Yet in*
> *other talks it often held me back in the middle of my*
> *speaking, but now it has opposed no word or deed of mine.*
> (*Apology 40a–b*)

Socrates' Daemon seemed to involve itself in the most trivial details of his life. For example, in *Euthydemus* Plato quotes Socrates as saying:

> *I was sitting by myself in the undressing room just where you*
> *saw me and was already thinking of leaving. But when I got*
> *up, my customary divine sign put in an appearance. So I sat*
> *down again, and in a moment the two of them, Euthydemus*
> *and Dionysodorus, came in . . .*[4]

It is clear from the writings that in all cases nobody else hears the voice of Socrates' Daemon. It is clearly an inner dialogue. However, it does seem that on occasion others were aware of the outward manifestation of a change in Socrates' behaviour. In the beginning of Plato's *Symposium,* Socrates is walking to Agathon's house for a dinner party (*symposium*). On his way,

Socrates meets one of his close friends, Aristodemus, and urges him to join the party even though he was not invited. As they walk to Agathon's house, Socrates lags behind, as if lost in thought. When Aristodemus arrives at Agathon's home, Agathon greets him at the door and asks where Socrates is. Aristodemus looks around, and Socrates has vanished. Agathon sends a slave to search for Socrates, who returns and gives the following report:

> 'Socrates is here, but he's gone off to the neighbour's porch.
> He's standing there and won't come in even though I called
> him several times.' 'How strange,' Agathon replied. 'Go back
> and bring him in. Don't leave him there.' But Aristodemus
> stopped him. 'No, no,' he said. 'Leave him alone. It's one of
> his habits: every now and then he just goes off like that and
> stands motionless, where he happens to be. I'm sure he'll
> come in very soon, so don't disturb him; let him be.'
> (Symposium 175a–b)

Agathon then ordered the slaves to start the dinner.

> So, they went ahead and started eating, but there was still no
> sign of Socrates. Agathon wanted to send for him many
> times, but Aristodemus wouldn't let him. And, in fact,
> Socrates came in shortly afterwards, as he always did – they
> were hardly halfway through their meal. (Symposium 175c)

It has been argued that many of these curious events in Socrates' life are proof that he may have been a temporal lobe epileptic. You will recall that one of the symptoms of TLE is an 'absence' whereby patients seem to withdraw into a world of their own. These *petit mal* episodes, now termed Simple Partial Seizures (SPS), may only seem like a short time to the observer, but to epileptics time can expand so that they can be in their dream-state for hours, if not days. The events described above imply such an 'absence'.

Indeed, a similar period of prolonged unresponsiveness is found in the *Symposium*. Alcibiades, one of Socrates' friends and admirers, talks about his experience with Socrates when they were on military campaign together years before.

> *One day, at dawn, he [Socrates] started thinking about some problem or other; he just stood outside, trying to figure it out. He couldn't resolve it, but he wouldn't give up. He simply stood there, glued to the same spot. By midday, many soldiers had seen him, and, quite mystified, they told everyone that Socrates had been standing there all day, thinking about something. He was still there when evening came, and after dinner some Ionians moved their bedding outside, where it was cooler and more comfortable [. . .], but mainly in order to watch if Socrates was going to stay out there all night. And so he did; he stood on the very same spot until dawn!*
> (Symposium *220c–d*)

Often a SPS is followed by a Complex Partial Seizure (CPS). This usually involves a brief loss of awareness and even a short period of amnesia. In *Phaedrus* there is a visitation of the voice just after Socrates had delivered a speech. The effect on him was such that he could not subsequently recall any part of the speech itself, just the voice. From this it is reasonable to conclude that the voice and Socrates' SPS/CPS episodes were linked.

Therefore I contend that Socrates was firmly at the TLE level of my Scale of Transcendence. It is not surprising that his Daemon was regularly in contact. Within Socrates' brain, glutamate was prising open his 'Doors of Perception', allowing the Daemon to shout through the gap. Indeed, I would add that Socrates' interest in religion was also a clue to his TLE. As we have seen with regard to Joan of Arc, Waxman-Geschwind Syndrome manifests itself with hyperreligiosity. Socrates had a strong belief in God as ruler of the world; as evidenced in warnings and revelations given in dreams, signs, and oracles. For him these all supported the belief that man himself can partake in the Divine. Of course if one had spent all of one's life in regular communication with a being that showed all the signs of divinity then such a belief would be not at all surprising. Indeed, as we have already seen Socrates believed, by experience, that his Divine Sign had prophetic abilities, a sure sign of god-like qualities.

One of the 'skills' of the Daemon is an ability to know the future life of its Eidolon. This knowledge is simply a memory of the last life and so, if one is literal, not a precognitive ability at all, simply a recollection of an event that has already taken place. It is only in the Bohmian IMAX of the Eidolon that the future is unknown. There is evidence that Socrates' Daemon used this knowledge on many occasions, sometimes confusing its Eidolon as to its motivations. A good example of this is reported in the *Phaedrus*. After Socrates delivers his first speech on love, he promises Phaedrus that he will not give any more speeches on the topic. Socrates is about to cross the river near where they are speaking and take his leave, when, all of a sudden, his Daemon speaks:

> *My friend, just as I was about to cross the river, the familiar*
> *divine sign came to me which, whenever it occurs, holds me*
> *back from something I am about to do. I thought I heard a*
> *voice coming from this very spot, forbidding me to leave until*
> *I made atonement for some offence against the gods.*
> (Phaedrus *242b–c*)

Could this be because the last time round something bad happened when Socrates crossed the river with Phaedrus? We have already seen that this is a skill that the Daemon uses time and time again. As with even modern Daemons a culturally-based explanation is made; an offence had been given to the gods and atonement had to be made.

The link between the gods and prophecy had long been accepted by the time of Socrates. The word 'prophecy' originally meant 'inspired utterance', which raises the question, inspired by whom? The ancient Greeks, including Plato and Socrates, had no doubt about this; the prophet or prophetess was simply the mouthpiece of another, all-knowing, entity. Within the Greek worldview the only possible source of this inspiration was the gods themselves, and in particular one god, Apollo.

The sanctuary of Apollo was located on a mountainside in central Greece. The god himself had decided upon this sacred spot. It was here, on one day in every year, that he would communicate with mortals. As time went on this period was extended to be the seventh day of any month. However, in an ancient form of locum work, Apollo would leave the task to another god, Dionysus, for three months of the year.

Apollo did not speak directly with mortals. He used a priestess, called the 'Pythia', as his mouthpiece. Indeed, even the utterances of the Pythia had to be translated by another priest before lesser beings were allowed to know the results of their question. It has never been fully explained why this was as it was, but there is a strong suspicion that the Pythia was usually deranged in some way and as such what she said would be, to the untutored ear, incomprehensible.

In this way the reputation of the Oracle at Delphi was assured. Famous characters from myth and history all made their way to its portals and all were given answers that were wrongly interpreted but with hindsight proved to be accurate. By the confusing use of grammar and the making of obscure references any outcome could be seen as correct. However, it is still surprising that whatever the outcome the predictions did, indeed, come true. It is again as if the Pythia herself was 'remembering' events from her own future by accessing the 'advice' of a disincarnate voice in her head – in this case the voice of Apollo.

The 'voice of Apollo' was soon to be heard in places other

than Delphi. These voices were 'heard' not by priestesses within a sanctuary but by wandering prophets who went under the collective name of the 'Sibyls'. These women were to be found at various times and at various locations across the classical world. However, they all seemed to use the same process to predict future events.

In his *Phaedrus*, Plato discusses in some detail this Greek fascination with prophecy, with particular reference to divine inspiration. Here he refers to the Greek term 'mania' which was seen as an essential mental state to contact the divine within the soul. Plato considered that there were various types of inspiration. One sort was religious:

> For the prophetess at Delphi and the priestesses at Dodona
> when they have been mad have conferred many splendid
> benefits upon Greece both in private and in public affairs, but
> few or none when they have been in their right minds . . .[5]

Another was creative:

> . . . Possession and madness comes from the Muses. This
> takes hold upon a gentle and pure soul, arouses it and
> inspires it to songs and other poetry, and thus by adorning
> countless deeds of the ancients educates later generations. But
> he who without the divine madness comes to the doors of the
> Muses, confident that he will be a good poet by art, meets
> with no success, and the poetry of the sane man vanishes into
> nothingness before that of the inspired madmen.[6]

And another was intellectual:

> . . . I need not mention Socrates himself – and all the rest of
> them; every one of you has had his share of philosophic
> frenzy and transport [manía kaì bakxeía].[7]

So here we have a specific link made between Socrates' intellectual abilities and his regular communication with his Daemon. This being was clearly a major influence in the life of the epileptic Socrates. However, in one of the greatest ironies of history, it was his Daemon that was to bring about the circumstances that led to his tragic death.

According to the writings of Xenophon, Socrates' frequent references to his 'divine sign' were the origin of the charges the state made against him in 399BCE. There were two counts in the accusation. These were 'corruption of the young' and 'neglect of the gods whom the city worships and the practice of religious novelties'. Central to the second accusation was his insistence on the reality of his Daemon.

In a fascinating comment Socrates states that he believes that not only is this being responsible for man's creative abilities, but also that this is related to precognition and clairvoyance.

> *I decided that it was not wisdom that enabled [poets] to write their poetry, but a kind of instinct or inspiration, such as you find in seers and prophets who deliver all their sublime messages without knowing in the least what they mean.*

If I am right then this is exactly what the Daemon does. As it has lived this life before it knows the future and will use this knowledge to protect its Eidolon. However, in certain circumstances the Daemon seems to abandon its Eidolon to its fate. We have already seen this take place with Joan of Arc and a similar set of circumstances were to play out during the trial of Socrates. I suggest that this may be because the Daemon knows that this is the high point of its Eidolon's existence and that when it has saved its lower self in previous life-runs the subsequent years made available by this 'temporal mutation' have brought disaster. For example, would Joan of Arc have become such an iconic figure if, instead of dying heroically at the stake, she had survived to become a bitter and twisted individual who brought disaster to France and her previously spotless reputation? We can never know but if my theory is correct her Daemon did.

I argue that the same thing took place during Socrates' trial. For some peculiar reason his 'Divine Sign' became absent for the first time in his life. This confused and concerned Socrates:

> In the past the prophetic voice to which I have become
> accustomed has always been my constant companion,
> opposing me even in quite trivial things if I was going to take
> the wrong course . . . yet neither when I left home this
> morning, nor when I was taking my place here in the court,
> nor at any point in any part of my speech, did the divine
> sign oppose me . . . What do I suppose to be the explanation?
> . . . I suspect that this thing that has happened to me is a
> blessing, and we are quite mistaken in supposing death to be
> an evil. I have good grounds for thinking this, because my
> accustomed sign could not have failed to oppose me if what I
> was doing had not been sure to bring some good result.[8]

Without this guide Socrates was left alone to present his defence. The very being whose self-evident reality had brought Socrates to such dire straits had suddenly absented itself. Although Socrates made some wonderful speeches it was clear that he would be found guilty – and so it was. The great man was sentenced to death. This came as no surprise and Socrates stated that he was 'well content' with the judgment.

According to Athenian law no executions could take place in Athens when the sacred ship was sailing to or from Delos. Because of an unexpected delay the ship could not return for a month. This brought about an unavoidable delay in Socrates' sentence being carried out. During this time he received many visitors to his cell. At any time throughout this period Socrates could have easily escaped and made his way to another of the Greek city states. His friend Crito had set up an elaborate plan that would have surely worked but Socrates refused to contemplate it, arguing that the verdict, although contrary to fact, was that of a legitimate court and must therefore be obeyed. It seems that although his Daemon had become non-communicative as regards verbal messages it was still active but only through subliminal motivation. However, there is one interesting section of Plato's *Crito* that suggests to me that the Daemon had simply moved to communicating through dreams.

Crito had been informed that the sacred ship had arrived back from Delos and that the execution would take place the next day. Clearly concerned, he made his way to Socrates' cell to find the philosopher asleep. When Socrates finally awoke Crito informed him of the bad news. Socrates' reply is fascinating. He says:

> *If it is the will of God, so be it. However, I don't believe that it will happen tomorrow. Just now, as you came to me, I was having a pleasant dream. A woman of uncommon beauty appeared to me, in a long white robe, called me by name, and said: 'In three days, you will arrive in your fertile Pythia.'*

It is after hearing this that Crito tells Socrates of his escape plan with Socrates making a very impassioned speech as to why he simply cannot take this route. He finishes off this speech with the following words:

> *Dearest friend Crito! I believe I hear this speech, as the Corybantes imagine they hear the sound of the flutes, and the voice rings so loudly in my ears, that I can hear nothing else over it.*

This is a very interesting comment. The Corybantes were dancers at the Oracle at Delphi. Their role was to assist the Oracle to make

> *'One night, at three in the morning, I woke up suddenly and then, I talked to someone. It's a mystery, don't try, you will not find (who that person was). It's somebody you will probably never meet. I can't explain that encounter myself. That person really exists but it all comes from very far. And then, during the hours that followed, I took the decision to come back.'*
>
> ZINEDINE ZIDANE (FOOTBALLER)

prognostications. Their dance was designed to drive them into full mania – indeed, it was known that in such ecstatic states some Corybantes would castrate themselves – and in doing so make prophecies themselves. Could it be that by using this very specific analogy Socrates (Plato) was implying a link between the 'voice ringing so loudly in my ear' and daemonic possession?

If what Socrates said to Crito was true then his Daemon, manifesting itself as a loud 'voice', ensured that the philosopher not only ignored the begging of his friend but was also condemning its Eidolon to death. Indeed, it could be reasonably argued that the beautiful woman that appeared in Socrates' dream was yet another manifestation of the Daemon insisting, quite precisely, that he would die: not on the next day, but in three days' time.

I have tried to find out if this prediction came true. Plato tells us that soon after this incident with Crito Socrates took his own life by drinking a cup of hemlock. I strongly suspect that the only reason that Plato would have included this curious dialogue would have been because the words of the 'woman of . . . beauty . . . in a long white robe' proved to be correct.

For over 2,000 years the life and death of Socrates has held an ongoing fascination for historians and psychologists. Although much has been written about his Daemon no really satisfactory answer has been forthcoming. For what it is worth, I would like to suggest that my 'Daemon-Eidolon Dyad' may go some way to explaining this mystery.

Of course, it can be reasonably argued that my two examples of 'the voices' are from many years ago and took place in a pre-scientific world. I would now like to fast-forward in time to some modern examples that follow exactly the same format.

The cleaved mind

The Irish writer Brian Cleeve, who died in March 2003, claimed that he wrote three books of metaphysical speculation under the influence of what he termed 'a presence'. These books, *The House on the Rock* and *The Seven Mansions* (both published in 1980), and *The Fourth Mary* (1982), attracted a cult following in Ireland and also aroused a considerable degree of debate.

This 'presence' was more than just a silent inner muse or an urge to write. Cleeve describes his initial experience in the opening paragraph of *The House on the Rock*. He writes:

> *I felt a pressure on my forehead. Like a band of pressure,*
> *from temple to temple, not heavy, but firm. I felt the coldness*
> *of a Presence, a sense of great suffering. A voice said, not*
> *aloud, but within my mind, I see all that was, and is, and*
> *will be. And then the voice said I shall teach you to hear,*
> *and to see, and you must write down what you have*
> *seen and heard.*

This is a powerful and affecting image of what takes place when the Daemon chooses to become immanent in the life of its Eidolon.

This being seems to have opened up Cleeve's eidolonic mind to a much wider, daemonic, perception of reality. He struggled to understand the messages that were being given to him. Rather like a sighted person describing a rainbow to a blind child the Daemon tried to convey the real nature of reality. Cleeve's Eidolon struggled to understand these concepts and attempted to put into writing the fires of perception burning in his brain. For Cleeve this seems more than just a feeling, it is a real dialogue. His Daemon actually talks to him as a voice in his head. It explains that the lower self can, with hard work, attain enlightenment but never wisdom. That is for the Higher Self only. In my first book I argue that the neurotransmitters that bring about schizophrenia do so because they allow eidolonic access to daemonic perceptions. This new super-sensitivity brings about a problem in the brain which is analogous to a camera film when it is over-exposed to light. It simply cannot deal with it. It is this that drives schizophrenics insane. Is this what Cleeve's 'presence' means by the following words?

Wisdom knows Perfection, the voice said. It is union with God.
Enlightenment is only a momentary vision of a fragment
of Perfection.
Enlightenment is seeing for a brief while. Wisdom is
possessing, for ever.
The one is swift moving, the other a deep stillness.

In his book *The Seven Mansions*, Cleeve tried to explain that man's consciousness is part of a much greater reality. This he termed the Real Mind. Cleeve used this to explain such phenomena as rein-carnation and past-life memories. He argued that the Real Mind can access the thoughts and perceptions of the many other beings that coexist in the same universe but at different times and places. This, to me, is very similar to the theories expounded by David Bohm in his 'Implicate Order' theory. Cleeve goes further than this as regards the implications of his 'presence'. In his book *The Invitation* he has a section entitled 'The Real World'. What is fascinating about this is that it seems to develop from a description of a series of curious dreams to a form of Socratic dialogue between the narrator, presumably Cleeve himself, and another entity that remains unacknowledged, its responses being shown in italics. There is one particular question and answer sequence that to me implies that Cleeve was aware, possibly unconsciously, of the Daemon-Eidolon duality. The narrator asks:

You have told us that every spirit living its human life has two selves – one is its own, 'real' self that it created as soon as it became aware of its own existence. The second, lesser self is its human self, that it chose when that human self was conceived – choosing it in order to live its human life?

The 'presence' replies:

Yes. You can compare this to your mind, that equals your spirit, your body, that can stand for your real self, formed by your mind, and your self, formed by your mind, and your clothes, that you choose so that you can go about your affairs, and that eventually you will discard. (You can even imagine someone, man or woman, for whom their clothes become more important than anything else, turning into human peacocks, draped in jewels and designer gowns, silk suits and shirts, existing only to be admired or envied by other fools.)

The Daemon then goes on to explain exactly what its role is in the life of its Eidolon. It uses the interesting analogy of a gardener and a wheelbarrow. It suggests that the Daemon is a gardener and the Eidolon is a wheelbarrow, by means of which the gardener develops the garden. When the wheelbarrow is no longer of use it is discarded. I interpret this as saying that the Daemon uses the Eidolon to change this life for the better. The Daemon manifests itself through the Eidolon to make changes and improvements. Thus when the Eidolon is reborn again the garden, analogous to the quality of that Eidolon's life, has been improved slightly. The new wheelbarrow is then utilized again to continue the development until, again, it wears out and needs replacing. To use the exact words of Cleeve's Daemon:

> *The spirit is the gardener. The soul is the garden. The body*
> *is something the gardener uses for a time and then discards,*
> *like a wheelbarrow, or a spade. He needs it, and is*
> *done with it.*

It may come as a surprise to discover that such communications are not that uncommon. A gentleman by the name of Albert Tanner, discussed in Colin Parsons' book *Encounters With The Unknown*[9], describes how for 30 years Tanner had a voice whisper messages in his left ear. These communications were of such a mundane nature that he quite naturally assumed that they were part of his own subconscious. However, on 28 April 1960, he was to realize that the source of the voice was most definitely not part of his mind. Tanner was in the process of boarding a plane to go on a business trip to North Africa. As he did so the 'voice' said, 'Do not go to Morocco.' It was so insistent in its tone that Tanner decided to not travel. On 1 May an earthquake hit the city he was to stay in and a tidal wave destroyed much of what was left.

From then on Tanner's Daemon became positively chatty. In 1961 he met a girl at a dance. He was on the point of proposing to the girl when the voice said, 'Do not marry her, she is ill.' She was in good health, but even if she were to be ill he still wished to marry her. A pre-marriage medical was to show that she was terminally ill with leukaemia. In what must have been a very sad meeting she refused to marry him and died soon afterwards. The voice was to comfort him during this difficult time by informing him that:

> *All life is immortal – only her body is dead – you will meet*
> *again if that is what you want.*

Of course Tanner, quite naturally, interprets this as meaning they will meet again in heaven or whatever. If I am correct in my analysis the Daemon's words should be taken literally. The voice is informing Tanner that they will meet again as they met in that life, in exactly the same circumstances. However, it is possible that circumstances will conspire to ensure that the leukaemia will be avoided.

The voice continued with its predictions. It told Tanner that he would marry a woman called Elaine. One suspects that the last time round Tanner had missed this opportunity and, in echoes of *Groundhog Day*, the garrulous Daemon did not want his errant Eidolon to miss out again.

Parsons is puzzled:

> *The mystery of Albert Tanner's helpmate is unfathomable in the light of current knowledge. It knows the future, but cares little about the quality of its information; it will supply advice of tremendous significance or comparative banality with equal aplomb.*[10]

Of course, Parsons was not aware of my 'Daemon-Eidolon Dyad'. I am sure that had he been so he would have considered it at least a partial explanation for the strange events.

Sometimes the voice seems to assist during circumstances that could be considered rather prosaic. Consider for a few moments the implications of what happened to Eric Laithwaite, Professor of Electrical Engineering at Imperial College of Science, Technology and Medicine, London.

In late 1974 Laithwaite was presenting the Royal Institution Christmas Lecture for Children. This event has taken place since 1825. By 1975 these events were shown annually on British television. Laithwaite was involved in the recording of his presentation entitled 'The Engineer through the Looking Glass'. On this particular occasion he was trying to explain that just because a result is not repeated in similar circumstances it does not mean it did not happen. To illustrate this he had a mechanism that would cause a ball to jump in the air once every 36 attempts.

The machine was set up to do this in an entirely random fashion so the ball could be seen to jump on any of the 36 opportunities. He switched the machine on twice: no jumps. As he began to switch it on for the third time he heard a voice in his head say: 'You know it goes next time.'

In astonishment he mentally replied: 'Does it?'

The voice said: 'Of course. Why don't you tell the children?'

He told them, 'But this time . . .' He switched on the current with his hand held out in readiness. Much to Laithwaite's surprise and amazement the ball jumped straight into it.

In my opinion this is an example of a bored Daemon that is jokingly involving itself in the life of its Eidolon. Obviously, this was of no great importance for Laithwaite, but it proved quite clearly the precognitive abilities of the 'hidden observer'.

I opened this chapter with a discussion regarding the experiences of Joan of Arc and her voices. As far as Joan was concerned the voices were of a religious nature. They were saints and the mission they had given her was of a religious nature. We have also seen that the mystic experience itself has its origins in my Daemon-Eidolon Dyad. So what does religion make of these experiences. Does theology recognize this duality?

Summary

Hearing voices is not as unusual as popular belief would have it. It seems that under certain circumstances the communication passes between the being that I term the Daemon and everyday consciousness. There is strong evidence to conclude that these voices seem to have knowledge that is denied to the hearer. I argue that this knowledge is, in reality, a memory on the part of the Daemon. It has lived this life before and therefore has access to past-life experiences. It uses this knowledge to guide and counsel its lower self, the being that I term the Eidolon.

[1] Foote-Smith, E. and Bayne, L., 'Joan of Arc', *Epilepsia* 32(6): 810–15 (1991)

[2] Sullivan, Karen, *The Interrogation of Joan of Arc*, University of Minnesota (1999)

[3] Wheeler, Bonnie and Woods, Charles T., *Fresh Verdicts on Joan of Arc*, Garland Publishing Inc., New York and London (1996) – Sullivan, Karen pp.85–111 in '"I Do Not Name To You The Voice of St. Michael": The Identification of Joan of Arc's Voices'

[4] Plato, *Euthydemus*, 272e–273a

[5] Plato, *Phaedrus*, 244b

[6] Ibid., 245a

[7] Plato, *Symposium*, 218b

[8] Cairns, H. & Hamilton, E., (eds), *The Collected Dialogues of Plato*, Pantheon, New York, p.24 (1961)

[9] Parson, C., *Encounters With The Unknown*, Robert Hale, London, (1991)

[10] Ibid., p.179

CHAPTER 4
Theology

I am He whom I love,
And He whom I love is I
We are two spirits
Dwelling in one body.

Al Halláj

Sunday's child

She felt strange. She looked at the group of people around her. Her father stood opposite, his head bowed in prayer. He was leading the usual prayer session, a regular occurrence in the deeply devout Harmon family. Even though she was only 17, Ellen knew that God had chosen her to be of special importance. As she prayed, her clasped hands rubbed against her nose. She felt the bump halfway up, a mute reminder of the accident that had nearly taken her life eight years earlier. The image of the angry girl imposed itself upon her thoughts. She saw again the stone come flying through the air towards her face, felt it smash into the side of her head. She tried hard to remember anything about the three weeks she had spent lying in a coma, her family anxiously clustered around her bed, but nothing would come. She did remember waking up, a slow hauling up back into the world of Maine in 1836. Since that time her recovery had been slow and difficult. She found it hard to concentrate and her memory was not at all good. She had been forced to give up school at 12 years of age. Even now she still could not write properly and such taken for granted things as drinking a cup of tea or coffee were almost impossible because of her shaking.

However, she had her dreams, vivid ones in which a being of light would talk to her and once had even introduced her to Jesus. That is why she always found that prayer calmed her. Her father's voice was reassuring and she felt comforted by the close presence of her twin sister and six other brothers and sisters around her. However, the feeling of strangeness seemed to increase. She felt that something was not right. Then it happened – she felt as if a ball of fire had hit her in her heart. She doubled forward as the searing heat engulfed her body. And then the voice of her dream companion broke into her waking world.

'Make Known to others what I have revealed to you,' it demanded.

Ellen then felt herself rising higher and higher outside her body. She looked back to see if her family were still there, far below her, but they had disappeared into the darkness. Ellen, however, continued floating into the most wonderful light. She then heard the voice speak to her again.

'Look again, and look a little higher.'

At this she raised her eyes and saw a straight and narrow path, cast up high above the world. On this path she saw many people who were travelling to a wonderful city, which was at the farthest end of the path. The vision then started to fade and she felt herself moving back down to earth. As she re-entered her body Ellen felt wave after wave of glory roll over her, until her body grew stiff.

She found herself surrounded by her family. She felt that she had been away for many hours but from the response of those around her it had been just a few seconds. As soon as she had fully regained her composure she knew what she should do. Heed the voice and use it to teach the righteous about God's plan for the world.

The young woman in question was Ellen Harmon. Within a few years she would marry and become Mrs Ellen White, one of the founders of the Seventh-day Adventist Church. For the rest of her life she experienced visions, heard voices and had precognitions.

In the period from 1844 to 1884, Ellen continued to have many waking visions. After 1884 they seemed to change in nature and content in that she primarily experienced prophetic dreams, or night-visions. These continued until her death on 3 March 1915.

It is, of course, impossible to obtain an accurate account of the total number of visionary experiences that Ellen White had been given, but her son James claimed that by 1868 she had experienced between 100 and 200.[1] Between 1868 and 1884 there are some 80 additional visions listed; and nearly 60 prophetic dreams after 1884 are enumerated in the *Comprehensive Index to the Writings of Ellen G. White*, besides 48 which are classified as of uncertain date. It would seem from all this that Ellen had been involved in at least 400 lifetime visionary experiences – perhaps many more. Ellen was convinced that nothing she wrote originated with her. She recorded:

> *In these letters which I write, in the testimonies I bear, I am presenting to you that which the Lord has presented to me. I do not write one article in the paper expressing merely my own ideas. They are what God has opened before me in vision – the precious rays of light shining from the throne. It is true concerning the articles in our papers and in the many volumes of my books.*[2]

Ellen White was clearly a very special person, one that even today has 8 million followers, 750,000 in the United States. However, she is far from alone. She had experienced a surprisingly common phenomenon, shared by religious mystics the world over. From St Paul with his experience of 'the voice of God' on the road to Damascus to St Catherine of Siena and from the Old Testament experience of Jeremiah when he felt the touch of Yahweh's fingers on his lips (Jer. 1:9) to the prophetic visions of Emmanuel Swedenborg, precognition and the hearing of voices have long been part of the religious experience. I suggest that it is to religion that we must now look to find evidence of my Daemon-Eidolon Dyad.

The divisible soul

The Kalabari people of the Niger Delta in West Africa have, like many other cultures, a fascination with why it is that we

'Each of us has a divine counterpart unfallen who can reach a hand down to us to awaken us. This other personality is the authentic waking self; the one we have now is asleep and minor. We are in fact asleep, and in the hands of a dangerous magician disguised as a good god, the deranged creator deity. The bleakness, the evil and pain in this world, the fact that it is a deterministic prison controlled by the demented creator causes us willingly to split with the reality principle early in life, and so to speak willingly fall asleep in delusion.'

PHILIP K. DICK (AUTHOR)

sometimes intend to do one thing and end up doing something completely different. To explain this, the Kalabari divide human consciousness into two independent beings. They have what they call the *biomgbo*, which corresponds to the conscious mind – the thing that calls itself 'me' – and the *teme*, a fascinating entity that seems to know the future circumstances of its *biomgbo*.[3] According to the Kalabari the *teme* knows what happened to the person in a previous life and tries to avoid the same mistakes being repeated. For example it might actively ensure that a man does not marry a particular woman even though his *biomgbo* is very keen on the lady in question. I believe that this curious belief system may be the best anthropological proof of my 'Daemon-Eidolon' duality that I have discovered thus far.

The Kalabari might be unique in the way they understand the relationship between the two elements that make up a person but the overall idea of conscious duality is one of the most persistent and culturally universal beliefs of humanity. On first encountering such a statement most people will naturally assume that what this really means is duality – the philosophical concept of body and soul. By this I mean that we all have a physical body that exists in time and space and then we have a non-physical identity that may, or may not, survive the death of the body.

This non-physical side is termed 'the soul'. However, a moment's reflection will make it clear that the soul is identical to the person. The consciousness that inhabits the body, an entity that is called 'me' or 'I', is indivisible. It is believed by many religions that when a person dies the 'I' continues as a self-aware consciousness that exists within another plane of existence: one that is not generally accessible to consciousnesses that are still alive. In many religious traditions there is a belief in a Last Judgment whereby the dead soul is held to account for the sins committed while alive. This judgment is handed down to a being that has all the conscious memories and self-awareness that it had when it was alive. As such when we use 'duality' in this way what we really mean is a singular, ongoing consciousness that continues after the death of the body. The two elements consist of an unconscious body and a conscious soul. This is not really duality at all. It is a singular consciousness and an unconscious body which is a collection of chemical elements that for a short period of time have been animated and have now returned to their inanimate state.

This is not the form of duality I wish to discuss. For me, real theological duality is where it is believed that the mind – the conscious part of the body – is dual. In other words it can be considered that we are triune beings that consist of a body and two minds.

Indeed, the ancient Egyptians considered that human beings consisted of three elements plus the body. The three entities were known as the *ba*, the *ka*, and the *khu*. The unconscious body consisting of earthly matter was termed the *khat*.

The *ba* entity called itself 'I' and was responsible for the animation of the body, the *khat*. The *ba* was the everyday personality that interfaced with the outside world, ensured that the *khat* was fed and watered and communicated with other *bas*. Motivating the *ba* and working closely with it was the *khu*. The *khu* was the holder of the thoughts, emotions, motivations and ambitions of the *ba*. As such it had no real independence from the *ba*. However, the *ka* was a totally independent being that shared the *khat* with its less perceptive compatriots. For the ancient Egyptians the *ka* was a semi-physical presence that shared the same physical location as the *khat*, but could sometimes be seen poking out around the edges in a slight haze. Indeed, and this will be of great interest later when we discuss the concept of *doppelgängers*, on occasion the *ka* could manifest itself outside the *khat* and be seen by its own *ba*.

The *ka* was usually depicted in tomb paintings as a small bird with a human face hovering over the body of the deceased. It was considered to be a form of guardian spirit: not a disincarnate spirit, but an entity that was also an element of the individual. This is an important concept: the *ka* and the *ba* are, in effect, the same being, but exist in different locations of time and space.

In modern psychological terminology the *khu* could be considered to reflect the subconscious mind, while the *ba* is the everyday being that we know as 'me'. However, the mysterious being known as the *ka* fails to fit into our cosy mind-body split. It seems to be part of, and yet independent from, the *ba*.

For me, this implies that the Egyptians clearly divided the personality into two closely-related but consciously independent beings and considered the body to be a third, non-conscious element. And they were not alone in this belief.

In the pre-classical period of Greek history it was believed that human beings had three elements to their make-up: a body, a *thymos* and a *psyche*. The *thymos* was the conscious self and the *psyche* was a form of soul. When death took place the body rotted and the *thymos* merged with the air. It was the *psyche* that continued to exist as a spirit-being in the Underworld, or Hades. Under certain circumstances a *psyche* could return to earth to live its life again, but only if it agreed to drink the waters of the River Lethe. This tributary of the Styx was also known as the River of Forgetting. The legend was that if the *psyche* drank of the waters of the Lethe its previous life-memories would be wiped clean. Having then done as instructed the *psyche* was allowed to return to earth to be reborn with a new *thymos* and body. The new triune being would then live its life again as the same person as last time and with no memories and therefore no awareness that it was reliving a life already lived.

It is impossible to say whether the Greeks took these ideas of the Egyptians and incorporated them into their own theology, but the similarities cannot be ignored. For them the body (equivalent to the Egyptian *khat*) and the *thymos* (*khu*) were the physical and non-physical aspects of the same entity, a being that in later Classical times they termed an *eidolon*. However, the *psyche*, like the Egyptian *ka*, continued as a totally independent entity which they were to call a *daemon*. In echoes that cannot be mere coincidence, the Greeks also saw the *daemon* as being a form of guardian spirit that looked after and, on occasion assisted, its *eidolon*. Indeed, the *daemon* had similar skills to its Egyptian equivalent. It also had a habit of poking out of the body, being perceived as what the Greeks termed an *aura*.

The earliest-known writer on the subject of this daemon-eidolon duality was the Sicilian-Greek Empedocles. For him the daemon, although semi-imprisoned in the body, is a divine being exiled from its rightful place among the gods. It exists totally independently of its lower self, or eidolon, and has great knowledge and power.[4] However, he suggested that certain individuals, through training or personal greatness, could become one with their own Higher Self and, in doing so, become a god. Indeed, Empedocles was convinced that he was one of these proto-gods. Legend has it that he flung himself into the crater of Mount Etna to prove his divinity to his followers. History does not record the outcome of this act, but one can only assume that it certainly assisted him in getting to the abode of his fellow gods somewhat quicker than the eidolons left observing his descent into the abyss.

When I came across the terms 'eidolon' and 'daemon' while researching my first book I found them curiously evocative of the two sides of split consciousness. Indeed, so taken with them was I that I used them in a capitalized form to name the two elements of my 'Cheating the Ferryman' theory. I feel that this works very well and from now on I will use the terms 'Daemon' and 'Eidolon' as generic terms describing the two elements of conscious awareness. For consistency I will from now on term the overall concept the 'Daemon-Eidolon Dyad'.

I am of the opinion that this Daemon-Eidolon Dyad is central to many ancient belief systems and has carried through into modern psychiatry and psychology. Let us do a swift review of the evidence for such an opinion.

For the Chinese of the Chou dynasty (1025–256BCE) these two elements were called the *hun*, which was yang-like and masculine and the *p'o* which was yin-like and feminine. In the early Vedic beliefs of India they were the *asu* and the *manas*. This has now evolved in modern Indian thought so that all people have a physical body, a 'subtle body' and a 'spirit'. For the ancient Zoroastrians of Persia, the Daemon and the Eidolon were termed the *urvan* and the *daena* respectively.

It can be argued that many of these religions had a cross-fertilization of beliefs and therefore it is not that surprising that there are similarities. However, many New World, Arctic and sub-Saharan beliefs also echo this duality. For example, in South America the Apapocuva-Guarani and the Mbua of Brazil as well as the Waica of the Amazon basin have curiously similar theories, as do the Ewe of Togo, the Mossi of Burkina Fasso and the Bambara of Mali. Most interesting are the beliefs of duality to be found in the shamanistic peoples of Siberia, specifically the Yukagir, the Khanty, the Mansi, the Samoyed and finally the Tunguz of the Yenisei River region.

What is of great interest are the similarities between these beliefs, particularly the belief that all human beings have a lower and a higher self. The two elements can communicate, but it seems to be a one-way process. It is usually the higher self – the Daemon – that does the 'talking'. The Eidolon seems to be a totally passive receiver of information. However, there are mystic traditions in which an Eidolon, through rigorous training, can open up the communication channels by itself. In this way it can access the knowledge and perceptions of its Daemon. The implication here is that the Daemon has knowledge not available to its lower partner, a knowledge that it is happy to impart if asked in the right way. The path of the mystic is to learn the right questions.

Each of these examples is supported by a rich and fascinating oral culture. However, for the present argument I would like to review the evidence for the Daemon-Eidolon Dyad as it is found within the written as well as oral traditions of Judaism, Islam and Christianity. Having done this, I will then focus on the fascinating beliefs of the Hawaiian Kahuna.

Judaism

For most of us brought up in the West the terms 'spirit' and 'soul' mean the same thing. Both are the non-physical elements of a human being. Those of a religious persuasion believe that these elements survive physical death and will continue in some other plane of existence. However, in the ancient Hebrew of the Old Testament the words soul and spirit are not interchangeable but are, in fact, two very different concepts.

In the Old Testament the 'spirit' was the element in human beings that 'did' things. It was active in the world, an agent for physical change. The 'soul' on the other hand was a passive thinker, an observer and evaluator of the world that 'felt' what was to be done or not done. What is of particular interest is that the soul could die, whereas the spirit was said to simply return to God.

That is not to say that the spirit and the soul were not closely related. Hebrews 4:12 says:

> *The word of God is quick, and powerful, and sharper than any two-edged sword, piercing even to the dividing asunder of soul and spirit . . .*

This belief is to be found in many parts of the Old Testament, but it is only commented upon in passing. This is because it represents an element of Judaic theology that is relatively unknown to the mind schooled in the Christian interpretation of the Bible and its teachings. This esoteric school is known as 'Kabbalah'.

The word 'Kabbalah' literally means 'tradition' and this implies that the beliefs and practices of the Kabbalists can be traced back to the earliest period of Judaism. This may or may not be the case. According to orthodox Kabbalists, the sacred book of Kabbalah, the *Zohar*, was written by a 2nd century CE rabbi called Simeon bar Yochai who used writings that went back to the time of Moses as his sources. However, the *Zohar* itself was first 'discovered' by Moses de León in the 13th century. Almost all modern Jewish academic scholars believe that de León himself authored the book. Whatever its origins this book had a profound effect on Jewish mystic thinking with many great Kabbalist schools being set up across the length and breadth of Europe.

It is fascinating to discover that within Kabbalistic thought we again encounter the triune nature of the soul. The lowest level, called the *Nefesh*, is in many ways equivalent to the unthinking, automatic nature of the physical body. Kabbalah scholar Brian L. Lancaster terms this the 'bodymind'.[5] The middle level is termed *Ruach* and is the consciousness that calls itself 'I': the equivalent of the Greek *thymos* or my new definition of the Eidolon. Not surprisingly the highest 'self', my Daemon, is represented in Kabbalistic terms as the *Neshamah*. This being is a portion of God that is trapped in this world but yearns to return to its rightful place. It acts as a guiding spirit that subliminally influences the life of its Ruach-Eidolon. According to the Zohar:

> . . . *the* neshamah *resides in a man's character – an abode which cannot be discovered or located. Should a man strive towards purity of life, he is aided thereto by a holy* neshamah, *whereby he is purified and sanctified* . . . (Zohar 1:62a)

Again it is interesting to note that the *Neshamah* and the *Ruach* are very much two sides of the same coin. Indeed, one of the goals of life is to endeavour to bring these two elements into close alignment. The *Zohar* says that the reflected light of God can only shine forth within the soul of man if he brings these two elements together:

> *The* neshamah *is above and the* ruach *is below and they join like male and female. When they are united they shine with a supernatural light, and in this union they are together called* ner *(lamp). The soul of man is the* ner *of God (Proverbs 20:27). What is* ner? Neshamah ruach. *(Zohar 2:99b)*

The implication here is that the *Neshamah's* role is to assist when it can in the life of its *Ruach*. Could this explain the mystery of the *maggid*? This was an angelic voice that dictated many of the writings of such renowned mystics as Joseph Karo and Hayim Vital. Karo called this being the 'answering angel'. Is it not reasonable to conclude that this 'voice' is that of Karo's *Neshamah*?

The Jewish convert to Islam, Abul Barakat, who died in about 1165, seems to say as much in the following quote:

> *This is why the ancient Sages, initiated into things the sensory facilities do not perceive, maintained that for each individual soul, or perhaps for several together having the same nature and affinity, there is a being in the spiritual world which throughout their existence watches over this soul and group of souls with especial solicitude and tenderness, protects, guides, defends, comforts them, leads them to knowledge, leads them to victory; and this being is what they call* Perfect Nature. *This friend, defender and protector is what religious terminology calls the* Angel.

That such a man could convert from Judaism to Islam may come as yet another surprise to the 21st century reader. However, for hundreds of years the followers of the Crescent and the Star of David had coexisted happily. Unlike Western Christendom with its labelling of the Jews as 'Christ Killers', Islam had no particular problem with the Jews. In general Muslims were extremely tolerant of Judaism, particularly in Moorish Andalusia where many Kabbalists were to be found. Indeed, one particular group of Muslims, the Sufis, found that their beliefs and those of the Kabbalists had considerable areas of overlap. It is to this group that we now turn.

Sufism and Islam

Judaism, or more specifically Kabbalah, teaches that the conscious soul of man has two elements, the *Ruach* and the *Neshamah*. Islam also has a very similar concept in that it too considers that the soul is an amalgamation of two seats of conscious awareness. In place of the *Ruach* the Muslims have the *Nafs* and for the *Neshamah* read the *Ruh*. Clearly these similarities are not total, but they do have many qualities in common – qualities they share with my Daemon and Eidolon.

For a Muslim the *Nafs* is the soul in its unregenerated state. By growing in awareness it can be changed into the more advanced being known as the *Ruh*. This is a being of deep spiritual dignity that sits midway between the angels and God. This being is of particular interest to the Islamic monastic order known as the Sufis.

Sufism is a mystical movement that is less legalistic than mainstream Islam. It attempts to bring about a more personal relationship with God. It is generally thought that the term originates from the Arabic word *suf*, which is literally translated as 'wool' because the early Islamic mystics from which Sufism evolved wore simple woollen robes called *jama i suf*. These garments were made of coarse wool mixed with horsehair and were worn next to the skin in imitation of Christian monks and hermits.

Sufis believe that along with his general teachings the Prophet

Muhammad (CE570–632) also taught at another level, imparting that knowledge only to his closest companions. These teachings have been handed down across the generations but have continued to be given only to those who are capable of understanding the symbolism of the message. A similar way of thinking applies to the Koran itself. This sacred book of the Muslims has both an 'outer' or apparent meaning and a secret or 'inner' meaning. Central to this belief is that the spiritually undeveloped person is trapped in a form of lifelong sleep in which reality is only experienced at the point of death. The Prophet is recorded as having said of man that 'when he dies he wakes'. The great Sufi master Rumi interpreted this by writing:

> The mind sees things inside-out. What it takes to be life is really death, and what it takes to be death is really life.

Or, as the Prophet said, 'Die before you die'.

In this way man lives in a state of forgetfulness of his true nature and that of reality itself. According to the Sufis of the Rifai this forgetfulness is called *nisyan*. Indeed, the term for man, *insan*, reflects this state of amnesia.

However, the Sufis believe that man is a dual being and that part of him does not suffer from *nisyan*. This element, the equivalent of my term the 'Daemon', is the *Ruh* and it is fully aware of its own past and future. This 'higher self' acts as a guide to its lower self. Indeed, Sufis see this relationship more like that of twins than abstractions such as the *Nafs* and the *Ruh*. In our unenlightened state – equivalent to my 'Eidolon' – we exist unaware of our 'Heavenly Twin', 'Angelic Spirit', 'Guide of Light' or, most importantly, 'Man of Light'. All these terms are used by Sufis to describe the entity I term the Daemon. The Western writer on Sufism, Henry Corbin, argues that this being is the equivalent of the 'guardian daimon'. In his fascinating work *The Man of Light In Iranian Sufism*, Corbin makes the following observation:

*. . . Plotinus (Enneads 3:iv) speaks of the daimon paedros
into whose care we are given, and who is the guide of the soul
throughout life and beyond death . . . Apuleius (De Deo
Socratis, 16) (deals) with the higher group of daimons to each
of whom the care of one human individual is entrusted and
who serves as its witness and guardian . . . Philo of Alexandria
calls the Nous (Divine Intellect) the true man, the man within
man . . . who dwells in the soul of each of us, now as archon
(ruler) and king, now of judge . . . on occasion he plays the
part of a witness, sometimes even of a prosecutor . . .*[6]

Corbin relates this 'daimon' to another Sufi theme of the 'Man
of Light' which is equated with Archangel Gabriel or the Supreme
Spirit (*Ar-Ruh al-Qudsi*), or perfect nature: in short, everyone's
'true' or 'higher' self. The aim of Sufism is for the lower self to
'wake up' and realize that it has a heavenly twin that exists as
close to it as its 'jugular vein' and that this heavenly twin is, in a
very real sense, a more spiritually advanced version of itself.

It is clear that both Sufism and the Kabbalah have many things
in common. It is as if they have both discovered universal truths
that are only available to those who are able to understand and
appreciate their subtle power. Can it be that there is an older
tradition that may have influenced both these great philosophies?
It seems that there is. A clue lies in another etymological root to
the word 'Sufi'. A 10th century author called al-Biruni proposed
that the root word was not *suf* (wool) but *'sufiya'*, a variation
on the Greek word *Sophia*: 'wisdom'. If this is correct then there
is a precise link between Sufism and the Christian schismatic sect
called the Gnostics.

Gnosticism

For the Gnostics 'Sophia' was not just a word but also the name
of a being which existed in an intermediate position between man

and the true God. These God-like beings were known as the 'Aeons' and they shared with God a location outside time and space called the Realm of Fullness, or 'Pleoroma'. However, Sophia accidentally brought about the creation of a flawed being called the 'Demiurge'. This being decided to create a universe in its own flawed image. The resulting imperfect reflection of the Pleoroma is our universe, a universe of the Darkness. All human beings exist in a universe that is not quite right – a universe that was not created by God, but by a being that thought he was God.

However, within every human being is a spark that belongs to the Light, the Pleoroma and the True God. This spark, the Daemon, is located deep within the soul of each human being and is trapped in this illusory universe of darkness. For the Gnostics, man had forgotten his true nature, exactly as the Sufis had described it in their concept of *nisyan*. However, all was not lost. If a man's lower self, his Eidolon, could realize his state through inner-knowledge – *gnosis* – he could see the universe as it really was and merge with his inner light, his higher self.

This belief in the higher self had been adopted by the Gnostics from the earlier beliefs of the pagan sages of the Mystery religions of Greece and Rome. This Daemon-Eidolon duality was central to the theology of such groups as the Stoics and the Platonists. For the philosophers of the Mysteries the Eidolon is the embodied self, the being that calls itself 'I'. This being labours under the illusion that it is a singular being. However, this self is false and man's true nature is the immortal Daemon.

The Stoic Epictetus made the following observation which was subsequently recorded by his pupil Arrian:

> God has placed at every man's side a guardian, the Daemon
> of each man, who is charged to watch over him; a Daemon
> that cannot sleep, nor be deceived. What greater and more
> watchful guardian could have been committed to us? So,
> when you have shut the doors, and made darkness in the

house, remember, never to say that you are alone; for you are not alone. But God is there, and your Daemon is there.

Here we see the idea that this other entity, the Daemon, is more than simply another facet of human nature. It is an independent being that watches over its lower self. That it has an ongoing consciousness is stated by the phrase 'cannot sleep'. Indeed, the implication is that the Daemon perceives even when the Eidolon sleeps.

The Gnostics seemed very aware of this duality of consciousness and the reasons for it. They realized that we are doomed to live our lives over and over again within this fake universe of the Demiurge. Our everyday lower self (Eidolon) is completely unaware that it has been here many times before and has done the same things many times over. It is again the issue of learning from these mistakes. The only way this can be done is by opening up the channels of communication between the ignorant self and the fully aware Higher Self. This can only be done through Gnosis – self-knowledge. Without Gnosis the Eidolon cannot merge with its Daemon and so move on. In the *Gospel of Philip* (63:11–21) this is clearly stated in the parable of the ass:

> *An ass which turns a millstone did a hundred miles walking.*
> *When loosed it found that it was still in the same place.*
> *There are men who make many journeys (lifetimes), but make*
> *no progress towards a destination. When evening (death)*
> *came upon them, they saw neither city nor village, neither*
> *creation nor nature, power nor angel (they were in isolation of*
> *the soul's afterlife). In vain the poor wretches laboured.*

The journey of the ass around the millstone is synonymous with the revolutions of the Eternal Return. It labours to get back to where it started and goes through the process again and again. As long as it is unaware that it has done it before it will never learn. However, if a part of the ass realizes what it is doing it can break free.

Certain writers have put this example forward as evidence that the Gnostics believed in reincarnation. A moment's reflection will show that is clearly not the case. If the parable of the ass was meant to illustrate reincarnation, then why use such a circular repetition as going round a millwheel? The ass is clearly the same ass and it is not 'reborn' as a pig or a dog. This ass goes round in circles with no break or change in species. To me this parable is presenting the Eternal Return.

Later the writer of the *Gospel of Philip* implies that after many cycles and the generation of many eidolonic lives the Daemon is allowed to move on and enter 'The Kingdom of Heaven':

> *[Jesus said] You who have joined the perfect, the light [The Daemon?] with the Holy Spirit, unite the angels with us also, the images [one's previous Eidolonic incarnations]. Do not despise the lamb [Eidolon], for without it, it is not possible to go to see the King. No one will be able to go to the King if he is naked. (58:11–17)*

The implication here is that to be clothed is to be 'covered' by all your past eidolonic incarnations.

Gnosis comes about when the Eidolon becomes fully aware of its Daemon. When this happens the two beings become a unitary consciousness – an undivided self.

The *Gospel of Thomas* (61 and 84) is absolutely clear about this. It states:

> *If he is undivided, he will be filled with darkness . . . When you see your likeness [Daemon], you rejoice. But when you see your images [Eidolonic incarnations] which came into being before you, and which neither die nor become manifest, how much will you have to bear!*

It is interesting that Thomas makes this curious statement that the 'images' neither die nor become manifest. For me this seems to be a way of explaining that these are discarded iterations of the person that will never die because somewhere in Everett's Multiverse they continue while at the same time they will never become manifest in this particular universe. (Put very simply, Everett's Multiverse theory, based on quantum mechanics, suggests that the 'real world' consists of multiple parallel universes in which everything that could happen does happen. So the same life is being lived in every possible way throughout the 'Multiverse'. However, the human observer normally only perceives one universe at a time. For a full explanation of why this bizarre explanation is accepted by the majority of modern particle physicists I suggest that you read chapter one of my previous book – *Is There Life After Death?: The Extraordinary Science of What Happens When We Die*.[7])

For the Gnostics, only by bringing the Daemon and Eidolon together could consciousness progress to the next level of existence. As we saw in Chapter 1, the psychologist Julian Jaynes argued that human consciousness was unitary until around the first millennium BCE when a splitting took place. Could this be what the Gnostics were all too aware of? Man needed to get back to this unitary state to evolve again. Thomas is again very clear on this matter. In verse 22 he writes:

> *Jesus said to them, 'When you make the two one, and when you make the inside the outside, and make the above like the below, and when you make the male and the female one and the same, so that the male not be male nor the female . . .*
> *then you will enter the Kingdom.'*

For the Gnostics it was clear that once this joining together was brought about man could become as a god within his own self-created universe. What else can be made of this statement, again taken from the *Gospel of Thomas*, verses 48 & 106:

Jesus said, 'If two make peace with each other in this one house they will say to the mountain, "Move away," and it will move away . . . When you make the two one, you will become the sons of man and when you say, "Mountain move away," it will move away.'

The idea that to engineer an open communication with one's Daemon can bring about enlightenment is very interesting when viewed in the light of the experiences of a later Gnostic by the name of Mani.

Mani, the founder of an eastern Gnostic religion in northern Babylonia, melded sections of traditional Iranian religion to create a new version, Manichaeism. He was born near Baghdad in CE216, into a family related to the Persian royal house. He had been brought up as a member of a sect known as the *almughtasila* ('those who wash themselves'). However, as a boy he received a revelation in CE228 from a spirit that he described as 'a twin'. He said:

I recognized him and understood that he was myself from whom I had been separated.

Mani described these visions as coming to him 'like lightning'. He likened this to what happened to St Paul on the road to Damascus. This is a very interesting description and one that we will encounter again and again when we discuss the nature of mystical experience. It is of particular importance in relation to the overall theory of 'Cheating the Ferryman'.

This 'heavenly twin' reappeared when Mani was 26 and this time his Daemon was keen for its Eidolon to know as much as it could allow it to. It told Mani:

Who I am and what my body is, and how my arrival at this world occurred . . . Who is my father on high and what order and commission he gave me before I put on this material body

and before I was led astray in this abominable flesh . . .
Who is my inseparable twin . . . He revealed it to me, the
boundless heights and the unfathomable depths.[8]

But there was more. This Daemon had another power that we will encounter many times in the pages to come – precognition:

I had revealed to me all that has happened, and all that
shall happen, everything that the eye sees, and the ear hears,
and the thought thinks. Through him I understand everything.
Through him I saw everything.[9]

Whatever was communicating with Mani, this entity seemed to have some very interesting ideas as regards the nature of matter and light. As we have already seen, Gnostics believed, and indeed still do, that we are beings of light that are trapped in an illusory universe of darkness. However, Mani had a curiously modern interpretation of this state of affairs. For him the purpose of religion was to release the particles of light imprisoned in matter. This is an amazing belief taking into account what we now know about matter. The mathematician Sir James Jeans suggested in the early 1930s that what we call light is really matter moving at its fastest possible speed, and that to move matter at this speed requires infinite power. As he pictured it, the moment this infinite energy is reduced and the speed of matter slows down, it ceases to be light and becomes 'matter'. He termed matter 'bottled light' and he termed light 'unbottled matter'. Can it be that Mani, writing over 1,700 years ago had awareness of the ultimate nature of matter? If this is so, then his teachings on the possible dual nature of human consciousness should be taken very seriously.

Mani was clearly a very interesting person and one that we will return to in Chapter 10 when we discuss the curious life similarities between his life and that of the 20th century science fiction writer, Philip K. Dick.

As a final point it is interesting to note that some of the Gnostic 'Gospels' apply the Daemon-Eidolon duality to Jesus himself. In one of the famous Nag Hammadi texts can be found the following passage where the narrator has the disciple John say:

> When all of his disciples were sleeping in one house at Gennesaret, I Alone, having wrapped myself up, watched from under my garment what he did; and first I heard him say, 'John, go thou to sleep,' and thereupon I feigned to be asleep; and I saw another like unto him come down, whom I also heard saying to my Lord, 'Jesus, do they whom thou hast chosen still not believe in thee?' And my Lord said, 'Thou sayest well for they are men.'

Gnostic teaching, as a mystery religion, was oblique in its symbolism. For them Jesus symbolized the Daemon in that he was a transposed being from the Realm of Light. Within the controversy known as Docetism, Jesus was a visible Daemon who by his very nature could not have a body. By contrast, according to Gnostic belief he did have an Eidolon, represented in the role of his twin brother Thomas. In *The Book of Thomas the Contender*, Jesus (Daemon) teaches Thomas (Eidolon):

> 'Brother Thomas, while you have time in the world, listen to me, and I will reveal to you the things you have pondered in your mind. Now since it has been said that you are my twin and true companion, examine yourself and learn who you are, in what way you exist, and how you will come to be. Since you will be called my brother, it is not fitting that you be ignorant of yourself. And I know that you have understood, because you have already understood that I am the knowledge of the truth. So while you accompany me, although you are uncomprehending, you have in fact already come to know, and you will be called "the one who knows himself"'.

The allegorical content is thinly disguised here. The name Thomas is Aramaic for 'Twin'.

The supporting evidence for duality within the three 'religions of the book', Judaism, Christianity and Islam is clear. However, it is evident that these three religions have had a good deal of cross-fertilization of ideas and theology. In order for my theory to hold true I need to present evidence of religious beliefs that are both geographically and culturally distant from Europe and the Middle East. How far do I need to go? Well I suspect that a small group of islands in the middle of the Pacific Ocean that were only 'discovered' by Europeans 230 years ago and not fully opened up to Western influences until 1820 could be the ultimate example of cultural isolation. This group of islands are collectively called Hawaii. Can I find evidence of Gnostic dualism in the old religion of these isolated volcanic islands? Surprisingly yes, and nobody was more surprised than me.

The Kahuna of the Hawaiian islands

I am a member of an organization known as The Scientific & Medical Network. This is an international association of like-minded individuals who are striving to create a mutual under-standing between the scientist and the mystic. Soon after my first book had been published I was invited by Evelyn Elsaesser Valarino, the Near-Death Experience researcher, to Geneva to give a presentation to the Western Switzerland Group of the SMN. The meeting took place in an old monastery called Cret Berard. The location and the company were equally splendid and the presen-tation seemed well received by the group. At lunch I sat next to a gentleman by the name of Jean-Luc L'Eplattenier. Jean-Luc was very complimentary regarding my 'Cheating the Ferryman' theory and then asked me if I was aware of the Kahuna of Hawaii. I replied that I had heard the name, but that was it. Jean-Luc then discussed his experiences in Hawaii and how similar to my

> *'The one thing that remains constant is that he (the prophet)*
> *is possessed of a power not himself that invades his nephesh,*
> *masters it, and makes it a vehicle for the accomplishment of*
> *Yahweh's will.'*
>
> JAMES MUILENBERG (BIBLICAL SCHOLAR)

theories were the teachings of the Kahuna. He explained how my ideas on Near-Death Experience and the nature of reality as an inwardly-generated illusion paralleled Huna beliefs. He then gave me a vivid description of a series of mind-expanding experiences he had had while visiting a Kahuna place of worship. However, this was as far as the discussion went. As my presentation had focused upon the quantum physics elements of my theory I had only mentioned in passing my Daemon-Eidolon Dyad theory and Jean-Luc had no reason to expand into other areas of Huna belief.

Three months later I was researching material for this chapter when I found that I needed more evidence for the triune nature of the human being: evidence from a culture that was neither European nor Middle Eastern. For some reason something Jean-Luc had said entered my mind. I cannot even recall now what it was, but I decided to study the Kahuna and there it was – everything I needed to prove that my theory is supported by beliefs outside those religions influenced by Gnosticism.

The word Huna means 'secret', 'a profound message' or 'that which is hidden'. As we have already seen, Gnosticism, Kabbalah and Sufism all share this idea of a 'hidden knowledge': learning that can only be imparted to those who are willing to train their minds to accept it. We can see a virtually identical esoteric school of thought among the peoples of both Hawaii and greater Polynesia, including the Maoris of New Zealand.

When white men first came to the Hawaiian Islands they found themselves faced with a philosophical tradition that was seemingly alien. However, if representatives of the Gnostic tradition had been on board those ships a curious familiarity would have been observed.

Huna was, and still is, a practical way of life based on intuitive knowledge and inner guidance, where understanding about the inner workings of oneself and the external world is gained through constant observation. Those who have mastered the philosophy of Huna are called *Kahuna* in Hawaii and *Tahuna* in Tahiti. These individuals are revered by the indigenous community and also by an increasing number of Westerners who feel a deep association with the philosophy of Huna.

What is of great significance is that these isolated societies at the other side of the world developed a philosophy of the nature of the soul that is virtually identical to the triune beliefs of Mediterranean philosophy. We again have a subconscious element, a conscious element and a super-conscious element. In Huna these are known as the *Unihilipi*, the *Uhane* and the *Aumakua* respectively. The characteristics of these three elements are absolutely identical to the *Nefesh*, *Ruach*, and *Neshamah* of Kabbalistic psychology and my concepts of the subconscious, the Eidolon and the Daemon. In a clarification of an issue not necessarily made clear in other philosophical models of the triune self, Huna teaches that the *Aumakua* has full awareness of the thoughts and instincts of both the *Unihilipi* and the *Uhane,* whereas the two lower members of the triune are only cognisant of their own perceptions.

In translation, the three Polynesian words *Unihilipi, Uhane* and *Aumakua* become even more interesting. *Unihilipi* means 'a spirit that remembers', *Uhane* translates as a 'ghost that talks' and *Aumakua* means an 'utterly trustworthy parental spirit'.

Prayer has a very interesting function within Huna tradition. When a Kahuna prays, he or she is praying to their own Higher Self, not to a supreme deity. The logic is simple: to give praise to, or ask personal favours of, a God is pointless. A God has no need for praise and has more important matters to deal with than the personal requests of a human being. It is from their own *Aumakua* that advice and assistance is sought.

In many ways the Huna model of the relationship between the *Uhane* and the *Aumakua* is the closest equivalent to my 'Daemon-Eidolon Dyad' that I have encountered. What particularly caught my attention was the belief that the *Aumakua* has a very novel way of assisting its lower self. According to Huna teaching the future already exists in a pre-formed state. This pre-moulded future can be experienced by the *Uhane* during sleep. With the help of the *Aumakua* the *Uhane* can dream the future and re-design it to follow a more agreeable course. Once this is done the future crystallizes and becomes fully formed and unchangeable. On awaking the *Uhane* just follows the time-line as designed by the *Aumakua*.

Could this be another explanation for *déjà vu*? One of the attendees at my talk in Cret Berard was the Swiss-based American Jungian analyst Dr Arthur Funkhouser. Art and I had been in touch for a few years and my visit to Geneva was the perfect opportunity for us to meet up. I had become aware of Dr Funkhouser through his fascinating theory regarding the *déjà vu* phenomenon. In his 'Dream Theory of Déjà Vu' Art suggests that a *déjà vu* is brought about when the subject subconsciously

'This is why the ancient Sages, initiated into things the sensory facilities do not perceive, maintained that for each individual soul, or perhaps for several together having the same nature and affinity, there is a being in the spiritual world which throughout their existence watches over this soul and group of souls with especial solicitude and tenderness, protects, guides, defends, comforts them, leads them to knowledge, leads them to victory; and this being is what they call **Perfect Nature**. This friend, defender and protector is what religious terminology calls the **Angel**.'

ABUL-BARAKAT (SUFI MYSTIC)

'remembers' a dream they had earlier. The sensation of recognition is simply a recollection of the dream (see also Prologue). Huna philosophy implies something very similar: the future is not only experienced in a dream but it is also designed and fabricated in that dream as well.

In my theory 'Cheating The Ferryman', I propose that the Daemon is fully aware of the future that lies in wait for its Eidolon. As it has already lived this life before, it can, through various communication methods (including dreams), warn its lower self of future dangers. If these warnings are heeded then the future will be sidetracked into another universe that will contain all possible outcomes brought about by that 'temporal mutation'. This is very similar to the teachings of Huna. For the Kahuna the future can also be changed before it happens and they agree with my theory that the agent that brings about these changes is the *Aumakua*/Daemon.

But the similarities between Huna and my 'Cheating The Ferryman' theory do not stop there. According to anthropologist Joshua Stone it is believed by the Kahuna that:

> . . . after physical death, the person would make a
> thought-form world of 'purgatory' in which they would live as
> in a dream, all such things they needed to live out.[10]

In my last book I suggested a very similar scenario. If my theory is correct then many of us exist in a three-dimensional re-creation of our lives. You will recall that I termed this 'dream state' the Bohmian IMAX. This seems very similar to the Kahuna belief that at death we all exist in a mind-generated 'purgatory'. If this is the case, then what is the status of dreaming within the Bohmian IMAX? Could it be that we are dreaming within a dream? Is this fascinating state the place where the Eidolon is able to encounter the Daemon on a level playing field? It is this possibility that I would like to address in the next chapter.

Summary

In this chapter I have presented a considerable amount of evidence from theology that there is a fairly universal belief that human beings consist of not one but three elements. There is the unconscious, bodily element that is an epiphenomenon of the physical body. It is rooted in matter and on death this element ceases to exist. The other two elements are closely related and contain the components of conscious awareness that we call 'the self'. Different cultures and different theological belief systems give different names to these elements, but the attributes of each can be shown to be virtually identical. It is therefore reasonable to conclude that there seems to be some deep-rooted universal truth in regard to this triune structure.

For many religious belief systems the link between the everyday world and that of the gods takes place during deep mystical experience. This can be brought about by opening up the channels of communication in the brain. I argue that this may be the intention, but what really takes place is that such rituals just allow easier daemonic communication.

CHAPTER 4 Theology

---

[1] Newfield, D.F., *Seventh-Day Adventist Encyclopaedia*, pp.1380–1

[2] White, E.G., *Testimonies for the Church*, Pacific Press, pp.66–7 (1948)

[3] Horton, Robin, 'Destiny and the unconscious in West Africa', *Africa*, vol.31, pp.110–16 (1961)

[4] Guthrie, W.K.C., *History of Greek Philosophy*, CUP, p.318 (1962)

[5] Lancaster, Brian L., *The Essence of Kabbalah*, Arcturus, p.39 (2006)

[6] Corbin, Henry, *The Man of Light in Iranian Sufism*, Omega, NY, pp.34–5 (1994)

[7] Peake, Anthony, *Is There Life After Death?: The Extraodinary Science of What Happens When We Die*, Arcturus, pp. 15-36 (2006)

[8] Lane-Fox, Robin, *Pagans and Christians*, Penguin, p.565 (1986)

[9] Simon, Bernard, *The Essence of the Gnostics*, Arcturus, p.99 (2004)

[10] Stone, Joshua David, *The Huna Teachings of Hawaii*, IAM University

CHAPTER 5
The Dream

Writing is nothing more
Than a guided dream.

Jorge Luis Borges

By the rivers of Babylon

It was getting later and later. Again and again the professor looked at the crumpled piece of paper in a vain hope that he might be able to decipher the message. In his hands was a hasty sketch made by a student member of an expedition the University of Pennsylvania had sent to Babylon a few months earlier. The drawing was of two small fragments of agate which were supposed to belong to the finger-rings of some ancient Babylonians.

It was now midnight and still the only thing he could decipher with any real certainty was that the first character of the third line on one of the fragments seemed to signify the sound 'Ku'. This was a small breakthrough. He knew that these characters were in use from around 1700 to 1140BCE and that during that period there had ruled an obscure king known as Kurigalzu. The professor wondered if there was a link. He then studied the other drawing. However hard he tried he simply could not classify the markings. By this stage his mind was close to shutdown and he decided that the best course of action was to go to bed and rest.

As he drifted off to sleep he found himself in a temple. Out of the shadows came a tall, thin priest of about 40 years of age. The priest beckoned him forwards and led him to the treasure chamber of the temple. In the corner was a small entrance leading to a windowless, low-ceilinged room, in which he saw a large wooden chest. He noticed that the floor had scraps of agate and lapis lazuli scattered across it. The priest then turned and addressed the dreaming academic. Much to the professor's surprise he spoke in American English. Why this should be so puzzled him because although he lived in America his first language was German. What surprised him even more was what the priest said:

The two fragments, which you have published separately upon pages 22 and 26, belong together. They are not finger-rings, and their history is as follows.

The priest informed the professor that he was right in his suspicion that King Kurigalzu was involved. He explained that the king had sent an inscribed votive cylinder of agate to the temple and had then decided that the priests had to make a pair of agate ear-rings for the statue of the god Ninib. The priests had a problem. They had no agate available to them so the only solution was to cut the votive cylinder into three parts, thus making three rings, each of which contained a portion of the original inscription. The priest explained that the first two rings had served as ear-rings for the statue and these were the fragments that the professor was having so much trouble with. He added:

If you will put the two together, you will have confirmation of my words but the third ring you have not found yet, and you never will find it.

With this comment the priest disappeared and the professor woke up.

He was desperate not to forget the words of the priest so he immediately woke his wife to tell her what he had been told. Later that morning he re-examined the fragments and put them together as instructed. Allowing for some missing letters he was able to read off the inscription. It read:

To the god Ninib, son of Bel, his Lord, has Kurigalzu, pontifex of Bel presented this.

The academic in question was Herman Volrath Hilprecht, professor of Assyrian at the University of Pennsylvania in the 1880s. Hilprecht was to find that his dream was even more amazing when, a few weeks later, he was given the opportunity to examine the original fragments. A very excited Hilprecht turned up at the Imperial Museum in Istanbul and requested that he be allowed to handle the two pieces. They were located in two separate glass cases and as they were thought to be separate rings they had never been associated together.

To the amazement and subsequent delight of the curators he was immediately able to join the two rings together. He had anticipated that they would match simply because his 'dream adviser' had told him that they were fragments of a votive cylinder. Indeed, what was astonishing was that the white vein of the stone showed on one fragment and the grey surface on the other.[1]

This may seem impossible. How can a dream-character have so much information available to it? If the priest was just a figment of Hilprecht's over-tired imagination how did it present the solution to a problem to which its waking mind clearly did not have the answer? If my theory is correct then Hilprecht's Daemon, using

'Well, as regards the dreamer, I can answer that, for he is no less a person than myself – as I might have told you from the beginning, only that the critics murmur over my consistent egotism – and as I am positively forced to tell you now, or I could advance but little farther with my story. And for the Little People, what shall I say; they are but just my Brownies, God bless them!, who do one-half my work for me while I am fast asleep, and in all human likelihood, do the rest for me as well, when I am wide awake and fondly suppose I do it for myself.' (From **Across The Plains**)

ROBERT LOUIS STEVENSON (WRITER)

its 'memory', knew what the answer to the problem was. If the Daemon is fully aware of the past-life of its Eidolon then to give such information is easy. In his last life Hilprecht probably failed to find the answer for a few years. Maybe somebody else made the link many years later and he read about it. If this was the case then in this version of his life the information was already there – the Daemon just had to present it.

This daemonic guidance through dreams is the first level of my Scale of Transcendence. As I discussed in Chapter 3 the Daemon becomes more immanent in the lives of people the higher up this scale they are. However, in dreams the Daemon does not need the neurotransmitter-facilitated avenues of communication that it uses to such an effect with migraine-sufferers, TLE-sufferers and schizophrenics. The subconscious mind seems open to all kinds of subtle communications. In this chapter I wish to review the evidence that dreams are the 'superhighway' of Daemon-Eidolon interaction.

All I have to do is dream

Dreaming is something that we all do. However, it is also one of the most mysterious psychological states. When we dream we are unaware that we are dreaming. This simple statement is fascinating because it implies that while experiencing a dream-state we cannot tell it from 'reality'. The illusion is totally real, even when strange things take place. A moment's reflection will show that this is amazing. If we cannot know that we are dreaming while dreaming how can we really know that our waking experience is any more real?

At its most basic, dreaming is defined as mental activity that takes place while we are asleep. However, many different kinds of mental activity take place during sleep which cannot really be defined as dreaming. For example, somebody might say that they didn't sleep well because they were worried about a big business presentation that they had to make the next day. Another might report that after a long day on a fishing boat their sleep was disturbed by a feeling that they were moving as if they were still on the sea. The first is emotionally related and is more of a feeling of anxiety than a rich, narrative-based full dream. The second is a reproduction of a sensation of rocking. Yet again it has no dream-like sensations and it lacks the emotional content of the first sleep-state.

However if, on waking, the subject describes that they dreamed that they cycled off Beachy Head and then flew over to France then this would be considered a real dream-state. It has all the surreal and non-logical aspects of dreaming. In the first two sleep states one thing will be absent that will be clearly evident in the third – Rapid Eye Movement, or REM.

REM, also termed paradoxical sleep, was discovered in 1953. It was ascertained that at certain times during our sleep cycle our eyes move rapidly backwards and forwards. What was also revealed is that our bodies go through several different periods of sleep each night. Each period can be broken down into five stages. Stage one sleep lasts for between one and seven minutes and is when we are feeling drowsy but can still be easily awoken. As we go into stage two sleep it becomes harder to wake us; we spend about 50 per cent of our time asleep in this state. Then, in the third and fourth stages, follows the deepest slumber. At this time our heart and respiratory rates decrease and our body temperature drops.

REM activity occurs during this fourth stage. It can take place from four to seven times a night. This is when we dream. It has been shown that 90 per cent of subjects, when awoken during REM activity, will remember the dream that was being experienced. This has been shown to be true of people who had earlier claimed that they never dreamed.

However, brain damage can change this. In the 1970s, neurologists recorded that patients who had sustained damage to the pons – a primitive brain region located in the brain stem – never achieved REM sleep. It was therefore assumed that dreaming was facilitated by the non-conscious part of the brain. Sleep specialist J. Allan Hobson could not accept this belief. He argued that most dreams have huge emotional intensity and must, therefore, be generated by the emotional areas of the brain such as the limbic system. Through a series of experiments he was able to show that when REM activity started it triggered the production of a neurotransmitter called acetylcholine. This caused the pons to send impulses to many areas of the brain, including the limbic system. Hobson called this the reciprocal-interaction model.

A few years later Mark Solms at New York University proved that pons damage did not, after all, destroy the ability to dream. He tested 26 people who had damage to their pons and found that only one did not dream. The confusion had arisen because although a damaged pons does not bring about REM activity, dreaming is not indicated by REM activity in these circumstances.

Solms went on to identify two areas of the brain in which damage would bring about the loss of dream activity. These were the white matter of the frontal lobes and the occipitotemporo-parietal cortex. Neither are anywhere near the pons. He argues that these parts of the brain are the areas responsible for processing memory, experience and ideas. For Solms and his supporters this explains the richness and emotional content of dreams, elements that the primitive pons could simply not supply.

What this means, in simple terms, is that dreams originate in areas of the brain that are involved in rational thought, not in the unconscious, irrational areas of the brain stem.

Today, neuroscientists, psychologists and psychiatrists support either Solms or Hobson, with the debate still raging on in the academic journals. However, in March 2007 a paper was published by the specialist journal *Neurology* that may not only assist in the resolution of this problem, but might also have direct relevance to my 'Cheating the Ferryman' theory, because it presents a whole new angle on the Near-Death Experience itself. The paper was written by University of Kentucky neurophysiologist Kevin Nelson, who suggests that the NDE experience is, in fact, a form of waking dream.[2]

For the study, Nelson and his team approached 55 individuals who had reported a Near-Death Experience. This was defined as a time during an episode of danger, such as a car accident or a heart attack, when a person experienced a variety of sensations including a sense of being outside the physical body, unusual alertness, seeing an intense light and a feeling of peace. The experiencers were asked a series of questions about their sleeping habits. One question was as follows: 'Just before falling to sleep or just after awakening, have you the sense that you are outside your body and watching yourself?'

Of the 55 subjects, 33 (60 per cent) answered 'Yes'. The team then asked the same question of 55 individuals of a similar age and background to the first group, but who had never reported experiencing an NDE. The 'Yes' answer was given by only 24 per cent of this group.

This was of great significance for Nelson and his team. The question was asked for a specific purpose: it was an attempt to evaluate how many of the NDEers also experienced the mental state known as REM intrusion. This waking-dream state takes place when REM experience blends into wakefulness during sleep transition. Sometimes this can lead to another curious psychological state known as sleep paralysis, together with visual or auditory hallucinations. Although once considered rare it is now believed that up to 25 per cent of people experience sleep paralysis at least once in their lives. This percentage figure was accurately reflected in the positive 24 per cent 'Yes' answer of the non-NDE group.

Nelson argues that during a medical crisis muscle paralysis combined with an out-of-the-body experience could show many of the prominent features of a Near-Death Experience. Of all the near-death subjects who reported having sleep paralysis, 96 per cent also reported having an out-of-body experience either during sleep transition or an NDE.

These results bring into question the whole belief that an NDE is evidence that human consciousness survives the death of the body. If such crucial elements of the NDE experience can be shown to be epiphenomena (the mind as a by-product of the living brain) then clearly these elements cannot continue to be experienced when the brain itself is dead.

According to my 'Ferryman' theory the moment of death is never reached by any conscious being. As such the theory is in no way invalidated by Nelson's findings. Indeed, it can be argued that 'Cheating the Ferryman' is supported by the fact that something very strange happens to consciousness at the point of death – but these unusual neurological states are still related directly to a living brain, not a dead one.

Central to 'Ferryman' is one element of the NDE that is not mentioned by Nelson, the Being of Light – the entity I call the Daemon. If I am right then this element of consciousness will still be involved in the sleep transition state because it is through dream-states that the Daemon manifests itself to those people outside my scale of transcendence.

In a fascinating parallel, the Indian psychoanalyst B.S. Goel seems to agree with me when he writes:

> All dreams reflect the desire of the jiva (individual
> consciousness) to merge with Shiva (cosmic consciousness).
> And since the jiva knows itself as the body, the spiritual
> desire manifests as a desire to please the body.[3]

Here again we have this duality of consciousness – for jiva read Eidolon and for Shiva read Daemon. Indeed, in a curiously apposite event Dr Goel, who had dabbled in Freudianism and Marxism, had a very vivid dream in which a being he called his 'guru' told him that his path had taken a wrong turning. Was this 'guru' yet another manifestation of my Daemon?

I argue that the Daemon has many channels by which it can

communicate with its Eidolon. However, with most 'normal' people the neurological pathways through which this communication takes place are blocked by the inhibitors suggested by the 'filter theory' of Huxley, Broad and Bergson (see Chapter 2). For migrainers, temporal lobe epileptics and schizophrenics these pathways are ever-widening, but without the assistance of certain psychedelic substances such as mescaline they remain blocked for the rest of us during waking hours. However, during REM activity a channel opens and the Daemon takes its opportunity. Is this the real identity of Hilprecht's 'priest' and Goel's 'guru'?

Proof of such an assertion can only be presented if dreams are really a channel whereby knowledge of the future is made available to the dreamer. If my theory is right then the Daemon knows exactly what will take place in the future life of its Eidolon. All it needs to do is communicate through the small opening brought about by REM activity. I will now present evidence from history to support such a supposition.

The gates of horn and ivory

It is clear that dreams sometimes seem to solve problems that the waking mind simply cannot. It is as if the Daemon is keen to assist but can only do so by using symbols. A classic example of this is the way in which German chemist Friedrich Kekulé discovered the complex structure of carbon.

Before 1858, organic chemists had no real idea of what the substances they worked with looked like at the molecular level. In that year Kekulé was staying in London. He had been to see his friend, Hugo Mueller, and was travelling on the last bus to his lodgings in Clapham. As it was quite late he fell into a sleep-like state that again seems very like a REM intrusion. As he did so he saw in front of his eyes many atoms dancing in the air. As they gambolled and spun he noticed how, on a regular basis, two smaller atoms would unite and form a pair and how they would then be surrounded by a larger atom and how even larger atoms would 'embrace' three or four of the smaller ones. He then saw these large aggregate atoms form a chain, dragging the smaller ones behind them but only when they were at the back of the ever-enlarging chain. His dream state was shattered when the bus conductor called out 'Clapham Road' and the atoms dissolved in front of him.

Such was the vividness of this dream that he was able to spend the rest of the evening making sketches of what he had 'seen'. This was the origin of his 'Structural Theory'. What his Daemon had visually told him was that certain carbon atoms could link together in chains, with hydrogen atoms and other atoms connected to them.

But his Daemon had now got a taste for chemical structures. In 1865 it enabled him to make what is widely regarded as the most brilliant piece of prediction to be found in the history of organic chemistry. This time Kekulé was living in Ghent. His small study had no natural light and he was made drowsy by the heat of a roaring coal fire. As on the bus eight years earlier he found himself dropping off to sleep: then his Daemon went to work.

Again Kekulé fell into a light dream and again he saw the atoms dance. However, this time they began twisting in a snakelike motion until, suddenly, one of the 'snakes' suddenly caught hold of its own tail. 'As if by a flash of lightning I awoke,'[4] he related.

In a moment he realized how the dream had shown him a cyclic structure for benzene. The dream had also demonstrated how the six carbon atoms could be joined together into a ring. What is simply amazing about this structure is how much it resembles the modern view, which is based upon the quantum mechanical concept of the electronic linking of atoms, although electrons were totally unknown until the turn of the 20th century, 40 years after Kekulé made his 'discovery'. How on earth did his Daemon know this?

Indeed, quantum theory itself was discovered with the help of another Daemon, this time the one that coexisted with the great

Danish physicist Nils Bohr. While still a student, Bohr had a vivid dream in which he was watching a horse race. As his dream-self looked down at the racecourse a voice in his head pointed out that the marked lanes on the racetrack kept the horses in a fixed route round the circular track. On awaking Bohr realized that this dream had shown him how it was that electrons had to follow a fixed and rigid orbit around the nucleus. The model of atomic structure had been discovered!

Sometimes the Daemon gets frustrated with the inability of its Eidolon to get the message and it repeats the dream over and over again until it registers. This is exactly what happened to the Swiss-born American geologist Louis Agassiz (1807–83).

When in America he worked on a vast exercise to classify all the known fossil fish. While doing this, he came across a specimen that lay within a stone slab. It was such a strange fossil that Agassiz simply could not figure out its actual shape. As it was embedded in the slab he could not extract it for fear of ruining it altogether. He was very frustrated about this but one night he had a dream in which he was presented with an image of the fish in perfect condition. However, because he was unprepared for such a vision he had no way of recording the image before it faded away with the morning light.

He assumed that he had lost the opportunity given to him by the dream. However, to his surprise the dream image was again presented to him on the following night. Although he was unprepared for the second night running he was ready on the third night. Again the image was presented and this time he had pen and paper ready by his bedside. When he awoke he drew his recollection of the image in the faint early dawn light. He then went back to sleep satisfied that he had captured the fish correctly.

On waking, he looked again at his drawing. He was surprised, and slightly worried, by the fact that his version of what he had been shown had remarkably different features to all the other specimens that he had recorded up to that time. Agassiz decided that he had to take a gamble. He went to his laboratory and extracted the fossil from its stone slab. Much to his amazement his dream-image was exactly correct in every anatomical detail. It was as if his subconscious had a future memory of him seeing the fossil in its full glory. Of course we know that it was his Daemon that remembered from his last-life rerun. It was just another little clue that our superior partner had left to posterity.

Sometimes the Daemon even shows amazing design and engineering skills. In 1789 the musical instrument designer Ernest Chladni was wrestling with the design of an instrument that he was sure would bring about a totally new sound. However hard he tried, his brain could simply not pull together the disparate elements needed to bring about his new sound. Just as Kekulé was to discover over half a century later, all that was needed was a small nap. Immediately, the hypnogogic imagery welled up from Chladni's subconscious. The channels of communication between Eidolon and Daemon were open. Straight away the Eidolon was presented with a perfect, three-dimensional image of the required instrument. The image was only available for a few seconds before Chladni awoke with a start, but it was not only still in his mind, he could also dissect it and view it from all angles. Within a few days his design was complete and he set about building the first prototype. On 8 March 1790 it was finished and several days later Chladni was able to play a few tunes on what he was to call a euphonium.

The euphonium has proved itself to be an interesting but fairly minor musical instrument. Some other inventions have had a much greater impact upon society. One such device is the sewing machine, an invention that was to make its inventor, Elias Howe, a very rich man.

In this case, Howe had perfected the machine, but couldn't come up with a needle design that would allow it to go through the cloth in the way that was demanded by the mechanism. Yet again the Daemon was there to ensure that this time round, and in this Everett Multiverse, Elias reaped the financial benefit. It created a dream whereby its Eidolon found itself being taken prisoner by a group of natives. As they danced around him Howe's lower self noticed that the spears that the natives carried all had small holes near the tips. This was what his new needles needed. The dream remained with him long enough after waking for him to jot down the design for further reference. It was exactly what was required and the rest was, as they say, history.

Sometimes the Daemon feels the need to disguise itself in dreams. It seems to realize that its Eidolon will only do as it requests if it feels at ease with the source of the information. In my opinion this is what happened to the poet William Blake. Throughout his life Blake insisted that he was being visited by angels, who advised and assisted him in his work. He described this as being 'under the direction of messengers from Heaven, daily and nightly'.[5]

A close reading of Blake's statements on this matter leaves one in no doubt that these were daemonic assists disguised as messengers, angels and, on one occasion, his recently dead brother, Robert. In February 1787, Blake's brother Robert died. Blake was distraught at this tragedy. He had remained constantly at his dying brother's bedside for two weeks and reportedly collapsed into a continuous sleep for three days and nights after his death.

At the time of his brother's death Blake was searching for a better way to print and publish his work. For a year he laboured in this quest without much success and then Robert appeared to him in a 'waking dream'. A contemporary describes the event:

> Blake, after deeply perplexing himself as to the mode of accomplishing the publication of his illustrated songs without their being subject to the expense of letter-press, his brother Robert stood before him in one of his visionary imaginations, and so decidedly directed him in the way in which he ought to proceed, that he immediately followed his advice.[6]

'Be it a daemon or a genius that often rules us for hours of crisis – enough stretched sleepless in a hotel in Spezia there came to me the prompting for the music for my Rhinegold; at once I returned to my melancholy home to carry out that immense work that fate of which now, above all else, binds me to Germany.'

RICHARD WAGNER (COMPOSER)

CHAPTER 5 The Dream

The new method of printing that 'Robert' suggested worked 'without the expense of letter-press.'[7] Whatever was suggested in this dream was certainly effective. Blake now found himself the master of his own production process. Yet again the Daemon had helped its Eidolon to effect a massive change in fame and fortune.

Sometimes the Daemon also acts as a form of dream-tutor. In his book *Le Sommeil et les rêves* (1861), French doctor Alfred Maury described how when he was learning English his Daemon corrected his English grammar. In his dream Maury was speaking to a young lady in English and he wanted to tell her that he had visited her that previous evening. He used the expression 'I called you yesterday'. The dream lady replied that this structure was not quite right. She explained that in correct English the words would be 'I called on you yesterday'. On waking, Maury was fascinated by the vividness of his dream recollection. He was interested to know if his dream adviser was right – after all, if a dream is purely a creation of the subconscious how could that subconscious know something that the conscious mind did not? Much to his surprise, when he checked the phrase out in a book on English grammar the imaginary lady had been quite right.

Again we have to ask ourselves how this can possibly be. Maury simply did not know the correct verb-preposition structure of that English phrase. Clearly somebody in his head did!

And it is not just foreign grammar. Srinivasa Ramanujan (1887–1920) was one of India's greatest mathematical geniuses.

He made substantial contributions to the analytical theory of numbers and worked on elliptical functions, continued fractions and infinite series. In 1914 he was invited to Cambridge by English mathematician G.H. Hardy and in the next five years proved over 3,000 theorems. However, he claimed that all his mathematical insights were given to him just before he awoke from sleep. In these semi-dream states he conversed with a being that he described as the Hindu goddess of Namakkal. The goddess would then present him with mathematical formulae that he would verify immediately on waking. In this example he describes how the vision worked:

> *There was a red screen formed by flowing blood as it were. I was observing it. Suddenly a hand began to write on the screen. I became all attention. That hand wrote a number of results in elliptic integrals. They stuck in my mind. As soon as I woke up, I committed them to writing . . .*[8]

All the examples I have given so far have involved Daemons who have given information that was unavailable or unknown to the receiving Eidolon. These Daemons have disguised themselves as disincarnate voices, disembodied limbs or as people within the dream itself. However, on occasions the Daemon wishes it to be known to its Eidolon that it is a being in its own right – a being with a personality and motivations of its own. A classic example of this is what happened to the French poet Jean Cocteau in 1937.

Cocteau has been called the most versatile artist of the 20th century. Yet because of the eccentricity of his behaviour and the obscurity of much of his work he has never really received the recognition he deserved. Many critics argue that this is because of his absolute belief in a supernatural force that guided him through his life. Cocteau argued that this power was to be found in the work of all the great artists. Clearly what Cocteau was trying to put across was the inner power of his Daemon – a being he called Heurtebise.

From 1913 onwards Cocteau was convinced that he was receiving guidance through his dreams. At that time he had only a subliminal awareness of this assistance. Indeed sometimes this subconscious assistance seemed both confused and confusing. The fruit of this subconscious muse was a work entitled *The Potomak*, which was not published until 1919. It took the form of a confusing mixture of a novel, a poem and an autobiography. What made it even stranger was that Cocteau had been 'instructed' to lace it with bizarre drawings that seemed to have little in common with the text. When asked to explain this mélange he said that it had been 'imposed upon him' by what he termed the 'parliamentarians of the unknown'. He implied that these beings dictated to him while he was asleep.

In 1925 he was to discover that his parliamentarians had a prime minister. He had just entered an elevator after visiting a friend. He was alone in the lift but he suddenly felt, right beside him, the presence of 'something both terrible and eternal'. He could not see anything but he knew it was there. And then it 'spoke' to him. It told Cocteau that 'my name can be found on the brass plaque'. Cocteau looked round and saw the name of the elevator's manufacturer engraved upon it – 'Heurtebise'.

Here we have a Daemon announcing itself literally as bold as brass. Once it had announced itself, it stayed with him for the rest of his life. It confirmed that it had been responsible for 'the parliamentarians', also telling him that from now on he had to carry out what the Daemon desired. As if giving him a subtle message about what its nature was, Heurtebise cast itself as a glazier in Cocteau's theatre production of his work *Orpheus*. What does a glazier do? He makes mirrors and reflections and if one looks in a mirror what is reflected but one's own image? Is this what Cocteau, or Heurtebise, was trying to impart: that he is a *doppelgänger*, a double?

However, it was in 1937 that Heurtebise was to show his precognitive powers. Cocteau was trying to write an updated version of the Arthurian legend. Ideas were simply not coming. He fell asleep exhausted and slept for many hours. As he started to awaken he found himself caught in what we now know as a REM intrusion. Another term for this state is hypnopompia. While in this state he experienced a profoundly vivid hallucination. He saw in front of him a theatre. The curtain went up and he watched with utter amazement as a whole three-act play was performed for him. The details of the characterization were deep and rich, the dialogue sparkling. Most of the characters were unknown to Cocteau as he knew little about the details of the Arthurian tales. The play ended, the curtain came down and the poet slid into a waking state. The images were so strong that he immediately put pen to paper and wrote the whole play.

It was only later, when he was checking the accuracy of the details, that he discovered that all the characters, and the circumstances in which they found themselves, were mirrored in the legends. Cocteau was stunned by this because the information was totally unknown to him at the time of writing.[9]

Was Heurtebise carrying out the threat he had made 12 years earlier – that the poet would be simply a channel for the creative desires of his own Daemon?

What I found particularly interesting about Cocteau/Heurtebise's work was the level of symbolism that could be seen in 'their' work, particularly the films. They seemed to be preoccupied with time's flow and on many occasions used the cinematographic device of playing back the film. Is this not exactly what my theory says happens in the final moments of our lives – an eternal return where time runs back and forth like a snake swallowing its tail?

I am also interested in drawing a parallel with Strindberg's vision in the Augustiner Tavern (see Chapter 2). Could it be that what Cocteau actually experienced was a Daemon-induced section of his own future life when he sat in a theatre and watched his own production of *The Knights of the Round Table*?

Was this more than just a waking dream? Could it be that Cocteau was in a very specific way being shown future events? If the Bohmian IMAX is a recording then future events have already been experienced by the Daemon and, under certain circumstances, these memories can be recalled before the events take place in this particular life rerun. This phenomenon is surprisingly common. It is called precognition.

Summary

Dreaming is the main area of subliminal communication between the Daemon and its Eidolon. It seems that the 'Doors of Perception' are far more ajar during sleep, even for individuals whose normal waking life contains none of the elements of my Scale of Transcendence (migraine, TLE or schizophrenia). During sleep the Eidolon delves deep into its own subconscious and in doing so meets up with its own Higher Self. When this takes place the Daemon can subtly place ideas or thoughts that can carry through to the waking life. These are usually conveyed using deep-rooted archetypes and symbolism. This is why dream interpretation has been such an important part of esoteric traditions. In the last hundred years or so Jungian analysis has spawned many imitations, all of which take a similar approach to the dream state.

I have presented examples of how the Daemon, in its role as dream-guide, shows knowledge that is simply not available to its Eidolon. Again this is evidence the Daemon has lived this life before and it simply uses that seemingly precognitive ability to guide the Eidolon along a different life path to that followed last time.

[1] Woods, Ralph L., *The World of Dreams*, New York, pp.525–30 (1947)

[2] Nelson, K. et al., 'Does the arousal system contribute to Near-Death Experience', *Neurology* (2007)

[3] Goel, B.S, *Psychoanalysis and Meditation*, Third Eye Foundation of India (1986)

[4] Benfrey, O.T., *Journal of Chemical Education*, vol. 35, p.21 (1958)

[5] Wilson, M., *The Life of William Blake*, Nonesuch Press, p.135 (1927)

[6] Ackroyd, Peter, *Blake*, Sinclair-Stevenson, p.111 (1995)

[7] Bentley, G.E., *Blake Records*, Oxford University Press, p.460 (1969)

[8] Raganathan, S.R., *Ramanujan, The Man and the Mathematician*, Asia Publishing House, New York (1967)

[9] Cocteau, J., from 'Proces de l'inspiration' in *Le Foyer des Artistes* (1947)

CHAPTER 6

Precognition

It's a poor sort of memory that
Can only work backwards
Lewis Carroll, Through the Looking Glass

Leonhard and his Hanna

This character was like no other for German novelist Leonhard Frank. His half-written novel was enlivened by an addition that exemplified all that was wonderful in a young woman. The person he had decided to call Hanna was a hot-blooded beauty with a flawless olive and rose-coloured complexion. In his creative fervour he had made her both graceful and slender with a great love of life. Hanna's character had sparkled out of his imagination and she quickly placed herself within the narrative of his novel *The Singers*. The year was 1927 and life was good for an intellectual writer at the leading edge of the Expressionist movement. Frank used to spend his time frequenting the coffee houses of Weimar Berlin, discussing ideas and theories with his friends. However, in 1929 something very strange was to happen to him – something that was to change his life.

He was sitting in his favourite haunt, the Romanisches Café, when he recognized one of his fellow clients. A young woman was sitting nearby. She was alone but was clearly waiting for somebody. This young woman was exactly as he had imagined Hanna. She had the same looks, skin and graceful movements that had haunted his book and his imagination. Here was the literal woman of his dreams. However, he was frozen with inactivity. What could he do? He could try and open a conversation, but he feared that such a move would be wrong. He was 48 years old whereas this refugee from his subconscious was no more than 20. To even speak to her would, in his opinion, probably bring about a courteous rebuff. His agony of forced inactivity was mercifully short. He watched as a young man rushed into the café and profusely apologized to the young woman. She smiled back at the interloper and the young couple, clearly in love, walked out of the café arm in arm.

The incident so haunted Frank that for the next few weeks he regularly visited the café, hoping against hope that she would return. He still had no plan but something deep within him was demanding that if the opportunity should arise again he would speak to her. However, it was not to be. She was never to return. Indeed, the political circumstances in Germany were to change so much that within three years Frank would find himself exiled from his homeland. As a Jew, a country infected by Nazism was a very dangerous place for him. By 1933, the Nazis were burning his books and he decided that he had to leave.

After spending a short time in Switzerland he moved on to Paris where the Nazis were to catch up with him again. In 1940, he was confined to an internment camp. He escaped on several occasions and was recaptured before he finally managed to flee Europe, ending up in the United States. All through these years of adversity the image of 'Hanna' haunted him.

However, he discovered America to be a fertile ground for his creativity and he found work as a Hollywood scriptwriter. He lived in New York, but found the oppressive summer heat too much for his central European sensibilities, preferring to spend the summer months out in the countryside. In 1948 he found himself staying at a farm that took in paying guests. It was then that the impossible happened. Sitting outside the farmhouse in a pose identical to the one that he remembered from Berlin in 1929 was his 'Hanna'. He simply could not believe that he was seeing her again in a place and a world so different from pre-war Berlin. What was he to do? He spent a day in an extended torment similar to that which he had experienced in those few minutes in the

Romanisches Café. Much to his relief she was still at the farm on the following day. This time he approached her. He introduced himself and explained how he had first seen her in Berlin and how she resembled a character from one of his novels. He told her that the character's name was Hanna. She said that she was called Charlotte. On impulse he leaned forward to kiss her. Naturally surprised, she pushed him away, saying that she was happily married to the young man that she had been with all those years ago. However, after avoiding him for three weeks she suddenly announced that she had fallen for him and that she would leave her husband, which she subsequently did. Later they married. Leonhard, after a long hard struggle, had found his 'Hanna'.

This 'ability' to write a fictional story based on actual future events is to be found in the work of many writers. In 1955 the English writer H.E. Bates was moved to write a short novel entitled *Summer In Salander*. In this work he has a shallow and manipulative woman by the name of Vane destroy the life of the antihero, Manson. Bates had a very specific mind's-eye picture of this woman. He saw her as being vain, as her name implies, and he had her manifest this vanity by possessing a whole set of expensive luggage. The letter 'V' was lavishly monogrammed on each piece. Clearly this image was one that Bates was particularly pleased with as he labours it in some detail. Bates had placed the story on a mythical island, which he called Salander. In his imagination he had unknowingly chosen a real island as the basis of his fictional creation – an island that two years later, in 1957, he visited. Whilst on the ship that was making its way to the island he spotted a set of expensive luggage awaiting the arrival of its owner. With amazement Bates registered that a large letter 'V' was clearly monogrammed on each piece and watched as his fictional character had her luggage off-loaded on to the island. He then spent the next three or four days observing the events in his story come to pass as the woman, as Bates puts it, 'proceeded to her spider act of destruction'.

What was happening here? Could it be that creative people take information from both the past and the future in order to create their stories or their art? If my theory that the Daemon is more immanent in the lives of creative people is correct then it is likely that it might use its 'helicopter' view of its Eidolon's life to take ideas from both the past and the future. As the Daemon has already lived this life before, it will recall future events while its Eidolon recalls past events. Of course, one can also argue that because writers are more aware of the daemonic part of their memory banks a dimly recalled past-life event can sometimes trigger a creative flow as much as something witnessed in the present. It is all well and good to surmise that this may be the case, but is there any scientific evidence to support such a suggestion?

The rabbits of Sysiphus

Philip K. Dick, the American science-fiction writer who died in 1981, will be referenced many times in this book. For those of you who have already read my first book this will come as no surprise. However, to anyone who is new to my theories this will seem strange. For you, my preoccupation with this fascinating writer will become clear as the book progresses.

For now I would like to make a second reference to a particular group of 'fictional' people that are referred to in many of Dick's novels. These individuals Dick terms 'precogs'. You will recall that I introduced these beings in Chapter 2. I explained that precogs have precognitive abilities – they can see the future. However, their clairvoyant abilities may sometimes only involve a very short timescale. I described the classic sequence in the film *Minority Report* where a precog helps Cruise's character stay out of his pursuers' line of vision by advising him to move in a particular pattern across the floor of a shopping mall. In following this pattern he is always obscured from the bad guys by the seemingly

> 'Now – the place being without a parallel in England, and there-
> fore necessarily beyond the experience of an American – it is
> somewhat remarkable that, while we stood gazing at the kitchen,
> I was haunted and perplexed by an idea that somewhere or other
> I had seen just this strange spectacle before. The height, the
> blackness, the dismal void, before my eyes, seemed so familiar as
> the decorous neatness of my grandmother's kitchen . . . I had
> never before had so pertinacious an attack, as I could but suppose
> it, of that odd state of mind wherein we fitfully and teasingly
> remember some previous scene or incident, of which the one now
> passing appears to be but an echo and the reduplication.'
>
> NATHANIEL HAWTHORNE (AUTHOR)

random movements of other people going about their own
business. I used this as an example of a controlled *déjà vu*
experience. However, it is also an example of another skill that
we may all have – short-term precognition. You may be surprised
to know that there is very strong experimental evidence to show
that this is an innate ability shared by all human beings. The
implications of this are simply astounding and may possibly be
the source of additional clues to the existence of the Daemon.

It all started in 1972, with an experiment that brought about
a most surprising result.[1] Subjects were asked to sit on a chair
and rest their arms, with palms turned upwards, on a table in
front of them. A cushion was then placed under each arm and a
contraption with three tappers on it was placed over them. These
tappers were positioned at the wrist, the elbow and the upper
arm. They were designed to give five taps to the wrist, two at the
elbow and three on the upper arm. Each set of taps was separated
by a short time interval. These ranged from 50 to 200 milliseconds (a millisecond is 1,000th of a second). It would, therefore,
take under a second to complete a full series of taps. What was
expected was that the subject would feel three discrete groups of

sensations as the tappers hit the arm at the wrist, the elbow and the upper arm. Much to the surprise of the experimenters, what the subjects actually felt was a group of taps travelling in a regular sequence over equidistant points up the arm. The sensation was described as having a small animal, like a rabbit, hopping up the arm. It was found that a variation in the interval between the taps (inter-stimulus interval: ISI) brought about a change in the perceived effect. If the ISI exceeded 200 milliseconds, the taps were perceived as being in their correct locations. With an ISI of 20 milliseconds or less, some taps 'disappeared'. The technical term for this is sensory saltation.

The question that the experimenters, Frank Geldard and Carl Sherrick, were forced to ask was a simple one – how did the brain know that after the five taps on the wrist there were going to be some taps near the elbow? In order to test this the experimenters, unbeknown to the subjects, adapted the sequence so that the taps were only delivered at the wrist. In every case the taps were perceived as would have been expected – all five on the wrist. The 'rabbit' never started running. But how did the brain know that there would be no follow-up taps on the elbow and the upper arm?

In every repeat of this experiment this phenomenon has been observed. The mystery is total and it has caused fascination and confusion ever since. It simply does not sit within our understanding of time and space. In Chapter 2 I presented the concept of the Cartesian Theatre as suggested by cognitive scientist Professor Daniel C. Dennett. It was the implications of Geldard and Sherrick's work that fascinated Dennett. He was to write:

> *Now, at first one feels like asking how did the brain know*
> *that after the five taps at the wrist there were going to be*
> *some taps near the elbow? The subjects experience the*
> *'departure' of the taps from the wrist beginning with the*
> *second tap, yet in catch trials in which the later elbow taps*

are never delivered, subjects feel all five wrist taps at the wrist as expected. The brain obviously cannot 'know' about a tap on the elbow until after it happens.[2]

This is why Dennett suggested the idea that the brain 'buffers' information. He proposed that the brain might, for some reason that is unknown, wait until all the taps are received before 'informing' consciousness that the event is taking place. Until the final tap is received all the sensations are stored at some way station between the arm and the seat of consciousness. However, as Dennett rightly points out, how does the brain know that the last message has been received? Would not the brain delay the release of the full message to consciousness just in case another, clarifying, one was about to be received? To this, I would add that I cannot see what possible advantage, evolutionary or otherwise, this little mental trick can give to the consciousness in question.

An easier, but far more contentious, explanation is that consciousness is, in some very real sense, ahead of, or outside, time. William James, the American psychologist, introduced the concept of the specious present – a small but finite chunk of space-time containing everything that the observer is consciously perceiving at that moment. H.F. Saltmarsh modified James' theory to explain precognition.[3] He supposed that the conscious mind's specious present was smaller than the specious present of the subconscious. Thus, Saltmarsh argued, it is perfectly possible that an event may lie in the future of the conscious mind but may also lie in the specious present of the subconscious mind, a theory vindicated by the work of Geldard and Sherrick. It is possible that this skill is always available to the 'other self' that functions as part of the subconscious in our normal waking lives. Indeed, to be subconsciously aware of what is about to take place a few milliseconds in the future could be of great evolutionary advantage. One could avoid the unexpected thrust of an animal's claws or horns or sense an imminent and dangerous natural event. A commonplace sensation that lends credibility to this ability is the curious way in which we seem to react to a loud noise or an unexpected sound a split second before we actually hear it.

Four years later Dr Stanislav Grof reported a series of experiments that seemed to show that this short-term precognition may be stimulated by chemicals within the brain itself. As we discovered earlier the human brain works using chemicals known as neurotransmitters. The behaviour and effects of these chemicals can be modified by the application of external drugs. LSD, or lysergic acid, is the most famous of these. Although it is a banned substance it has been used by psychologists to test the brain's response to such substances. Grof reported that under certain circumstances persons under the influence of LSD also show an ability to look slightly into the future. He wrote:

> Occasionally, LSD subjects report . . . anticipation of events
> that will happen in the future. Sometimes, they witness
> complex and detailed scenes of future happenings in the form
> of vivid clairvoyant visions and can even hear the acoustic
> concomitants that are part of them; the latter range from
> ordinary sounds of everyday life, musical sequences, single
> words, and entire sentences, to noise produced by motor
> vehicles and various alarming acoustic signals (the sound of
> fire engines, ambulance sirens, or blowing car horns). Some
> of these experiences manifest various degrees of similarity
> with actual events occurring at a later time.[4]

However, one can reasonably argue that what takes place during an LSD 'trip' is a hallucination and as such any experiences reported through this medium have to be approached with a fair degree of caution.

A year after these experiments, in 1977, a universally-experienced visual curiosity was to show that mind-expanding drugs or unusual nerve-based perceptions were not needed to demonstrate that human beings show short-term precognitive abilities. The American philosopher Nelson Goodman had long been fascinated by a common visual effect experienced by all human beings. If two lights are flashed through a small aperture in a darkened room at short intervals, an observer perceives not two lights but one single light moving backwards and forwards. The way in which a stationary object can be perceived as moving was first noted by the Czech psychologist Max Wertheimer. Wertheimer was so fascinated by this phenomenon that he founded a whole school of psychology based around its implications. He called this effect the PHI phenomenon, following on with a whole series of other similar perceptual curiosities named after Greek letters.

In one of those flashes of inspiration, Goodman wondered what would happen if one of the illuminated spots was red and the other green. What colour would the 'single' moving light be when perceived by an observer? He approached the psychologists Paul Kolers and Michael von Grünau and asked them if they could set up an experiment to find out. Common sense says that one of two possible scenarios would take place. In the first one, the subject would perceive two flashing lights, one of red and one of green, and the illusion of movement would be lost. If not, then the second scenario would be perceived. This is more complex but still acceptable. When the red light was switched on the subject would see a red light moving towards the location of the green light. At the point that the green light was illuminated the subject would see the red light turn into a green light. Indeed, if the subject did not know the colour of the second light he could only become aware of that colour when the second light was switched on. However, and this is the creepy bit, for all subjects the colour change takes place abruptly, midway between the two light source locations. How can this be? The subject cannot 'know' what the second colour will be before the second light is turned on. That event is in the immediate future for both the subject and the experimenter.

This unexpected result stunned Goodman. He was later to write:

How are we able to fill in the spot at the intervening place-time along a path running from the first and second flash before the second flash occurs?[5]

Again Daniel Dennett is at a loss to explain such a temporal anomaly. Writing many years later in 1992 he was still puzzling over the implications.

Unless there is precognition in the brain, the illusory content cannot be created until after some identification of the second spot occurs in the brain.[6]

In a very similar experiment to the Kornhuber example in Chapter 1, Benjamin Libet of the University of California and Bertram Feinstein of the Zion Neurological Institute in San Francisco pooled their knowledge to experiment directly on an exposed human brain. Running along the top of the brain is a strip known as the somatosensory cortex. It has long been known that individual points in the body can be made to feel sensations by the direct stimulation of this strip. For example, the stimulation of a point on the left somatosensory cortex can produce the sensation of a brief tingle in the subject's right hand. Libet was keen to compare the time course of such sensations to those more normally induced by direct stimulation. He did this by applying a brief electric pulse to the hand itself. He then asked the conscious patient what had come first, the hand tingle that started right in the cortex or the hand signal that was sent to the brain from the hand. Logic says the cortex message would arrive first, because it does not have to travel so far. In each case the message took a considerable time (500 milliseconds) from the onset of stimulation to what is termed 'neuronal adequacy'. What was found was that the tingle in the hand was felt before the tingle produced by the brain.

In later experiments Libet connected non-surgical subjects to an EEG (electroencephalograph) and asked them to flex their wrists at any moment they felt the urge. It seems that when you or I decide to make any form of physical movement there is a sharp drop in electrical activity in the brain. This is in order to clear the way for a neural event and it can be detected by an EEG. As with the open-skull experiment, Libet found that the electrical event was taking place in the brain a good half-second before the subject reported consciously experiencing any impulse to make a move.

Libet found these results astonishing and as such wrote the following:

> *The brain seems to be able to compensate for the lag in its processing. It can refer everything that happened backwards in time to the moment it [the stimulus] first arrived at the brain so that, subjectively, it feels as if we are living in the immediate present.*

Daniel Dennett, commenting on these results, was even more specific, stating that this experience:

> *automatically referred backwards in time . . .*[7]

and went on to say:

> *Most strikingly, Libet reported instances in which a patient's left cortex was stimulated before his left hand was stimu-lated, which one would think would surely give rise to two tingles; first right hand (cortically stimulated) then left hand. In fact, however, the subjective report was reversed; first left, then right.*[8]

The implications of this experiment are far-reaching and raise a serious challenge to the belief that human beings consist of nothing more than the brain itself. Something that is not dependent upon brain processes is making decisions and perceiving stimuli outside the material and chemical processes that make up the brain. Could this be the proof that we are made up of mind and matter? Sir John Eccles became a Nobel laureate for his research into neurophysiology and has long been a proponent of this belief (termed Cartesian dualism after the great French philosopher, René Descartes). In relation to the astounding findings of Libet he made the following comments:

> *This antedating procedure does not seem to be explicable by any neurological process. Presumably it is a strategy that has been learnt by the self-conscious mind . . . the antedating sensory experience is attributable to the ability of the self-conscious mind to make slight temporal adjustments, i.e. play tricks with time.*[9]

Here, we have a world authority on neurophysiology admitting that the human mind, or certain elements within the human mind, can 'play tricks with time'.

Why these experiments, and some interesting and very similar ones that have taken place since, are not better known is, to me, simply amazing. I can only assume that the implications are so odd that they have been quietly brushed under the carpet in the hope that they will eventually be forgotten. The reason for this may simply be that they are too paradigm-challenging to be given greater exposure. However, it may also be that the military wished to keep the whole thing under wraps until they decided how useful human short-term prescience may be to them.

In support of this contention is the fact that in May 2002 NATO was seen to be interested in this little-known ability of the human mind. The international defence organization had set up a three day conference at the Slovak Academy of Sciences at Tatranská Lomnica. Giving a presentation at this conference was Dick J. Bierman of the University of Amsterdam. Bierman was there to discuss a series of experiments that he and Dean Radin had devised in the late 1990s, the results of which were quite startling.

Bierman and Radin had taken a group of volunteers and attached sensors to their left index and middle fingers. By quantifying the level of skin conductance the sensor could measure the volunteers' level of emotional arousal. They were then placed in front of a computer screen that had been programmed to present a randomly-generated sequence of images. The pictures had been carefully selected to be either very calming or highly emotional. Each volunteer started the experiment by pressing a key on the keyboard. After 7.5 seconds a picture was displayed on the screen for a specific exposure period. Before, during and after exposure the subject's skin conductance was measured at 5 samples per second.

The results clearly demonstrated that there was a significant difference in skin conductance response between emotionally calm and emotion-arousing stimuli. Indeed, this is what one would expect. However, and this is a hugely significant however, skin conductivity responded to a particular type of picture before it was shown on the screen!

Bierman explained that only one conclusion was possible: that the human mind is somehow able to scan the emotional content of its immediate future.

You will recall that earlier in this chapter I made an allusion to Philip K. Dick's precogs. It seems that I am not the only one to notice the similarities between these fascinating clues to our precognitive abilities and the work of this great writer. The science writer Mark Anderson, clearly unaware of exactly who was responsible for these interesting fictional characters, was moved to write the following:

Bierman's work may have revealed a crude ability to sense the future, much like the 'precogs' in the forthcoming Stephen Spielberg movie Minority Report, *even if the skill only spans a few heartbeats.*

The results of Radin and Bierman's experiments have been so impressive that many other scientists have been queuing up to test the effect out for themselves.

One such scientist was Dr Kary Mullis, a Nobel Prize-winning chemist. After having experienced the sensation of pre-sentiment he was quoted by the British newspaper, the *Daily Mail*, as saying: 'It's spooky, I could see about three seconds into the future. You shouldn't be able to do that.'[10]

In the same article Professor Brian Josephson of Cambridge University stated that the evidence seemed compelling and he added, 'What seems to be happening is that information is coming from the future.'

All the fascinating experiments outlined above seem to show, and it is impossible to come to any other conclusion, that some part of the human mind can predict, like Philip K. Dick's precogs, what is about to occur in the short-term future.

In his book *Man and Time*, the playwright J.B. Priestley collected many examples of time not behaving as it should. One involved a young man in the terminal stages of a critical illness. He developed an ability to perceive events a second or two before they actually took place. It was as if part of him was actually living a few seconds ahead of everybody else. Colin Wilson, citing Priestley, describes what took place:

> *[The mother] said that during her son's illness he suddenly remarked, 'A dog is going to bark a long way off.' A few seconds later she heard the faint bark of a dog. He then said, 'Something is going to be dropped in the kitchen and the middle door is going to slam.' Within seconds both things had happened. When she told the doctor about it he said that he had known of this happening before and that her son's brain was working 'just ahead of time'.*[11]

This is identical to the findings of Radin and Bierman. Here we have a seriously ill young man with the ability to scan the immediate future and sense it in the present, or at least the 'present' of the observer.

So we have seen that short-term precognition can take place under laboratory conditions or during extreme illness. Does this happen in the world of normal perception? Surprisingly, the answer is 'yes'. Evidence that the human mind can track backwards in time has been given support by anecdotal reports regarding dreams. It seems that in certain circumstances dream scenarios are created by a stimulus that occurs after the dream has finished.

In the 1980s, at the request of the research organization The Koestler Institute, members of the public sent in examples of curious coincidences that had occurred to them. Brian Inglis recorded many of these in his fascinating book *Coincidence: A Matter of Chance or Synchronicity?* One of these responses however did not involve coincidence, but time. The correspondent, Rian Hughes, wrote:

> I dug out an old alarm clock – it had always been faultless
> in the past, but had not been in use for some years – to
> wake me up for a morning appointment. My dreams, early
> that morning, concerned boxing. Despite my protestations, I
> was to go several rounds with an enormous bruiser who
> looked ready to settle the business without bothering about my
> puny frame. Forced into the ring, I took a deep breath – then
> the bell went. I woke up. The bell was the alarm clock –
> ringing once and once only (a 'ding'), at exactly the right
> time in my dream (or my dream had led up to the time the
> clock went off exactly). It had never rung only once before.[12]

It is clear from this that Hughes' mind somehow 'back-created' the whole dream, which was stimulated by the similarity between the alarm sound and that of a boxing bell. No other explanation is possible. Our subconscious mind exists outside the temporal flow.

> *'In 1948 I had a most interesting experience in a sixteenth century hacienda in Bolivia. While going through the building with the owner I suddenly found myself in an area I had seen in a dream which had recurred many times over a period of twenty years. To the astonishment of the owner I accurately described the layout and appearance of an entire wing before he had opened the door leading into it. Since that time I have not had this dream.'*
>
> CARROLL B. NASH (PSYCHOLOGIST)

The million pound question is whether you can indeed 'phone a friend' as a popular British quiz series suggests. However, this friend with all the answers, both past, present and future, is not on the other end of a telephone line. It is as close to you as can possibly be. It shares your brain with you. We have now seen evidence upon evidence that we all have a life-long partner, an entity that I call the Daemon. If my 'Cheating the Ferryman' theory is correct, then we know exactly why this being has such powers. For most of us it tends to be fairly aloof in its dealings with its lower partner. However, for Leonard Frank and H.E. Bates their respective Daemons seemed keen to use their precognitive knowledge to assist in the creative process and, as we shall now see, these writers are not alone in having a subtly active 'Daemon of Creativity'.

The clairvoyant muse

In his book *Ways of Escape*, the writer Graham Greene suggested that many novelists write about future events that they are subconsciously aware of. He suggested that Émile Zola, when writing about imprisoned miners dying of poisoned air, was drawing on some form of 'future memory' of his own death when he was smothered by fumes from his coke stove. In a chilling personal anecdote, Greene postulates that his fictionalized account of the preoccupation of one of his characters with trouble in Indo-China, written in 1938, was precognitive. He was to find himself, 14 years later, standing by a canal in the small Vietnamese town of Phat Dun and looking down at scores of Viet Minh bodies. In 1938 such a situation was unthinkable.

Is this subliminal inspiration due to direct daemonic guidance or is it simply that the artistic Eidolon unconsciously accesses the 'memory' banks of its Higher Self and finds inspiration? As we have already seen we all may have an ability to see the future, albeit a few seconds in advance. Possibly the neural pathways are different for some creative people and they sense the more distant future.

For example, what can we make of the experience of John Burke, a freelance writer, who wrote of the following series of events that took place in the early 1970s? Burke was in the process of researching background material for a fictional book set in the Fens. He and his wife had decided to go to Wisbech to get the feel of the region. What took place there is of such relevance to my theory that I feel that I should quote Burke in full:

> In our discussions on the story I had realized that a subsidiary
> character, father of one of the main male characters, would
> have to be made more substantial than first envisaged. At that
> time I did not know Wisbech other than from passing through
> it (rather, round it); but off the top of my head, having read
> somewhere that it had once been a thriving port, I invented a
> local merchant whose interests expanded until he could afford to
> have a couple of coasting vessels built for him in Sunderland,
> and build up contacts with Holland and Germany. He bought
> himself a Georgian house on the outskirts of the town, became
> Lord-Lieutenant of the County, and ultimately Lord Mayor of
> London, leaving the firm in the hands of his son (an essential
> feature for our plot).

On the day of our arrival we had planned to saunter round
the town talking and simply soaking up the atmosphere before
exploring further afield. Unfortunately the soaking became a
physical one: it began to snow heavily, and we sought refuge
in the little local museum. I was on one side of the room
when my wife called me across: 'Look at this – here he is!'
What my wife had discovered in a large glass case was the
character I had invented. Every detail was correct even down
to the relevant dates, with only one exception: he did not
become Lord Mayor of London – merely High Sheriff.

One could reasonably argue that Burke could have known these facts but forgotten them. The information was readily available. However, in Rudyard Kipling's case this was not possible. In his autobiography *Something of Me*, Kipling stated quite categorically that most, if not all, of his stories were either directly dictated or subliminally influenced by a being that shared his mind with him. Interestingly enough, he calls this being his Daemon.

In 1906, Kipling wrote a series of short stories published in an anthology entitled *Puck of Pook's Hill*. In one story, 'The Old Men at Pevensey', he tells the tale of two characters, Hugh and Richard, who live in Pevensey Castle in Kent. The year is 1100 and they are living in dangerous times. As a plot device, Kipling has to give the characters a place to hide some chests full of gold coins. He decided that he needed to create a sea-water well in the walls of the castle. He knew that this did not exist, but he could think of nowhere else that the gold could be hidden. If this tale was Daemon-inspired, then this being was deliberately giving clues to its own future memory because in 1935 a sea-water well was found in exactly the location suggested by Kipling, or more accurately, Kipling's Daemon.

However, his Daemon was not finished yet. In another story in the same anthology Kipling tells the tale of a group of Roman soldiers manning Hadrian's Wall. The story, entitled 'On the Great

Wall', describes in some detail how the Seventh Cohort of the Thirtieth Legion defended themselves against the Picts by using arrows. He had no idea at the time whether that particular legion had been anywhere near Northumbria and at the time there was absolutely no evidence that Roman legions had used arrows as weapons. Again his Daemon was on form. In *Something of Me* he wrote:

> *Years after the tale was told, a digging-party on the Wall sent me some heavy, four-sided, Roman-made 'killing' arrows found in situ and – most marvellously – a rubbing of a memorial-tablet to the Seventh Cohort of the Thirtieth Legion! Having been brought up in a suspicious school, I suspected a 'leg-pull' here, but was assured that the rubbing was perfectly genuine.*

That there was a 'leg-pull' going on is fairly clear. What Kipling did not realize was that the leg-puller was, in a very real way 'Something of Me'!

I would now like to finish this chapter with probably one of the most prosaic cases of daemonic intervention that I have come across. Having said that, I continue to be amazed at the sheer simplicity of the event but how supportive it is of the whole Daemon-Eidolon Dyad.

I recently received a fascinating communication from a reader of my first book, Tom Jones. Tom, who now lives in China, has spent most of his life having daemonic experiences but it was only after reading *Is There Life After Death?* that he was in a position to make sense of what was happening to him. Suddenly, he understood that many strange, and seemingly unrelated, incidents all had a common cause.

Tom considers that his Daemon is continually monitoring the immediate future and cites one classic example of just how absolutely practical this being can be. A few years ago Tom was working in a steel mill in Los Angeles. Tom explained to me what happened:

I was walking under the many pipes along the ceiling with an open coffee cup in my left hand and a notepad in my right hand. Suddenly, of its own volition I watched as my right hand quickly and smoothly (almost casually) moved across my body and covered the coffee cup. Immediately a large glob of oil landed on the notepad, instead of my coffee!, and then my right hand moved back to its previous position. It was like I was a spectator! It just happened by itself! There was NO WAY I could have seen the oil falling, I have a weird habit of walking with my head down all the time.

This is exactly the skill that Philip K. Dick's precogs show in the movie *Minority Report* – being just ever so slightly ahead of time.

So there we have it. There is strong experimental evidence to conclude that we all have precognitive skills. We seem to be able to subconsciously access part of our Daemon's past-life 'memory' banks. Some of us are more attuned to this. The more creative we are the more immanent in our subconscious is our Higher Self.

However, Tom's Daemon seems to have some other, very curious skills. These include an ability to become visible to its Eidolon. In 1979 Tom was working in Egypt. One evening he was in a light sleep when the following curious event took place:

While working in Egypt in 1979 I was in my apartment sleeping when I opened my eyes, or so I thought, and saw MYSELF walk through the wall and come towards my bed. This second 'me' then sat on the bed and rotated its legs which 'clicked' into mine and then lay down, again with a 'click' and then I opened my physical eyes in total shock!

CHAPTER 6 Precognition

CHAPTER 6 Precognition

> '[The mother] said that during her son's final illness he suddenly remarked, "A dog is going to bark a long way off." A few seconds later she heard the faint bark of a dog. He then said, "Something is going to be dropped in the kitchen and the middle door is going to slam." Within seconds both things had happened. When she told the doctor about it he said that he had known of this happening before and that her son's brain was working "just ahead of time".'
>
> J.B. PRIESTLEY (PLAYWRIGHT)

For me this is Daemonic immanence of the highest order. In this situation the Eidolon encounters something more mysterious – an encounter with one of the great mysteries of both psychology and literature, the legendary 'Double-Walker' or *doppelgänger*. In the next chapter we will see how this staple of fantastic literature is, in fact, a recognized psychological state and is yet more evidence for my Daemon-Eidolon Dyad.

Summary

The ability to see the future has been claimed by many individuals over the centuries. However, the evidence implies that in most cases accurate predictions seem to be based upon simple statistical chance. The more predictions that are made, the more likely it is that one will come true given sufficient time. Predictions are also notoriously, some would argue wilfully, obscure. It is virtually unknown for a professional clairvoyant to make a specific prediction that states in advance the events as they will actually unfold.

However, this does not mean that precognition does not take place – it is simply that in most, if not all, cases the Eidolon has no control over it. The Daemon seems to deliberately instigate images within the brain of its Eidolon. These are quite precise and usually intensely personal. It is as if the Daemon does not wish to change the big issues. Indeed, it is reasonable to conclude that we would never know if the Daemon was successful in changing future events by giving its Eidolon the opportunity to change the future. This is because the original future ceases to exist in our universe. We will simply never experience the events as they should have been.

There is strong evidence that all human beings have the ability to monitor the contents of their own immediate future. This can be explained by the delay in which information of the external world is 'buffered' before it is presented to eidolonic consciousness. It can be argued that this is not really precognition but simply a delay in processing. What this buffering does imply, however, is that the brain, in a very real sense, records sensory experience.

[1] Geldard, F. & Sherrick, C., 'The Cutaneous Rabbit: A Perceptual Illusion', *Science*, 178 (1972)

[2] Dennett, D.C., *Consciousness Explained*, Penguin (1993)

[3] Saltmarsh, H.F., *Foreknowledge*, G.Bell (1938)

[4] Grof. S., *Realms of the Human Unconscious: Observations from LSD Research*, E.P. Dutton, NY, pp.177–8 (1976)

[5] Goodman, N., *Ways of Worldmaking*, Hackett, p.73 (1978)

[6] Dennett, D.C., 'Temporal anomalies of consciousness' in Y. Christen & P.S. Churchland (eds), *Neurophilosophy and Alzheimer's disease*, Springer-Verlag, Berlin, p.5 (1992).

[7] Dennett, D.C., *Consciousness Explained*, Penguin, p.155 (1993)

[8] Ibid.

[9] Popper, K.R. & Eccles, J.C., *The Self and its Brain*, Springer-Verlag, Berlin, p.364 (1977)

[10] *Daily Mail*, 'Is This Really Proof That Man Can See Into The Future?', article, May 4 (2007)

[11] Priestley, J.B., *Man And Time*, Aldus, p.203 (1964)

[12] Inglis, B., *Coincidence*, Hutchinson, p.167 (1990)

CHAPTER 7

The Mystery of the Double

A figure in the terrible distance moved towards me
As relentlessly as day advances upon night,
Nearer it came and slower I went out to meet it.
It was myself.

Leonard Clark, Encounter

Shelley's encounter

The view from the terrace was magnificent. Percy could see right
across the Gulf of Spezia towards the forbidding Castle of San
Giorgio in Lerici. The hot June sun splashed the whole vista in
sparkling Italian light. He could hear the chatter from inside the
house as his wife, Mary, and his two friends, Edward and Jane,
excitedly discussed the proposed sea journey that Edward had
planned for early July. Edward had suggested that they take Percy's
undecked yacht *Ariel*, formerly the *Don Juan*, across the bay to
visit his friend Leigh Hunt in Leghorn. Looking out at the placid
waters he decided that this seven- or eight-hour journey would
be wonderful. He was jerked out of his thoughts by the sudden
sensation that he was not alone. Turning round, he expected Mary
to be there, hopefully with a cooling glass of lemonade. He had
been right about the presence but very wrong about the identity
of the person now standing in front of him. Percy gave out a
silent scream as he looked straight into the eyes of himself. The
double stared back then silently pointed out to sea. Percy, rigid
with fear, could still hear his friends, only a few yards away, but
he could not call out for help. The fetch then stopped pointing
and turned to gaze again at the terrified poet. Its mouth opened
and it asked one chilling question: 'How long do you intend to
be happy?' – and then it vanished.

This incident took place in June 1822. It was the poet Percy Bysshe Shelley that had faced his double and what he had seen that day was yet another, and probably the most fascinating, aspect of Daemon communication. It is as if under certain circumstances the Daemon can create an image of itself which is projected out into the visual field of its Eidolon. As is usual with these communications something was about to happen and the Daemon had to communicate quickly. What is particularly interesting in Shelley's case is that it spoke, but in some form of riddle. Why this was so is unclear because it did have a message of great importance to give. When it pointed out to sea across the Gulf of Spezia, it was trying to convey the idea that something was going to happen out there. And it did.

On Monday 1 July 1822 Shelley and his friend Edward Williams did as planned and sailed *Ariel* from Lerici to Leghorn. The journey was fine and they spent a week with Leigh Hunt. They began the return journey on 8 July, but as they made the crossing a huge storm blew up. Ten days later the bodies of Shelley and Williams were washed up on the shore between Pisa and Spezia.

Was this the reason for the cryptic message of the Daemon double? Clearly, if my theory is correct then Shelley's Daemon would have known that the trip across the gulf would end in tragedy. Is it possible that it forced itself to appear on realizing that the trip was about to take place? I would argue that this was an act of desperation on the part of Shelley's Daemon. My reason for thinking this is because there is strong evidence that it had been trying other channels in the months running up to the fateful trip.

In the spring of the previous year, Shelley had been devastated by the death of his close friend John Keats. Deep in mourning, he wrote what is probably one of his greatest poems, *Adonais, An Elegy on the Death of John Keats*. This is a long poem with over 400 lines. However, it is the final eight that send a shiver up the spine when read in the light of the events of July 1822:

. . . my spirit's bark is driven,
Far from the shore, far from the trembling throng
Whose sails were never to the tempest given;
The massy earth and spherèd skies are riven!
I am borne darkly, fearfully, afar;
Whilst, burning through the innermost veil of Heaven,
The soul of Adonais, like a star,
Beacons from the abode where the Eternal are.

I suggest that you read these words as you imagine the terrifying last few minutes of Shelley's life. He would have been far from the shore, looking back at the ripped sails of *Ariel*, as a violent tempest thundered around him. The images he evokes in the poem seem frighteningly prescient.

Was this Shelley's Daemon again communicating through creativity? Shelley had long acknowledged that his poems were not directly of his own creation. In an earlier piece he had written:

. . . the mind in creation is as a fading coal which some
form of invisible influence like an inconsistent wind,
awakens to transitory brightness.

This unseen influence would sometimes seem even more immanent in Shelley's creative process.

Shelley seemed quite sure that this 'dictator' was a presence or a consciousness different from himself. He describes in chilling detail the nature of this relationship in his poem *Hymn to Intellectual Beauty*:

Sudden, thy shadow fell on me:
I shrieked, and clasped my hands in ecstasy!

Indeed, may this not be a poetic description of the pre-seizure aura of temporal lobe epilepsy? Could it be that Shelley, like so many other creative individuals, 'suffered' from this mysterious illness? If this was the case then yet again my theory is supported by reported personal experience.

It has long been believed that Shelley suffered from epilepsy. If my theory is to have any credibility this is not sufficient. I have to show that he had epilepsy focused on the temporal lobes. One of the known symptoms of TLE is an awareness of some form of psychic duality. Clearly, his experience with his *doppelgänger* ticks that box. Indeed, I think I have found evidence that Shelley had perceived the image of his own Daemon before the incident of 1822. In 1820 he published a drama entitled *Prometheus Unbound*. In Act 1 can be found the following passage:

> Ere Babylon was dust,
> The Magus Zoroaster, my dead child,
> Met his own image walking in the garden.
> That apparition, sole of men he saw.
> For know there are two worlds of life and death:
> One that which thou beholdest; but the other
> Is underneath the grave, where do inhabit
> The shadows of all forms that think and live
> Till death unite them and they part no more;

Clearly, something personal has stimulated this writing. Remember, this is two years before his death, but Shelley is already fascinated by duality. Indeed, it is possible that Shelley even used my terminology. In an epic poem, amazingly entitled *The Daemon of the World*, he differentiates between a being that he calls the Daemon and another that he terms 'the Spirit'. When he first introduces the Spirit, he describes how both the Daemon and the Spirit exist in something he calls 'the car':

> It ceased, and from the mute and moveless frame
> A radiant spirit arose,
> All beautiful in naked purity.
> Robed in its human hues it did ascend,

Disparting as it went the silver clouds,
It moved towards the car, and took its seat
Beside the Daemon shape.

For a moment consider that Shelley was using 'car' to describe the corporeal body. If this is the case then the poet is describing my 'Daemon-Eidolon Dyad'. Of course this is pure conjecture on my part. Indeed, I could get really carried away with this and point out that one homonym of 'car' is 'ka', the third element of the Egyptian trinity of the *ba*, the *ka* and the *Khu*. However, but significantly, the Egyptians considered the *ka* to be a form of *doppelgänger*!

As we have already seen, *déjà vu* is considered a classic sign of a TLE aura. If I can find evidence of *déjà vu*-like experiences in the writings of Shelley to add to his perception of duality, then my case is strengthened considerably. Well, it seems I have.

In 1810, Shelley was out taking a stroll near Oxford. He was in the countryside and the high banks of the old track way had obscured his view. However, as he turned a corner he was struck by a very strange sensation. He wrote:

> *The view consisted of a windmill standing in one among many plashy meadows, enclosed with stone walls; the irregular and broken ground, between the wall and the road on which we stood; a long low hill behind the windmill, and grey covering of uniform cloud spread over the evening sky . . . The scene surely was a common scene . . . the effect which it produced in me was not such as could have been expected. I suddenly remembered to have seen in some dream of long . . .*[1]

At this point Shelley stopped recording his feelings. He was later to add: 'Here I was obliged to leave off, overcome by thrilling horror.'

What else can this be interpreted as other than a *déjà vu* experience? If so, then we have two major elements of TLE. The third is recognized as being hyperreligiosity or a great interest in the mystic and the numinous. A glance at any of Shelley's poems will clearly show this to be the case. He might have been expelled from Oxford in 1811 for his strident atheism, but clearly as he aged he moved towards some kind of mystical pantheism.

In my opinion, Shelley's epilepsy was TLE. If so, this would effectively explain his *doppelgänger*/Daemon experience because, however strange this may seem, *doppelgängers* are a recognized symptom of certain forms of 'illness' involving the temporal lobes.

What Shelley experienced on the terrace of the Casa Magni is technically known as autoscopy. Put simply it is the seeing of one's own double. The word derives from the Greek word *autos* which means self and *skopeein*, the Greek verb 'to see'. Thus it simply means 'seeing self'.

A fascinating, and very personal example, was described by the British psychic Rosalind Heywood. It was late one evening and she was feeling particularly selfish. Her husband was fast asleep beside her, but she was keen to wake him up and demand his 'attention'. As she was about to shake him into consciousness the following curious event took place:

> *Before I could carry out this egoistic idea I did something*
> *very odd – I split into two. One Me in its pink nightie*
> *continued to toss self-centredly against the embroidered*
> *pillows, but another, clad in a long, very white, hooded*
> *garment, was now standing, calm, immobile and imperson-*
> *ally outward-looking, at the foot of the bed. This White Me*
> *seemed just as actual as Pink Me and I was equally conscious*
> *in both places at the same time. I vividly remember myself as*
> *White Me looking down and observing the carved end of the*
> *bed in front of me and also thinking what a silly fool Pink*
> *Me looked, tossing in that petulant way against the pillows.*
> *'You're behaving disgracefully,' said White Me to Pink Me*
> *with cold contempt. 'Don't be so selfish you know that*
> *he is dog-tired.'*

Pink Me was a totally self-regarding little animal, entirely
composed of 'appetites', and she cared not at all whether her
unfortunate husband was tired or not. 'I shall do what I like,'
she retorted furiously, 'and you can't stop me, you pious white
prig!' She was particularly furious because she knew very well
that White Me was the stronger and could stop her.
A moment or two later – I felt no transition – White Me
was once more imprisoned with Pink Me in one body. And
there they have dwelt as oil and water ever since.

Autoscopy has two forms. The first involves the sensation that
one is outside one's own body and viewing it from that external
location. The second, in many ways much more disturbing, is
when one remains in one's own body but one sees another,
separate individual, who is absolutely identical to oneself – a
doppelgänger. This second form of autoscopy is known as
heautoscopy. Clearly, in the cases of both Shelley and Heywood
the experience was one of heautoscopy.

Although reported many times in medical journals and
psychiatric text books, there has never been a satisfactory
explanation put forward as to the mechanism of autoscopy. If it
is simply an image projected by the brain then how is it done?

I suggest that the *doppelgänger* is an integral part of our
psychology and is simply yet another manifestation of the being
I call the Daemon. In the pages that follow I will present my
case that the Daemon can, under certain circumstances, project
its own image into the visual field of its Eidolon and in doing
so have another tool by which it can change the Bohmian IMAX.

Ring in the changes

In 1954 the psychiatrist O.E. Sperling reported the fascinating case
of a child named Rudy who had a particularly vivid hallucinatory companion whom he called 'Rudyman'. He demanded a chair
for him to sit on and would ask permission from Rudyman to

> *'On other occasions when I have been aware of the duality in myself, the split seemed to be because a hidden part of me wanted to act on information that the conscious part did not possess.'*
>
> ROSALIND HEYWOOD (MEDIUM)

do certain things. If he was asked to eat his soup, he would report that he first had to consult Rudyman on the topic and then he would say, 'Rudyman said I should eat the soup.' Whenever his parents gave him an order, Rudy always reported that he needed to have a consultation with Rudyman as to whether to obey. Sperling observed that the child's father's name was Herman and that Rudyman was a combination of Rudy and his father's name. He also noted that many of Rudyman's characteristics, such as his height and his loud strong voice, suggested that Rudyman had features of both the child and the father. However, a counter-argument could be suggested and that is that 'Rudyman' was exactly what his name implied – Rudy as a man. Could this be another example of the Daemon manifesting itself as an authority figure in the life of its much younger Eidolon?

The implication here is that the Daemon, having already lived this life before, is aware of what is going to happen in the life of its Eidolon. We have seen many examples of how this might be the case. However, here we have a subtle, but very telling, variation on this idea. In order to manipulate the life-journey of their Eidolon some Daemons manifest themselves not as a *doppelgänger* but as an older version of the subject.

In the early 1950s a very curious incident was reported by psychologist Milton Erickson, an event that may give scientific support to my outrageous claim. In his paper 'A Special Enquiry With Aldous Huxley Into The Nature And Character Of Various States Of Consciousness', Erickson describes how a 26-year-old student had requested that he be placed in a trance state for exactly two hours. During this period the young man intended to observe quietly and note his experiences.

From Erickson's viewpoint in time and space the young man was in a deep-trance state for two hours. However, on being brought out of the trance the subject claimed that from his viewpoint he had been away for years.

He explained that as he had drifted into the trance he had found himself on an unfamiliar hillside. As he looked round he saw a young boy and he immediately knew that the child was six years old. He knew this for one simple reason. The young boy was himself as he had been 20 years earlier. When he recovered from the shock of this revelation, he was hit by another one. He 'knew' that the child was hungry. He found that he was sharing the feelings and sense-inputs of his younger self. He knew the child fancied a chocolate cookie. And then it hit him – he remembered the incident. The hillside was suddenly familiar as were the pangs of hunger. He was back in time, reliving an incident in his own past from the viewpoint of an observer. As the minutes went by, the student realized that this was no short-term reverie. He was going to be following his own life as a higher consciousness for some time. Indeed, he was right. As Erickson subsequently wrote:

> My subject reported that he 'lived' with that boy for years, watched his successes and his failures, knew all of his innermost life, wondered about the next day's events with the child, and like the child he found to his amazement that even though he was 26 years old, a total amnesia existed for all events subsequent to the child's immediate age at the moment, that he could not foresee the future any more than could the child. He went to school with the child, vacationed with him, always watching the continuing physical growth and development. As each new day arrived, he found that he had a wealth of associations about the actual happenings of the past up to the immediate moment of life for the child self.[2]

Eventually the time came for 'them' to decide on whether to go to college or not. This was not an easy decision, but the 'hidden observer' knew that it was of great importance. If the now teenage boy did not go to college then the observer would not have been hypnotized and the regression would not have taken place! Much to the observer's relief, the decision was made and a college was decided upon. The observer had spent many years with his younger self but suddenly there was an overwhelming urge to go back whence he came. With great concentration he hauled himself back into consciousness; the world melted around him and a laboratory came into view. This new world felt as real as the world he had just left. He could feel an armchair surrounding him and he caught, in the corner of his eye, somebody moving around. His confusion slowly dissipated and he recalled who he actually was. He realized that the person he could see was Dr Erickson, and he called out to him in great excitement. He was back from the most amazing experience.

Erickson was to describe the event, saying that his subject:

> . . . explained that the experience was literally a moment by moment reliving of his life with only the same awareness he had then and that the highly limited, restricted awareness of himself at 26 was that of being an invisible man watching his own growth and development from childhood on, with no more knowledge of the child's future than the child possessed at any particular age.[3]

If this is then the case it is reasonable to conclude that two independent – but literally and metaphorically related – centres of conscious awareness co-existed in the same brain. Could this be what was taking place with Rudy and Rudyman?

This may also help to explain a curious incident that happened to the German mystic Jakob Boehme, the fascinating German mystic who seemed to perceive in great detail the nature of both my Bohmian IMAX and the Pleorama. Boehme's relationship with his Daemon may have started very early in his life. While still a very young man Jakob was sent away from home and was apprenticed to a cobbler. One day he was left in charge of the shop while the owner went on an errand. The young Jakob was totally alone and became a little concerned when a stranger appeared in the shop. When he wrote about this incident many years later Boehme described the man as emitting light, particularly from his eyes.

As we have already seen this luminosity seems to indicate the Daemon in its guise as the 'Being of Light'. Indeed, this person seemed to know a good deal about the young man in front of him, including his name. The man told Jakob that although he was little now he would one day grow and become a man 'so uncommon that the world will marvel'. Holding the young man

'The more we examine the mechanism of thought, the more we shall see that the automatic, unconscious action of the mind enters largely into all its processes. Our definite ideas are stepping stones: how we get from one to the other, we do not know: something carries us; we do not take the step. A creating and informing spirit which is with us, and not of us, is recognized everywhere in real and in storied life. It is the Zeus that kindled the rage of Achilles: it is the muse of Homer; it is the Daimon of Socrates . . . it shaped the forms that filled the soul of Michelangelo when he saw the figure of the great Lawgiver in the yet unhewn marble . . . it comes to the least of us as a voice that will be heard; it tells us what we must believe; it frames our sentences; it lends a sudden gleam of sense or eloquence . . . so that . . . we wonder at ourselves, or rather not at ourselves, but at this divine visitor who chooses our brain as his dwelling place, and invests our naked thought with the purple of the kings of speech or song.'

OLIVER WENDELL HOLMES (PHYSICIAN AND WRITER)

in his gaze of light the stranger told Jakob that his future would be great, but that he would suffer many trials and persecutions for his beliefs. With this the man disappeared in a flash of light.[4] Was this strange visitor none other than Boehme's Daemon?

As far as the Eidolon is concerned life is experienced in a totally linear fashion. The future becomes the present and then disappears into the past. It consists of expectation, experience and recollection with consciousness existing in an ongoing moment that moves inexorably from the past into the future. If I may use an analogy, it is as if the Eidolon sits inside the carriage of a moving train. Behind the train is the past and the future lies ahead. What the Eidolon sees out of the window is the present. The Daemon travels on the same train, but it has a totally different viewpoint. It sits on the roof of the train and can see exactly where the train is going. Not only that but it has already made the journey before so it can remember each twist and turn of the route. It also knows how far ahead is the destination, the end of the line or, most fittingly, the terminus.

Not only that but the Daemon is conscious at all times and is aware of things that the Eidolon is not. Can this be what happens when we experience the well-known 'cocktail party effect'? This happens when a person's attention is focused on one thing, such as listening to a conversation at a party. All the other sounds and voices are placed in the background. However, if somebody mentions that person's name they will immediately be aware that this has happened. How can this be? Clearly, something or somebody is monitoring us at all times, but whatever its identity it is categorically not the Eidolon. I believe that this 'scanning' is done by the Daemon.

In support of this belief I present evidence from the journals of 'Quaerens'. It is acknowledged that the science of neurology started on 10 January 1894 when the surgeon John Hughlings Jackson performed an autopsy on a mysterious Victorian gentleman. The man was mysterious because in his papers and subsequent books Jackson identified this man as 'Dr Z' or by the name 'Quaerens' (Latin for 'seeker'). Why this was the case is because Quaerens was from a well-to-do family and had worked as a physician in London. Subsequent investigations have revealed that the patient was Dr Alfred Thomas Meyers, a physician at the Belgrave Hospital in London.

The man had committed suicide at the age of 42. As his family doctor Jackson had known the man for many years and in that time had kept a meticulous record of the strange mental states Meyers had experienced. Not only that, but Jackson had access to all of Meyers' (Quaerens') journals and diaries.

These journals made fascinating reading because Meyers had regularly recorded the fact that he suffered from extreme *déjà vu* experiences together with many of the other psychological states that we have now come to recognize as symptoms of temporal lobe epilepsy. However, at that time no link had been made with that particular area of the brain. When Jackson examined Meyers' brain he found a large scar on the left temporal lobe. He immediately deduced that this was the cause of the peculiar 'dreamy states' that Meyers had reported.

I have found evidence that on many occasions a *petit mal* seizure would bring about a total loss of consciousness on the part of Meyers' Eidolon. However, at this time his Daemon would take over and continue some form of awareness while Meyers was 'away'. For example, the epileptic doctor describes the following fascinating event:

> I was attending a young patient whom his mother had brought
> me with some history of lung symptoms. I wished to examine
> the chest, and asked him to undress on a couch. I thought he
> looked ill, but have no recollection of any intention to
> recommend him to take to his bed at once or of any diagnosis.
> Whilst he was undressing I felt the onset of a petit mal. I
> remember taking out my stethoscope and turning away a little

to avoid conversation. The next thing I recollect is that I was sitting at a writing-table in the same room, speaking to another person, and as my consciousness became more complete, recollected my patient, but saw he was not in the room. I was interested to ascertain what had happened and had an opportunity an hour later of seeing him in bed, with the note of a diagnosis I had made of 'pneumonia of the left base'.[5]

I am assuming that most of the readers of this book will be Eidolons. The Daemon may subliminally influence its Eidolon to do things it would prefer to do, but in general all sensory-motor issues are motivated by the Eidolon. As such the Daemon is mostly just along for the ride: it is simply a passenger with all the driving done by its lesser partner. Indeed, the same situation applies with verbal communication. As we have seen from split-brain experiments the non-dominant hemisphere is generally non-verbal. However, these roles may be reversed during a TLE-induced 'absence'.

In the case cited above we have a correct medical diagnosis made while Dr Meyers was clearly unconscious. This is very interesting. For me this suggests that during a TLE 'absence' it is only the Eidolon that absconds – the Daemon seems to take over both the sensory-motor and verbal aspects of conscious awareness. In effect the Daemon seamlessly replaces the Eidolon and becomes the interface between the mind and the external world.

Interestingly enough, there have been some rare cases when the Eidolon remains conscious during a *petit mal* seizure and for a few seconds perceives the world through the sense apparatus of its Daemon. During this time, the person perceives a dual consciousness that usually only takes place in the final few moments of life, or during a Near-Death Experience. Such a case was reported by psychologist Pierre Gloor in a paper published in 1982. The subject was a 32-year-old man who suffered from epilepsy that originated in both his left and right temporal lobes.

Interestingly, the seizures originating in the left temporal lobe gave no aura-warning and the subject fell into a short 'absence' lasting for a few seconds. He then recovered consciousness, but was confused for some time afterwards. The seizures originating in his right hemisphere were much more common and involved some fascinating *déjà vu* experiences. Of course, what I find particularly interesting is that the focus of these particular seizures was the right, non-dominant, hemisphere – the location, in my opinion, of daemonic consciousness.

I would therefore argue that this man, or more accurately, his Eidolon, was, during his seizure, given access to the sensory perceptions of his Daemon. According to Gloor the subject, during this second seizure type, experienced:

> . . . *a sudden unpleasant, churning sensation in his stomach,*
> *a pounding headache, and a sudden feeling of 'déjà vu'*
> *associated with the illusion that he could predict what would*
> *happen next. He became anguished, looked depressed, and*
> *often remained depressed after the seizures.*[6]

Gloor uses the term 'illusion that he could predict what would happen next', which clearly implies that the psychologist was sure that this precognitive ability was in no way a real psychological state. However, the patient was quite sure that it was fully real. This is how Gloor describes the event:

> *The patient pressed the 'seizure button' and a nurse came in*
> *with a flashlight. She asked him whether the attack was like*
> *the preceding ones, to which he replied: 'Yes, and you are*
> *coming in right now, it is all part of it; I mean as soon as I*
> *pressed it [i.e., the seizure button], I almost did not, because*
> *I knew you were going to come in. It is as if I were reliving*
> *all that is happening now. I just knew that you were going to*
> *come in with the flashlight on. In a minute there will be*
> *more people as if it all happened before, just reliving all this.*

The more I know what is going to happen the farther it goes
and the dizzier I feel . . . it makes me feel strange or weird.'
He then suddenly stopped speaking.[7]

For the patient this short-term precognition was totally real. He felt that time itself had become warped and twisted. He was perceiving reality as it really is. In my opinion this rare psychological state is known by many terms – The Oceanic Feeling, The Mystic Experience and The Peak Experience, all aspects of the Bohmian IMAX.

In my opinion, the case for believing that the Being of Light, the *doppelgänger*, the Double and the Daemon are all aspects of the same entity is fairly realistic. We have seen case after case that supports such a position. I would further contend that the voices, the Muse and the Protector, are all again aspects of this intriguing element of human consciousness. However, I also consider that there is another form of double that is not the Daemon, but is evidence of another, as yet unmentioned, part of 'Cheating the Ferryman' – a philosophy known as the Eternal Return.

In double-time

What this philosophy proposes is that life is cyclical not linear. Put simply, this means that everything we experience in this life we will experience again and again. It may come as a surprise when I say that this proposition has been taken very seriously by many philosophers, scientists and artists across the ages. For example, in 1813 the German writer Johann Wolfgang von Goethe attended the funeral of fellow writer and philosopher Christoph Martin Wieland. The death of this much-respected man stimulated a fellow mourner, Johannes Falk, to ask Goethe where he thought Wieland's soul could be found. After some reflection the great man embarked upon a lengthy and detailed reply. During the course of this statement Goethe made the following interesting statement:

> *I am certain that I have been here as I am now a thousand times before, and hope to return a thousand times.*

In this way the German writer was confirming his belief in a personal eternal return, a return that would take place not just once but many hundreds of times. Could it be that he in some way knew this to be an absolute truth in that he was one of those few human beings who was in some way aware that his life was a mere projection? I make this statement because in his autobiography *Poetry and Truth*, part 3, Book 11, he described the following curious event:

> *I was riding on the footpath towards Drusenheim, and there one of the strangest presentiments occurred to me. I saw myself coming to meet myself on the same road on horseback, but in clothes such as I had never worn. They were light grey mixed with gold. As soon as I had aroused myself from the daydream the vision disappeared. Strange however it is that eight years later I found myself on the identical spot, intending to visit Frederika once more, and in the same clothes which I had seen in my vision, and which I now wore, not from choice but by accident.*[8]

Let us review this whole event in the light of the information we now have. Goethe sees himself as he will be in eight years' time. In my opinion this incident implies that both Bohm's concept of enfoldment and my theory of a three-dimensional life review may be correct. As far as my theory is concerned this incident is a simple programming error. For a second Goethe slips out of his 'review' and perceives an event that to him is yet to happen but which within the timeless zone of the life review has concurrent existence. As regards Bohm's theory (see Chapter 2), incidents like this are bound to occur as areas of enfolded reality touch upon each other. In my opinion Goethe perceives this event because, as he says, he has been through his life many times and as such has become more subconsciously aware of what is really happening to him.

In a very real sense, Goethe's Eidolon and Daemon inhabit both bodies but at different times. However, depending upon which observational point his eidolonic consciousness inhabited then that is where Goethe sensed he was. In the first incident the Eidolon was conscious as a young man and in the second as a much older person. However, the Daemon was present on both occasions.

A very similar event took place in 1749 and was experienced by another German, the composer Christoph Gluck. Gluck had been visiting friends in the Flemish city of Ghent. After a hearty meal he decided to bid his friends goodnight and walk from the tavern to his lodgings a short distance away. As he made his way through the streets he noticed a figure walking ahead of him. He was surprised to observe that the figure seemed to be following exactly the route that he was following but always a few seconds ahead. Gluck also felt that there was something about the figure that was strangely familiar. On catching another glimpse of his mysterious companion he was disturbed to notice that not only was the person the same height and build as himself, but he was also wearing exactly the same clothes. His ill-at-ease feeling turned to fear as he saw the figure approach the front door of his lodging house, produce a key, enter and close the door. This was simply too much for Gluck. He turned around and ran back to the tavern. His friends were still there and were surprised to see him back. Gluck explained what had happened and begged to stay the night with one of them.

The next day Gluck and his friends made their way back to the lodgings. As they entered the house they were aware of a

'Immediately after this I was seized with a strange distemper, which neither my friends nor physicians could comprehend, and it confined me to my chamber for many days; but I knew, myself, that I was bewitched, and suspected my father's reputed concubine of the deed. I told my fears to my reverend protector, who hesitated concerning them, but I knew by his words and looks that he was conscious I was right. I generally conceived myself to be two people. When I lay in bed, I deemed there were two of us in it; when I sat up I always beheld another person, and always in the same position from the place where I sat or stood, which was about three paces off me towards my left side. It mattered not how many or how few were present: this my second self was sure to be present in his place, and this occasioned a confusion in all my words and ideas that utterly astounded my friends, who all declared that, instead of being deranged in my intellect, they had never heard my conversation manifest so much energy or sublimity of conception; but, for all that, over the singular delusion that I was two persons my reasoning faculties had no power. The most perverse part of it was that I rarely conceived myself to be any of the two persons. I thought for the most part that my companion was one of them, and my brother the other; and I found that, to be obliged to speak and answer in the character of another man, was a most awkward business at the long run.'

JAMES HOGG (POET AND EPILEPTIC)

commotion inside. A group of people were looking into the open door of Gluck's room. As he looked past them he saw a huge roof beam lying across a smashed and broken bed. Up above was a massive hole in the ceiling. During the night the roof beam had come crashing down on the bed in which Gluck would have been sleeping. It was clear that if he had been asleep he would most certainly have been killed.

What had happened here? If Gluck's double had been a simple hallucination, it would not have been able to open a door and enter a building. Of course the logical answer is that it didn't. The Daemon simply melded its perceptions with its Eidolon and projected the image into Gluck's brain. It is possible that in Gluck's last life he was, in a very real sense, the illusionary figure he saw ahead of him. The original Gluck entered the lodging house, went to bed and died as the beam crashed down. His Daemon was determined that this was not going to happen this time.

What is fascinating about this particular example is that in 1749 Gluck was 35 years old, but at that time he was still unmarried and although he had written a few operas much of his work lay ahead of him. Had he died that night such great musical pieces as *Orfeo ed Euridice*, *Alceste* and *Iphigénie en Tauride* would have been lost forever. These works were profoundly influential and they changed the entire structure of opera. Indeed, it has been acknowledged that it was Gluck's new operatic format that allowed Mozart to create his masterpieces. Had Gluck died that night in 1749, music as we know it might have been very different. In an alternative 'Everett Multiverse' (see Chapter 4), it probably is.

I suggest that there are two possible explanations for this event, both of which support my thesis. Firstly, I have presented evidence that the double, *doppelgänger* or fetch are all manifestations of the Daemon. I argue that this is yet another channel of communication that this being uses to warn its Eidolon of forthcoming events. In most cases the *doppelgänger* is a harbinger of death. It seems to be able to project an image of itself into the visual field of its lower self. The technical term for this is metachoria and it is a recognized psychological state. I consider that this manifestation is closely related to the Being of Light regularly reported in cases of Near-Death Experience. The role of this Daemonic metachoric experience is simply to prepare the Eidolon for death. This is in no way an intervention to change future events. It is simply a preparatory message. However, this is not always the case.

Sometimes the Daemon wishes to change the future by giving a subtle warning.

A second, more intriguing, explanation is that what Gluck actually saw was his own future self existing a few seconds ahead of time. In the case cited earlier, when Goethe saw his own future self, the time distance between the perceiver and the perceived was many years. However should this be possible then the amount of time between the two events need not be years and could, indeed, be only a few seconds. As such Gluck perceived his own future self as he would be very soon. But this idea is even more interesting in that I suggest that the metachoric 'future' Gluck existed in an alternative 'Everett Multiverse' – a universe in which he died as the beam crashed on to his bed. In other words, it was some form of weird trans-dimensional timeslip in which an alternative future was presented back in time in order to bring about a change in the past. I am very aware that this suggestion makes the plot twists of the movie *Back to the Future* seem very straightforward, but nevertheless it is entirely explicable according to the theory of 'Cheating the Ferryman'.

It is reasonable to conclude that Gluck's *doppelgänger* was simply a visual variation on the aural Protector-Daemon that I discussed in Chapter 3. However, it does seem that this particular apparition was closely linked with the possible death of its Eidolon. It is to the relationship between the Daemon and death that I now wish to turn.

Death's pale horseman

For the natives of Alsace in France, the perception of one's *doppelgänger* means that death is near. In Teutonic folklore, seeing one's 'angel' was also a portent of impending death. This relationship occurs over and over throughout the folklore traditions in different parts of the world. Here in the British Isles we have the being known as the fetch.

> 'It often seems to me as though an invisible genius were
> whispering something rhythmical to me, so that on my walks
> I always keep in step to it.'
>
> JOHANN WOLFGANG GOETHE (POET AND AUTHOR)

There are many examples of this link. In 1890 there was a young man who worked as a bookbinder in the city of Strasbourg. He was strong and in prime fitness and was known for his down-to-earth opinions about the supernatural. One evening he went down to the cellar to draw a tankard of wine. On opening the door to the cellar he saw himself crouching in front of the cask and drawing the wine. When he approached, the spectre glanced round with an air of indifference and then disappeared. The young man tottered up the stairs, pale and tremulous. Later that evening he began shivering. He retired to bed with a high fever. He died a few days later.[9]

Clearly this association has been built up over many centuries and therefore the link between a *doppelgänger* and death has to be taken seriously. I contend that as death approaches the Daemon will become more active in the life of its Eidolon. How effective this can be, however, is directly related to the Eidolon's location on my Scale of Transcendence. The Daemon finds communication fairly difficult for the majority of humanity, resorting, as we have seen, to dreams and vaguer hunches. However, an effective Daemon may be able to project an image of itself, or indeed of any person or object it decides will be effective, into the visual cortex of its Eidolon. Although manifested in the brain, this image can be presented in such a way that it is perceived as a projection into the external world. This is why doubles and *doppelgängers* are never seen by anybody other than the people themselves. In a very real sense the double is a hallucination, but one with a source outside the observer.

As we have seen, the Daemon is intimately tied up with the

apparent death of its Eidolon. If I am correct in this belief then daemonic/*doppelgänger* encounters will be regularly reported by people close to death. Let us now review the evidence for such an assumption.

According to a 1607 manuscript entitled 'The relation of the Lady Southwell of the late Q (een's) Death', Queen Elizabeth the First saw her own Daemon just before she died in March 1603. The manuscript reads:

> She fell downright ill, and the cause being wondered at by my Lady Scroope, with whom she was very private and confidential, being her near kinswoman, her Majesty told her (commanding her to conceal the same), 'that she saw own night her own body exceedingly lean and fearful in a light of fire'. This vision was at Whitehall, a little before she departed for Richmond.

What is of particular interest here is that Queen Elizabeth's Daemon was surrounded by a 'light of fire'. To me this is a clear indication that the 'Being of Light' reported in many Near-Death experiences and the Daemon are one and the same entity.

The link between the double and approaching death is supported by many reports. One of the most interesting was described by the archaeologist Wellesley Tudor Pole. He found a German deserter from the French Foreign Legion deep in the Sahara Desert. The man had been without food and water for a long time and was in a very bad way. Tudor Pole tried to help as best he could but it was clear that the legionnaire was beyond help. Suddenly the man looked beyond Pole . . .

> . . . and cried out in broken French [I translate], 'Why, there is myself coming to meet me. How wonderful.' Then he fell back and died and we reported the incident on reaching Bou Saada the next day.[10]

What is particularly interesting is that this incident has Tudor Pole wondering about whether there can be 'truth in the theory of twin souls, two parts to one whole, who some day will be united'. This suspicion is reinforced by a case cited by Sir Auckland Geddes in an address delivered to the Royal Medical Society on 26 February 1927.

The case, he says, is 'the experience of a man who passed into the very portals of death and was brought back to life by medical treatment. The record was taken down in shorthand by a skilled secretary as life was re-establishing itself'. The account here is abridged.

> *On Saturday, 9th November, a few minutes after midnight,*
> *I began to feel very ill and by two o'clock was definitely*
> *suffering from acute gastroenteritis, which kept me vomiting*
> *and purging until about eight o'clock . . . By ten o'clock*
> *I had developed all the symptoms of very acute poisoning;*
> *intense gastrointestinal pain, diarrhoea; pulse and respirations*
> *became quite impossible to count, I wanted to ring for*
> *assistance, but found I could not, and so quite placidly gave*
> *up the attempt. I realized I was very ill and very quickly*
> *reviewed my whole financial position. Thereafter at no time*
> *did my consciousness appear to me to be in any way dimmed,*
> *but I suddenly realized that my consciousness was separating*
> *from another consciousness which was also me. These, for*
> *purposes of description, we could call the A- and*
> *B-consciousnesses, and throughout what follows the ego*
> *attached itself to the A-consciousness. The B-personality*
> *I recognized as belonging to the body, and as my physical*
> *condition grew worse and the heart was fibrillating rather*
> *than beating, I realized that the B-consciousness belonging to*
> *the body was beginning to show signs of being composite, that*
> *is built up of 'consciousness' from the head, the heart and the*
> *viscera. These components became more individual and the*

B-consciousness began to disintegrate, while the A-consciousness, which was now me, seemed to be altogether outside my body, which it could see. Gradually I realized that I could see not only my body and the bed in which it was, but everything in the whole house and garden, and then I realized that I was seeing not only things at home but in London and in Scotland, in fact wherever my attention was directed, it seemed to me; and the explanation which I received from what source I do not know, but which I found myself calling to myself my mentor, was that I was free in a time-dimension of space, wherein 'now' was in some way equivalent to 'here' in the ordinary three-dimensional space of everyday life.[11]

Literature is full of examples of people who seem to know that they are about to die. It is as if the Daemon suddenly becomes aware of its own individuality and starts to be more involved in the life of its lower self. What I find curious with this is why does it not make a greater effort to try and save its life? It is as if some situations, particularly involving illness (rather than accidents), simply cannot be changed by a different course of action. There is nothing the Eidolon can do to stop death. Could this explain the strange death-related precognitions?

For example in 1958 a doctor named Arnold Cowan wrote to the *British Medical Journal*. Dr Cowan reported that a patient of his, suffering from cancer, told him on a Tuesday that he should not make his usual Thursday visit to see him as he would be dying at 2.30 the following afternoon. He learned later that his patient had summoned the members of his family to say farewell after lunch on the Wednesday. His wife being detained for a few moments, he sent a message for her to hurry up so that she would not miss the event. At 2.30 precisely he sighed, raised both hands above his head, smiled and passed away.[12.]

If this account is to be believed then it is reasonable to conclude

'He was sitting at the desk in his study. His servant had strict orders not to enter while his master was working. Suddenly it seemed to Maupassant as if someone had opened the door. Turning round, he sees to his extreme astonishment his own self entering, who sits down and rests his head on his hand. Everything Maupassant writes is dictated to him. When the author finished his work and arose the hallucination disappeared.'

OTTO RANK WRITING ABOUT GUY DE MAUPASSANT

(AUTHOR AND EPILEPTIC)

that these two consciousnesses coexist during life only to split at the point of death – exactly as proposed by my 'Cheating the Ferryman' theory.

So what evidence do I have from literature to support such an idea? I would now like to introduce to you yet another guise of the Daemon – the Being of Light.

Summary

Doppelgängers and doubles are not creatures of fiction but aspects of a very real, and well-documented psychological state known as autoscopy. However, although regularly observed this phenomenon remains a total mystery to modern neuroscience. I suggest that the double is simply an internally-generated image that the Daemon places within the conscious awareness of its Eidolon. This can be seen as a final act of desperation on the part of the Higher Self – possibly the daemonic equivalent of shouting.

There seems to be a strong link between *doppelgänger* experiences and death. To see one's double is, for many cultures, a harbinger of doom. If my theory is correct then this is not at all surprising. The Daemon knows that death is close and it wishes to communicate this fact to its Eidolon. It is difficult to understand the motivations of the Higher Self at this time. In most cases the *doppelgänger* communicates nothing by its presence. Clearly there are exceptions such as that reported by Gluck, but this is unusual.

In my opinion this is because the Daemon at this stage in its Eidolon's life is getting ready to manifest itself in its most important role – that of the Being of Light so regularly reported in the Near-Death Experience.

CHAPTER 7 The Mystery of the Double

[1] Shelley, P.B., 'Speculations on Metaphysics', *Prose Works Vol. II*, p.193 (1909)

[2] Erickson, M., 'A special enquiry with Aldous Huxley into the nature and character of various states of consciousness', from *Amer. J. Clin. Hyp.*, 8, 14–33

[3] Ibid.

[4] Knopf, Alfred A., *Men Who Have Walked With God*, Cheney Sheldon, p.242 (1945)

[5] Hughlings, Jackson J., *The Selected Writings of John Hughlings Jackson*, vol. I, ed. J. Taylor, Basic Books, New York, p.463 (1958)

[6] Gloor et al., 'The role of the limbic system in experiential phenomena of temporal lobe epilepsy', *Annals of Neurology* 12, p.132 (1982)

[7] Ibid.

[8] Davies, R., *Doubles, The Enigma of the Second Self*, p.121, Robert Hale, London (1998)

[9] Feinberg, Todd E., *Altered Egos: How the Brain Creates the Self*, OUP, p.82 (2001)

[10] Tudor Pole, Wellesley, *The Silent Road*, C.W. Daniel, p.112 (1960)

[11] Tyrell, G.N.M., *The Personality of Man*, Pelican, pp.197–8 (1947)

[12] Cowan, A., 'Premonition of Death', *British Medical Journal*, ii, 1041, p.914 (1958)

CHAPTER 8

The Being of Light

There is a fear that there is an afterlife
but no one will know where it's being held.

Woody Allen

The Morse Code

The woman was confused. The last thing she remembered was
being wheeled down to the operating theatre and then losing
consciousness as the general anaesthetic took effect. Wherever she
was now it was not in a dream. Everything was super-vivid as if
her senses had been turned up a few levels. She felt that she was
out of her body and floating in space. However, she knew that
space was a dark and cold place. This was warm and comforting
and she was surrounded by an intense light that for some reason
did not hurt her eyes. This is it, she thought to herself. I am dead.

Through the light she could detect a movement. It was a person
but like no other she had ever seen. This being had a radiance
that was even greater than the light that surrounded it. She felt
overcome by love as it approached her. It spoke to her. The voice
was both inside her and around her and was soft and gentle.

Then something very strange happened. The being took her
through the whole of her life in a full 'past-life review'. She
experienced it all in what seemed like a few seconds. But things
then became stranger again because the person then described to
her events that were yet to take place. The woman was amazed
at these visions and was even more amazed when, towards the
end of the experience, it showed her a photograph of a man. It
said that the man's name was Raymond Moody, adding: 'When
the time is right, you will tell him about this experience'.

The woman then found herself back in a pain-wracked body.

During the operation she had suffered heart failure and a lung collapse. She had been clinically dead and only swift action on the part of the surgeon had brought her back to life.

Her recovery was slow but effective. By the end of 1971, she was fit enough to go back to her normal life. As the years passed the memory of her Near-Death Experience faded, but it was always in the back of her mind.

On 31 October 1975 she was at home with her family when there was the sound of children's laughter outside and a loud knock on the door. Gangs of youngsters were roaming the streets dressed as witches, wizards and ghouls. It was Halloween and 'trick or treat' was in full swing. She smiled at her husband and grabbing at a handful of sweets they walked towards the door.

On opening the door they saw a group of children. 'Trick or treat!' the children gleefully shouted and they were given the sweets as a reward for their costumes. The woman, being new to the area, took the opportunity to chat to some of the children. She asked them their names. Each child proudly announced who they were, until she eventually came round to an older boy standing at the back with his mother.

'And your name, young man?' the woman asked.

'Raymond Avery Moody, the third,' the young boy announced proudly.

The woman was taken aback. She asked him to repeat his name, then she went white. The boy's mother came forward and asked if the woman was all right. She introduced herself as Louise Moody, wife of Dr Raymond Moody.

'I must talk to your husband,' the woman replied, turning back into the house to grab her coat, her hands shaking in anticipation. The name Raymond Moody was the exact name that the being had told her about four years earlier.

Later, she arrived at the Moody's house. On being introduced to Dr Moody she could hardly believe her eyes. Standing in front of her was the man from the photograph she had been shown in her experience. She explained to him the events in the hospital, her past-life review and her encounter with the being. Moody explained to her that this was indeed a strange coincidence because he was an expert in a new field of research called Near-Death Experience, or NDE. When she told him about the photograph Moody was astounded and was keen to know more.

For Moody this incident in late October 1975 was an incidental, and unexpected, coda to ten years' research. It had all started when he was a young philosophy student at the University of Virginia. He was sitting with 20 or so others in a seminar given by Professor John Marshall. The subject of the seminar was the philosophical issues related to death. Marshall told the group about Dr Ritchie, a locally-based psychiatrist who had been pronounced dead with a case of double pneumonia but had then been successfully resuscitated. While he was 'dead', Ritchie had the remarkable experience of passing through a tunnel and seeing beings of light. Marshall asked the students what this experience implied about the subjective nature of death.

A few months later, Moody had the opportunity to hear Dr Ritchie describe in person how in 1943 he had been in a hospital in Texas with a respiratory infection. As he lay in bed, Ritchie said, he suddenly felt very ill. The next second he was spitting up blood and he swiftly lost consciousness. What happened then stunned him – he found himself looking down on his own body. He turned round and walked into the corridor. As he did so he was approached by a ward boy. The boy ignored him, which was strange, but what happened after that was even stranger. As Ritchie stood there, the young man walked straight through him and continued along the corridor. Totally shaken, Ritchie approached another man and tapped him on the shoulder. The man completely ignored him.

He turned back into his room and desperately tried to get back into his body but with no success. Then the room seemed to get brighter and brighter – it was bathed in an intense white light

'I had been awake for a number of hours. My level of body tonus was fairly high and my mind clear to dream-images so that I believe I was not asleep but rather in some kind of trance-like state. At that time I was not conscious of my personal identity, nor of prior experiences, nor the external world. It was just that out of nowhere I was aware of my own thought processes. I did not know, however, that they were thought processes or who I was or even that I was an I. There was sheer awareness . . . sheer existing. After a time a "wondering" started to fill my awareness: that there was something more than this, a gap, an emptiness. As soon as this "wondering" was set in motion there was immediately a change in my awareness. In an instant, as if in a flash, full awareness of myself and reality expanded around me. To say that "I woke up" or "I remembered", while perhaps correct, would miss the point of experience entirely . . . suddenly all the specifications of reality had become apparent to me. At one moment my awareness was devoid of all structure and in the next moment I was myself in a multivaried universe of time, space, motion and desire.'*

RONALD SHOR (HYPNOTIST)

that was 'brighter than a thousand arc lights'. Out of the white light walked the figure of a man. Suddenly Ritchie found himself confronted by the most radiant being he had ever seen. As Ritchie was a religious man he thought that this man must be Jesus. The being then seemed to bring about a full review of Ritchie's life from the moment of his birth to the present. He saw 'every event and thought and conversation, as palpable as a series of pictures', as he described it to Moody.

Then Ritchie woke up in his own body, to the astonishment of the physician who had just signed his death certificate. An orderly who had been preparing the body for the morgue noticed feeble signs of life in the corpse and called the doctor, who hastily injected adrenaline directly into the heart. Although Ritchie had not taken a breath for nine full minutes, he showed no symptoms of brain damage. The commanding officer at the hospital called the Ritchie case 'the most amazing circumstance' of his career and signed an affidavit that George Ritchie had indeed made a miraculous return from virtual death on the night of 20 December 1943.

Although he was fascinated by this case, Moody simply filed it away in his memory and completed his Ph.D. in philosophy. He then began teaching philosophy at the University of Virginia. During a seminar, one of his students described a Near-Death Experience that was virtually identical to the one described by Ritchie four years earlier. In 1972, Moody entered medical school and by that time he had found other students who had experienced similar mental states during near-death situations. Over the next few years he collected about 150 similar cases. Clearly, he needed to publicize his findings.

A few months after the Halloween incident described above, Moody was to take the publishing world by storm. He wrote a book entitled *Life After Life,* a book that was to become an international bestseller. Moody had called the phenomenon Near-Death Experience and soon the abbreviation NDE needed no further explanation.

Many other writers and researchers were to follow in Moody's footsteps and soon dozens of books had been written on the subject. Clearly Moody had found something of profound significance.

According to pollster George Gallup jun., eight million adults in the United States have undergone a Near-Death Experience. This is one person in 20. These figures are even higher than those discovered by Moody himself whose 'straw-poll' of his lecture audiences resulted in figures of one in 30. Clearly this is a significant psychological state. So what exactly is the Near-Death Experience?

The Near-Death Experience

From his research, Moody was able to derive a set of nine traits that define the NDE experience. He made it clear that not all subjects experience all nine. Some may only encounter one or two. However, at least one must be present for the experience to be considered an NDE. The nine traits are: a sense of being dead; peace and painlessness; an out-of-body experience; the tunnel experience; people of light; rising rapidly into the heavens; a reluctance to return; a past-life review and an encounter with a being of light.

In the Gallup poll report mentioned above, 26 per cent reported an out-of-body sensation, 32 per cent underwent a life review and 23 per cent sensed the presence of another being; the tunnel experience was reported by 9 per cent. What is interesting, but not part of Moody's nine traits, was that 23 per cent of the respondees said that they had experienced heightened visual perceptions and 6 per cent claimed precognition.

Moody's book attracted considerable interest within the medical profession. Dr Martin Sabom, a cardiologist, was keen to see if he could find any evidence for the NDE from his patients. Sabom was in a perfect position to check this out. He specialized in the resuscitation of patients who had suffered cardiac arrest. Because of this, he recognized the inherent difficulty of determining whether or not a resuscitated patient had been clinically dead.

So he carefully defined what criterion he would apply. This was 'any bodily state resulting from an extreme physiological catastrophe . . . that would reasonably be expected to result in irreversible biological death in the majority of instances and would demand urgent medical attention.'

Of the 78 patients interviewed by Sabom, 34 (43 per cent) reported an NDE. Applying Moody's nine traits the results were interesting. 92 per cent reported a sense of being dead, 53 per cent described an out-of-body experience, 53 per cent had felt themselves rising into heaven, 48 per cent had experienced a 'Being of Light' and 23 per cent had undergone the tunnel experience.

All reported a reluctance to return. The other 'traits' not mentioned are included within the general definitions.

After Raymond Moody, the best-known name in the field of NDE research is probably Kenneth Ring. As well as continuing the work of Sabom and Moody, Ring has also been involved in some fascinating research into one particular area – the NDE experiences of people born blind. Ring and his co-worker, Sharon Cooper, identified 21 blind individuals who had experienced an NDE. Of these ten had been born blind, nine had lost their sight before the age of five and two were severely visually handicapped. Interestingly, ten of the subjects claimed that they 'saw' their body below them during the NDE. These ten all reported the usual Moody traits, including flying down a tunnel towards a bright light and having an encounter with a Being of Light.[1] One of the most interesting subjects was a 43-year-old married mother of three children called Vicki Umipeg.

Vicki had been born extremely prematurely and too much oxygen had been given to her after her birth. This had destroyed the optic nerve in both of her eyes. As a result of this miscalculation she had been blind since birth. During her life Vicki had suffered two NDEs. The first was when she was 20 and it was brought about by an attack of appendicitis. However, it was the second that is of great interest. She was involved in a car crash when she was 22 years old. In her NDE she 'saw' herself as she hovered above the hospital bed. At that point, she noticed that a section of her very long hair had been shaved off. After this she felt herself float through the roof and then she saw street lights and houses below her. She then found herself in a field covered with flowers. In this field were people she had known but who were long dead. Suddenly, a radiant figure walked towards her. She took this figure to be Jesus, although he never identified himself as such. This Being of Light gave her a full 'life review' that she saw in full colour and in great detail. After this the being told her that she must return in order to 'bear her children'. This greatly excited Vicki because at that time motherhood was only a dream. With that she found herself slammed back into her body and she experienced once more the heavy dullness and intense pain of her physical being.[2]

Here again we see most of the elements of the classic NDE but experienced by a person that had never experienced the world of vision and colour. This case has been cited many times as a classic case that virtually proves the objective reality of the NDE – this and the case of Maria and the tennis shoe.

In April 1977, a female migrant worker was admitted into Seattle's Harborview Medical Center in Washington State, USA. She had suffered a heart attack and so was quickly rushed up to the coronary care unit. Even worse, three days later she suffered a second, massive, heart attack. Fortunately, specialist staff were on hand and she was successfully resuscitated.

Later that day a social worker called Kimberley Clark called in to check how Maria was. Maria, although still ill, was very excited and was keen to tell Clark that she had experienced a strange series of sensations while she was unconscious. She described how she had witnessed her resuscitation from a position outside and above her body. She then said that she had become distracted by something above the emergency room entrance, which made her 'will' herself outside the hospital. She accurately described the area surrounding the emergency room entrance, which Clark found curious since a canopy over the entrance would have obstructed Maria's view if she had simply looked out of her hospital room window.

Floating in the air outside the window she spotted something strange on a third-floor window ledge at the far side of the hospital. Again she realized that she could 'will' herself to another location because she suddenly found herself right next to the object that had caught her attention. It was a man's tennis shoe, specifically a dark-blue, left-foot shoe with a worn-out patch over the little toe and a single shoelace tucked under its heel. With this image in her mind, she found herself back in her body as the crash team seemingly saved her life.

Clark was fascinated by this and agreed to try and see if Maria had actually seen something that existed outside her imagination. She inspected the outside of the hospital, but could see nothing from ground level. She then re-entered the building and began a room-to-room search of the floor above the one on which Maria's resuscitation had taken place. She could see nothing, even when pressing her head against the window to get a better view. Eventually, and to her great surprise, she did find the shoe. She entered one particular room on the third floor of the north wing and spotted the shoe, but from her vantage point inside the hospital she could not see the worn-out toe – which would have been facing outwards – or the tucked-in shoe lace.[3]

Clearly, these two examples seem to present irrefutable evidence that the NDE is a very real experience. This implies that conscious awareness can exist outside the brain.

All very interesting, I hear you say, but what has all this to do with my Daemon-Eidolon Dyad? Well, I believe that certain elements of the NDE not only provide strong evidence for the Dyad but also for the whole 'Cheating the Ferryman' thesis. These elements are the Being of Light (BOL) and the Past-Life Review (PLR). However, other elements of the NDE seem, at first sight, to contradict both my theories. If, as I believe, the NDE is brought about by the brain then without a brain conscious awareness cannot be. As such the phenomenon of floating outside the body simply cannot take place. Consciousness exists within the brain, so perception from a point outwith the brain simply cannot occur unless our science is totally in error. How can anybody 'see' without an eye to process the light or hear without an eardrum to vibrate and send the signal to the brain?

Can it be that the NDE experience is, in fact, some form of elaborate hallucination brought about by the body's reaction to approaching death? There is a good deal of evidence to suggest that this might be the case. It is to this that I shall now turn.

The flood of evidence

Death must be the most stressful event in a person's life. Suddenly the reality of one's mortality is clear. This must be particularly acute in circumstances where the person knows that their death is absolutely inevitable – for example, an impending car crash, falling from a cliff, drowning or seeing a potentially fatal wound on their body.

Apart from our conscious awareness the body itself knows that death is possible. The brain receives various messages informing it that something is terribly wrong and that its time as a living organism might be very short. It takes extreme action to preserve life or, if that is impossible, to ensure that the approaching death experience can be as trauma-free as possible. To do this the brain floods itself with a cocktail of internally-generated chemicals called endorphins.

Endorphins act in very similar ways to morphine by bringing about pain reduction along with a feeling of euphoria and bliss. One side-effect of a large amount of endorphins in the brain is the possibility of seizures. These occur in two important areas of the brain, the limbic system and the temporal lobes. It is known that these are the areas in which the endorphins and their receptors are most commonly found. In this way the endorphins bring about many of the symptoms of a Near-Death Experience.

However, in recent years new research has shown that all the symptoms of an NDE may be brought about by another chemically-induced mental state; one that reproduces with great accuracy all of the elements of the NDE. This work has been mostly been done by Dr Karl Jansen of the Maudsley Hospital in South London. If he is right, then the nature of the NDE may have been explained.

Jansen contends, in his now famous article[4] and his subsequent summation[5], that the hallucinogenic anaesthetic ketamine can reproduce all the features of the Near-Death Experience. Ketamine was used as an anaesthetic on wounded United States soldiers during the Vietnam War. Although very effective it was never used on civilians because it had some very peculiar side-effects. One soldier described these as follows:

> *[I] found myself as a bodiless point of awareness and energy*
> *floating in the midst of a vast vaulted chamber. There was a*
> *sense of presence all around, as though I was surrounded by*
> *millions of others, although no one else could be seen. In the*
> *center of the chamber was a huge, pulsing, Krishna-blue mass*
> *of seething energy that was shaped in a geometric, mandalic*
> *form. Then suddenly, I was back in my body, lying on my*
> *bed. 'Wow,' I thought, 'it's over. How abrupt!' I tried to sit*
> *up. Suddenly, my body was gone again and the room*
> *dissolved into blackness of the void, my reality being quickly*
> *pulled out from underneath my feet, like a hyperspatial*
> *magician's tablecloth trick.*[6]

However, under controlled conditions many experiments have taken place in which volunteers have taken various amounts of ketamine and reported their experiences. Many hallucinatory states have been reported, including rapid trips down dark tunnels into light, seeing a being or beings, out-of-body experiences, mystic states and memory recall. In *Psychedelic Drugs Reconsidered*, a monograph written on the general effects of psychedelic drugs, the effects of ketamine were described thus:

> *. . . becoming a disembodied mind or soul, dying and going*
> *to another world. Childhood events may also be relived. The*
> *loss of contact with ordinary reality and the sense of*
> *participation in another reality are more pronounced and less*
> *easily resisted than is usually the case with LSD. The*
> *dissociative experiences often seem so genuine that users are*
> *not sure that they have not actually left their bodies.*[7]

Ketamine, once in the brain, attaches itself to a glutamate receptor called the N-methyl-D-aspartate or NMDA receptor for short. You will recall that glutamate is one of a group of chemical substances known as neurotransmitters and is known to be the key neuro-transmitter within the temporal lobes, the hippocampus and the frontal lobes. So when ketamine is introduced into the brain, it disrupts the flow of this crucial chemical messenger.

It is useful to imagine these receptors as tiny harbours with several docks. What ketamine does, in effect, is to blockade the harbour, therefore stopping any glutamate getting through to its receptors. Generally, glutamate is not harmful but under certain circumstances vast amounts are generated, causing what is termed a glutamate flood. Excessive amounts of glutamate can lead to the death of brain cells by a process called excitotoxicity. What happens is that glutamate opens the harbour even wider and in doing so allows water to rush in, causing the neuron cell to literally burst apart. This process of cell-death can also be brought about by a lack of oxygen (hypoxia), low blood sugar (hypogly-caemia) and, significantly, epilepsy.

The circumstances that lead to a glutamate flood exist at times of extreme threat or crisis, particularly during life-threatening situations. However, it is counter-productive when a potentially damaging flood of chemicals enters the brain, particularly if the life-threatening situation proves to be a false alarm.

Jansen believes that during a real Near-Death Experience the glutamate flood is prevented by the internal generation of a substance that protects the NMDA receptors by binding to one of the 'docks' in the NMDA 'harbour'. This 'dock' is called the PCP receptor. This substance must, by its very nature, have a very similar effect to ketamine on the psychological state of the person involved. This endogamous (internally created) drug is the trigger for natural Near-Death Experiences.

In 1984, endogenous substances that bind to the PCP receptor were found in the brain. One of these was a peptide called alpha-endopsychosin.[8] Peptides are a peculiar group of neurotransmitters discovered in the 1970s. Initially found only in the intestine it caused great surprise when they were also discovered in the brain. What was even more curious was that small amounts of one type (TRH) can induce euphoric states and this has been used as an anti-depressant. Another (beta-endorphin) causes muscular rigidity and immobility (catatonia), while the wonderfully named luteinizing hormone-releasing hormone (LHRH) is reputed to stimulate libido. Alpha-endopsychosin is a member of an ever-growing group of internally generated drugs that are called endogenous morphines – the endorphins that we discussed earlier.

These are the body's own opiates and, as well as controlling pain, they can also bring about euphoria and hallucinations. However, up until the discovery of alpha-endopsychosin, endorphins were found to lack the potency needed to cause the powerful perception-altering effects – although they were believed to be responsible in some way for NDEs[9,10]. Indeed, it has been shown that endorphins secreted as a response to stress have a sudden rise and a slow decay over several hours – probably longer than a typical NDE.

However, it has now been shown that endopsychosins have exactly the same effect as ketamine in stopping the glutamate flood. As such it is reasonable to believe that the conditions that trigger an NDE may also trigger an endopsychosin flood to protect cells. From this, it would seem that the NDE is, in reality, a side-effect of consciousness caused by a purely physical reaction – a reaction to the great stress of realizing that one is about to die!

As we have seen, glutamate is the major neurotransmitter of the temporal lobes. It has long been accepted that endorphin release in this part of the brain can bring about an epileptic seizure and some researchers have shown that the death of brain cells due to excitotoxicity may also be brought about by an epileptic seizure. As such the same neuroprotective system that brings about the increase in NMDA blockers during the glutamate flood scenario of an NDE may also take place as a seizure approaches. In other words, the psychological hallucinations experienced by a person having a Near-Death Experience may be similar, if not identical, to the aura symptoms of a person with temporal lobe epilepsy.

As such, it is reasonable to conclude that as soon as a person starts to die the endorphins bring about an epileptic seizure within the temporal lobes – in other words, a massive TLE attack – which in turn sets up the NMDA barrier that brings about an NDE.

So here we have strong neurological evidence to suggest that many NDE experiences are brought about by brain activity. It is, therefore, reasonable to conclude that during the NDE the person never actually leaves their body at all. They only sense that they do.

Now in my opinion this does not disprove the reality of the NDE experience. All that it does is to present a process by which the NDE may be experienced. Indeed, such an interpretation reinforces, rather than weakens, my 'Cheating the Ferryman' thesis which argues that the existence of personal immortality does not rely on the assumption that we all have a physical body and a discarnate soul.

However, a major weakness of the 'Cheating the Ferryman' thesis is that many NDEers report that they experience a discarnate existence beyond the confines of the body during the NDE. If my theory is correct then this does not happen. A dying person's consciousness remains, as it always has been, locked within the confines of the brain. Even if one accepts the argument that the brain is some form of receiver (that is, that consciousness exists elsewhere) consciousness still needs a brain to modulate the signal in the same way that without a television set a TV programme cannot be seen.

So does the case that the mind can exist – and perceive – outside the confines of the body really stand up to close analysis or is it, as the neurologists say, all brought about by brain chemicals?

To try and understand this conundrum I would now like to review, in the light of these findings, the two cases we discussed at the start of the chapter: the case of the tennis shoe and the blind NDE experiencers.

Two classic cases?

The Harborview case has long been presented as the final proof that the NDE involves the 'soul' or spirit of the NDEer leaving the body of the dying person and floating around while still retaining all its sensory inputs such as sight and hearing. As we have seen, there is strong evidence to conclude that this is a hallucination brought about by events in the brain. However, if Maria really did see that shoe on the roof, then Jansen and the other neurologists will be shown to be wrong.

In 1994, two researchers from an organization then known as the Committee for the Scientific Investigation of Claims of the Paranormal (CSICOP) took themselves to the Harborview Medical Center to see for themselves the location and circumstances of the 1977 'Maria' case. Now it is only fair to point out that this organization has a hidden agenda, one that has become less hidden in recent years after a name change. Now known as 'the Committee for Skeptikal Enquiry' (CSI) it exists to actively question the evidence for any belief in the paranormal. As such any counter-evidence presented by CSI is actively presented with a view to disproving what took place in 1977. Hayden Ebbern and Sean Mulligan were keen to interview Kimberley Clark and, if possible, Maria herself. They were surprised to find that not only could they not trace Maria but they could find nobody who knew her. Of course this was a good 17 years after the events of 1977 so it is not really that surprising, particularly as Maria was a migrant worker.

Ebbern and Mulligan pointed out that Maria had been in hospital for three days before her experience and they suggested that she would have reasonably had time to familiarize herself with the layout of the building and the nature of the equipment that was being used to monitor her condition. As such, her description of this equipment and the events that followed her cardiac arrest could have been gained from mere observation rather than an out-of-body experience.

They then turned their attention to the shoe. Ebbern and Mulligan took themselves outside to ascertain just how difficult it would have been for somebody at ground level to see a shoe poking out of a third-floor window ledge. They placed a running shoe of their own at the place Clark had described and then went outside to observe what was visible from ground level. To their surprise they found it very easy to see. What made this all the more interesting was that in 1994 there was a good deal of new construction going on underneath the window in question and the two researchers had to view the window from considerably further away than would have been the case in 1977. Indeed, the shoe was so conspicuous that, when they returned to the hospital a week later, 'someone not specifically looking for it had seen it and removed it.'[11] The authors argue that, if the shoe was as obvious as it was in 1994, then it was likely that it would have been a talking point and that Maria could have overheard staff or visitors talking about it. Of course it would be reasonable to contend that if the staff were so meticulous in 1994 that they quickly removed the shoe then why, if the shoe was even more obvious in 1977, did not somebody similarly remove it?

Ebbern and Mulligan then tested out Clark's claim that the shoe was impossible to see from inside the building unless the person pressed their head against the windowpane. In fact they found that all one needed to do to see the shoe was to take a few steps into the room. From that position the shoe was clearly visible. They concluded that a patient lying in bed in that room would have had a clear, and unobstructed, view of the offending article of footwear. It is reasonable to conclude that anybody spending time in this room would have surely commented on the shoe to visitors and hospital staff. Yet again it is likely that this would have been a general topic of conversation during Maria's stay.

One of the stronger aspects of the case is Maria's description of the shoe, particularly the worn-out toe and tucked-in shoelace, both of which, according to Clark, were not visible from inside the building. Ebbern and Mulligan commented:

> We had no difficulty seeing the shoe's allegedly hidden outer side . . . [Maria's shoe] would have been visible, both inside and outside the hospital, to numerous people who could have come into contact with her. It also seems likely that some of them might have mentioned it within earshot . . .[12]

Clearly, the authors were very keen to question Clark's motives. They pointed out that she didn't report the case for seven years and had, in their opinion, clearly embellished some of the details. To this they added the idea that by removing the shoe from its original location evidence was destroyed that would have supported Maria's out-of-body claim. Indeed, the very fact that this is Clark's report on what Maria told her (with, I presume, no supporting witnesses) does rather weaken the case.

I readily concede that members of an organization such as CSI have a vested interest in debunking such cases. However, I am somewhat saddened to find that this case is regularly presented in articles, magazines and books as a classic case without any reference to the CSI paper. Indeed, I had long believed this to be irrefutable evidence for the discarnate nature of the NDE and have acknowledged it as such in many of my lectures.

I would now like to turn to the other strong case, that of blind NDEers having vision during their NDEs. From a personal viewpoint I find these cases particularly moving and I would desperately like to believe that in some way the blind can see when experiencing an NDE. Indeed, it is my hope that within the magical possibilities now opening with regard to quantum physics and consciousness studies it may be that by some process yet unknown the brain can override a lack of visual pathways. Possibly, the clue lies in such psychological mysteries as blindsight.

On the face of it the Ring and Cooper research, which I referred to earlier, seems extraordinarily compelling. If it is really true that the blind have out-of-body experiences during an NDE, then clearly they will not be using their eyes to see. As with any other sighted NDEer, whatever is perceived during these extra-corporeal adventures does not involve the retina, the optic nerve or the visual cortex. Here, we have a totally new way of sensing the world around us.

In his 2003 book *Religion, Spirituality and the Near-Death Experience*, Mark Fox takes a very dispassionate look at this fascinating element of the NDE. Fox first questions the veracity of the evidence because of the known problems that congenitally blind people have when, for whatever reason, they can suddenly see. The brains of such individuals have never had the chance to develop an understanding of the new signals being received from the retina. It takes a long time to accommodate this new data. Fox gives the example of a 52-year-old man who, after a lifetime of blindness, received corneal grafts. Up until that time he had understood the world around him through tactile means. Confronted by a world that was very different from his inner understanding of its workings he simply could not cope. Two years later he took his own life.

Fox therefore finds it hard to accept that Ring and Cooper's NDE subjects have no such problems. Apparently, they can immediately understand the three-dimensional nature of the visual world that is suddenly presented to their consciousness. They can readily identify objects about which they have no previous comprehension.

One particular case that I had difficulty with was where one of the blind subjects claimed that although she had 'omnidirectional awareness' she was colour-blind. I simply cannot understand how somebody who had never seen colour before, or indeed anything, could know that she was 'seeing' a world with an absence of colour? Blue or red can never be explained to a blind person because there is no comparison. One cannot say that 'blue is like the colour of the sky' to somebody who has never seen the sky. It rather reminds me of the very sad story I heard many years ago. A blind child asked her mother: 'What colour is the wind?'

'Provided one has the slightest remnant of superstition left, one can hardly reject completely that one is the mere incarnation, or mouthpiece, or medium of some almighty power . . . One hears – one does not seek; one takes – one does not ask who gives: a thought flashes out like lightning; inevitably without hesitation – I have never had any choice about it. There is an ecstasy whose terrific tension is sometimes released by a flood of tears, during which one's progress varies from involuntary impetuosity to involuntary slowness. There is a feeling that one is utterly out of hand, with the most distinct consciousness of an infinitude of shuddering thrills that pass through one from head to foot . . . There is an instinct for rhythmic relations which embraces an entire world of forms . . . Everything occurs quite without volition, as if an eruption of freedom, independence, power, and divinity. The spontaneity of the images and similes is most remarkable; one loses all perception of what is imaginary and simile… This is my experience of inspiration. I have no doubt that I should have to go back millenniums to find another who could say to me: "This is mine also!"'

FRIEDRICH NIETZSCHE (PHILOSOPHER)

Fox argues that what the blind NDEers reported was socially and culturally influenced and that their experience was part of the overall NDE 'fantasy' brought about by the influence of endorphins. This is not to say that it was not real to them, but it was a hallucination all the same.

NDEs are quite rare occurrences. Blind NDE cases must be, by extrapolation, rarer still. However, it seems that there is a link between the Maria case and that of the blind Vicki Umipeg that I discussed earlier. It seems that Vicki turned up at an NDE support group in Seattle. Running this support group was a social worker called Kimberley Clark-Sharp. This was the same Kimberley Clark who had reported the Maria case a few years earlier. Kimberley was so fascinated by what Vicki told her that she immediately contacted her friend Kenneth Ring. Fox comments that the chance of these two cases being from the same hospital was 'incredibly statistically improbable'.[13]

I am of the opinion that something very real did happen to these blind people and that they genuinely believed that they could see. However, whether they did actually see anything is open to debate. One can reasonably argue that blind people also 'see' in their dreams. These inner-worlds will have a visual logic to them that may be identical to those of us fortunate to have sight. As such an NDE may simply reproduce these inner landscapes and project them on to an external world.

However, I must strongly state that I believe that Maria's NDE and those of Ring and Cooper's blind research subjects were very real NDEs and stand as strong evidence for all of the other components of the classical NDE, with the exception of the out-of-body features. Most of the elements of the NDE experience can be explained neurologically, with one main exception – the identity of the Being of Light.

Charon's partner?

Moody's trick or treat encounter that opened this chapter is described in his 1988 book *The Light Beyond*, a fascinating review of his subsequent work in the field of NDE research.[14] What interests me about this particular event is that although Moody describes it he does not attempt to explain it. This raises many questions for me. For example who, or what, is the being that the woman encountered and, more importantly, how did it know the future?

So far I have attempted to give a reasonably scientific explanation for the Near-Death Experience. I have suggested that most of the elements can be explained by neurology. However, this cannot explain how Moody's neighbour met a being who knew that in the future she would meet Moody himself. Neurology cannot explain how the Being of Light that visited Ring's blind subject, Vicki, knew that she would become a mother, although clearly this was a possibility, nor cannot it ever explain the story that opened this book, the future dream of the young boy who saw through his own future eyes a room and a family that were not to exist for 20 years.

As we have seen, this mysterious 'Being of Light' is a central part of the whole NDE. It seems to have a particularly crucial role to play in the process. Indeed, it is interesting to observe that it is the only part of the experience that seems to introduce itself into the consciousness of a dying person before they pass into the zone of being 'clinically dead'.

Time and time again we have reports of dying people suddenly reacting as if they see a person in the room. They sit up, smile, and sometimes speak to something that cannot be seen by the observers.

In my opinion, the BOL is none other than the Daemon that we have been discussing throughout this book. It is simply the final manifestation of our lifelong partner.

If my 'Cheating the Ferryman' thesis is correct, then in the final moments of our life something very strange happens. This chapter has dealt with the subjective experiences of individuals who have survived and avoided the final descent into death. They have had a literal Near-Death Experience. A Real-Death Experience (RDE) is very similar in many ways, but it has a few crucial differences. One can never return from an RDE. I feel that it is analogous to the phenomenon known as the event horizon that surrounds a black hole.

A black hole is a star that has a gravitational pull so great that even light cannot escape. As you will no doubt be aware, every large object exerts a gravitational pull on smaller objects around it: the greater the mass, the greater the gravitational attraction. The earth's mass gives it such a pull that a smaller object needs a velocity of 11.2 kilometres per second to escape its attraction. However, the earth is a mere tiddler when it comes to other objects out in space. For example, to escape the sun's grip you would need a velocity of 617 kilometres a second. A black hole is an object with a mass so great that the required escape velocity is greater than the speed of light. Within the boundaries of modern physics nothing can travel faster than light, so nothing can ever escape from the grip of a black hole. Surrounding a black hole is the 'event horizon'. Now what is strange about an event horizon is that from the viewpoint of an observer a spaceship that approaches the event horizon will be seen to stop right at the horizon and never enter the hole. However, those unfortunates on the spaceship go over the horizon and are sucked into the black hole.

In an RDE, the person passes over into an alternative universe from which they can never return. Just like crossing over an event horizon, once in there is no escape. Those who have an NDE come very close but bounce back. As such they experience some of the aspects of a RDE but in a very different format.

Indeed, the event horizon analogy works in another way – a total reversal in actual fact. In the 'Cheating the Ferryman' theory, from the viewpoint of the dying person they never fall into the black hole, whereas from the viewpoint of an observer the dying person dies (falls into the black hole). Just as the spaceship is forever seen on the edge of the event horizon so it is that, from the viewpoint of the dying person, they never reach the point of death.

Confused? If you haven't read *Is There Life After Death?: The Extraordinary Science of What Happens When We Die*, then you most certainly will be. Indeed, I am sure that many who have read my first book are also not quite sure what I mean by 'Cheating the Ferryman', so I will try and explain. If I am successful then you will understand who the Daemon is and why it knows the future. So here goes.

So what really happens at the point of death? We have some knowledge from Near-Death Experiences but these, it can be argued, are trauma brought about by the potential reality of the real thing. The body prepares itself for death by giving the person positive thoughts rather than negative fears. As such it could well be that the proliferation of supportive evidence since the publication of Moody's *Life After Life* could be simply the fact that each person who reports the similarities experiences them in that way because that is what is expected. As I said above nobody has ever actually come back from beyond the point of death so we are still left with supposition.

However, I am of the opinion that the Near-Death Experience is not only a real phenomenon but is closely related to what actually happens. The problem with it is that it is a mistake. Let me explain.

Each report we have of a Near-Death Experience involves a potentially fatal situation that was not foreseen in any way. We have car crashes, plane crashes, accidents and potential murders. What we do not have is examples from people who knew, with absolute certainty, that death was about to take place at some time in the future. Indeed, with the exception of an execution, and even then errors can be made, the moment of death can never be predicted. Self-evidently, those with terminal illnesses approach death with foreknowledge, but in all cases death actually takes place. Also, it is usual that the approach to that death is made in a cloud of pain-killing drugs.

In terms of classic Near-Death Experiences there is foreknowledge of imminent death but with a very short lead-time. The standard example is a car crash where the victim sees the potential collision a second or two before the actual impact. In these cases many of the classic symptoms are reported: time dilation; the meeting with the Being of Light; the tunnel experience; and the Past-Life Review. Indeed, it is particularly interesting to note that the greater the time interval between the victim's expectation of certain death and the event itself the more likely it is that a Past-Life Review is experienced. The old wives' tale that a drowning man sees his life pass before his eyes is evidence of this.

In support of my interpretation of these events I wish to point out that the first real research into NDE was stimulated by a climbing accident in which the Swiss geologist Albert Heim[15] fell 70 feet while climbing in the Alps. The duration of the fall was long enough for him to experience a full Past-Life Review. After surviving the experience he went about collecting reports from his fellow climbers. Of the 30 cases that he reviewed the vast majority had experienced Past or Panoramic Life Reviews.

The likelihood of experiencing an NDE is even greater when the time available for reflection is extended. This is particularly the case when it comes to survivals from skydiving accidents. In these cases Past-Life Reviews are extremely common. The reason the incidence is higher in this context is simple: the mechanism that stimulates the NDE is panicked into thinking that actual death is about to take place. However, on realizing that it was not to be, the memories of the event become confused and clouded. As with other traumatic episodes in one's life, memory places a comfort blanket around it. The question is who is responsible for this mistake and why do they make it?

I am sure that you know who I believe to be responsible for this error and I am not about to disappoint you. Yes, it is the Daemon but a Daemon of a particular sort. I term this being a trainee. This may be confusing but please bear with me.

In this book, we have seen example after example showing the existence of the being I call the Daemon. We have discussed neurology and theology and have shown time and time again the precognitive abilities of this being. We have seen why it is that some people are more aware of their duality than others. We now know from examples of the lives of writers, poets and painters that the Daemon shares our life with us.

However, in many cases the Daemon itself is unaware that it is different from its Eidolon. Imagine how this can come about. The Daemon shares every thought and feeling of its Eidolon and as such cannot perceive itself as an independent entity. Indeed, it is reasonable to conclude that for all intents and purposes a human being at this stage of its existence is anything other than a unitary being. That is why most readers of this book are not aware that 'I' constitutes a 'we'. Life goes on and both potentialities coexist in ignorance. It is only at the moment that death seems imminent that the split occurs and the Daemon suddenly realizes that it is independent. This self-awareness may be brought about by an initial flood of chemicals into the brain, but it still comes as a bit of a shock. I believe, and unfortunately I have absolutely no proof of this, that at that point the whole self is only aware of its Daemon personality and the Eidolon is an unthinking *tabula rasa*. Suffice it to say that the Daemon realizes what its purpose is. It sees death approaching and instinctively sets a Past-Life Review in train.

However, for reasons that will become clear in due course, the Daemon has misunderstood the clues. It realizes quickly, as part of its sudden self-awareness, that the time is wrong. In an unforgivable, but essential, anthropomorphism, imagine the Daemon with its finger on the start button of the 'Life Review DVD IMAX Machine'. It sees death approaching and starts the review. It then suddenly realizes that it has got it all wrong – it panics and presses the 'fast forward' button. The Past-Life Review then rushes past the senses of the Eidolon in its entirety but, in respect of the temporal perception of the Eidolon, at phenomenal speed. The Daemon may then show itself to its Eidolon and make some form of excuse such as 'It is not yet your time', or some similarly anodyne comment. The Eidolon then blacks out and wakes up in a hospital bed or in pain at the roadside.

In this way I can explain why it is that the Past-Life Review is perceived by the Eidolon as taking place in a split second. It is simply a fast-forward!

So much for the Near-Death Experience but what then happens when the real thing takes place? Well, the run-up is identical. The Daemon realizes who it is and what it should do but on realizing that death will take place it keeps its metaphorical finger on the 'play' button. The real Past-Life Review begins. However, something else happens as well.

At the moment that death becomes unavoidable, chemicals are released into the brain that influence how the Eidolon perceives time. It begins to slow down. As we have seen the human brain is very flexible in its perception of temporal flow. Drugs, mood and metabolism all contribute to time's perceived duration. It is a recognized fact that massive chemical changes take place in the body at the point of death. What is also recognized, but little known, is that these chemicals are virtually identical to those released during an epileptic seizure.

In this way psychological time, for the dying person, begins to slow down. In effect they 'fall' out of the time perspective of any observers who may be witnessing the death. For the dying person each second may take twice as long to pass as the previous second. As such their consciousness moves away from the observer's, whose seconds continue to be seconds.

Imagine the scene at a road accident. The paramedic is desperately trying to save the life of a badly injured man. She realizes that he is about to die. Six seconds before he does so, the endorphins and/or glutamate chemicals flood his brain and release his Daemon. As he lies on the ground his psychological time becomes affected by the endogenous drugs. The time between the sixth and fifth second for the concerned paramedic takes, in her perception, one second. However, for our dying man the very nature of time is changing. For him that second takes two seconds to pass. The next half-second (which is another second for the paramedic) takes four seconds and the next quarter-second (again another second for the paramedic) takes eight seconds. Within three seconds of 'normal time' our two people exist in totally different time-worlds. The dying man is still back in the first second and existing in an ever-shrinking 'chronon' of time. His individual seconds are dividing as time progresses. In the same sense, but far more real, that the hare (in Zeno's Paradox) never overtakes the tortoise, so it is that the dying man never reaches his actual point of death. The curiosity, however, is that in the temporal world of the paramedic the man dies.

I can imagine that some readers will still have a problem with this idea of ever-decreasing 'chronons' of time. However, the proposition is in keeping with basic science. What we have here is a literal interpretation of the scientific concept of half-life only in this case it is a real life that we are talking about. You will recall from your schoolday physics that radioactive substances decay in such a way that they lose half of their radioactivity in a given period of time. For example the radioactive isotope cobalt-60, used in radiotherapy, has a half-life of 5.26 years. Thus, after that interval a sample that originally contained eight grams of cobalt-60 would contain only four grams of cobalt-60 and would emit only half as much radiation. After another interval of 5.26 years, the same sample would contain only two grams. So far so good.

However, in a real example of Zeno's Paradox, after a further 5.26 years the cobalt-60 weighs only one gram and at the end of the following period it decreases to half a gram. However – and this is a crucially important point – the amount of cobalt-60 never reaches zero, it just halves every 5.26 years from now to eternity. Put simply, it suffers from the same problem as Zeno's hare: it never arrives. And so it is with our life-force. We also have a real half-life that within our own perception is a full-life. As with Einstein and his realization that it is time that must give in terms of relativity theory so it is that time must also give in the world of near-death.

Our dying man has moved out of time and, it must be said, space, and is inhabiting a world within his own mind. He has, in effect, unlimited time but what is this time for? In answering this question we must return to the Daemon.

The Daemon is now aware of what its task is to be. It is responsible for ensuring that the Past-Life Review takes place, but not as it is known from the reports of NDEers. In the real run that is stimulated by an actual death situation the review takes place at normal speed, in a minute-by-minute equality. Each minute of the life record is perceived by the Eidolon as an actual minute. Put another way, the Eidolon lives its life again in real time.

During this 'second life' there is one major difference from the first one. We go through this second life as a dual, not a unitary, being. The Daemon is now conscious of what it really is. In the first life-run the Daemon is trapped in the non-dominant hemisphere of the brain. It is conscious but not aware of its own independence. In the final moments of the first-life the glutamate flood wakes it up. When the second life starts it knows what it is from the first few moments. But it also knows something else – the whole future life that its Eidolon is going to live. It can look from its vantage point and see all the trials and tribulations that they both will have to face. Its skill is in deciding which trials and tribulations it will allow to take place and which ones it will avoid.

The reason for this is simple; the second life rerun is only one of many. Like Phil Conners in the film *Groundhog Day*, there are multiple lives to be lived and all possible paths can be taken. The Daemon knows this, so just as Conners explores certain avenues in his ever-repeating day so does our 'Hidden Companion'.

As we have seen throughout this book, the Daemon can be very active in somebody's life or very quiet. This is because it is learning the route. It may experiment and take its Eidolon off on a different life track. If it ends in the premature death of its Eidolon it doesn't matter because at the point of death a new life starts again. You will again recall that Phil Conners commits suicide many times and just ends up waking up again. Then he starts to have fun!

This is how hunches, clairvoyance, precognitive dreams, spirit guides and guardian angels all work. They are simply all manifestations of our resident Higher Self. And *déjà vu*? Well, that simply is what it seems to be, no clever psychoneurological explanations are needed. It is simply what it seems to be. A memory!

I am hoping that suddenly all the examples and anecdotes that have been presented to you in this book are suddenly making sense. Take the opportunity to re-read some sections knowing what you now know. Apply 'Cheating the Ferryman' to what is described and you will understand exactly what was taking place.

However there is one drawback for the Daemon if it knowingly makes its Eidolon take a different route. Just like its lower self the Daemon has not followed this road before. As such any new events that will be encountered will be novel to both parts of the Dyad. The Daemon can no longer show any precognitive abilities and warn about future dangers. It may suspect that this might be a problem – after many lives it will develop considerable wisdom – but it will not know with absolute certainty.

How do I know this? Well, so far we have had examples of guidance and support from historic daemons. I would now like to move on to a far more active variation – the life savers.

Summary

There is clearly a relationship between the *doppelgänger* phenomenon and that of the Being of Light. They are both aspects of the Daemon as its Eidolon approaches death. If the Eidolon is experiencing death for the first time then the whole scenario of splitting into two beings is just as surprising to both components. Up until that point 'they' have been a unitary being. Suddenly, the Daemon feels itself detaching itself and at the same moment knows that it has to act as a calming influence on its highly traumatized lower self. It is possible that at the point of original death the Daemon has not mastered the ability to disguise itself as a religious figure, a deceased family member or any other 'friendly' figure. It just appears as itself. This may help to explain the death-double reports.

The Daemon is also responsible for starting the Bohmian IMAX. If it is doing all this for the first time it may simply confuse a potential death situation with the real thing. It starts the rerun then realizes that it has made a mistake. It panics and presses the metaphoric 'fast-forward' button of the IMAX recorder. The Eidolon suddenly sees its past-life flash before it at super-fast speed. This is a classic NDE experience. The Daemon then makes some weak excuse such as 'It is not your time, you must go back', and the Eidolon finds itself back in the 'real' world.

I think this may help explain why after a Near-Death Experience many people change and become more attuned and spiritual. Indeed, there is considerable supporting material that shows that many NDEers develop precognitive or mediumistic skills. This is because the Daemon has been woken up early and the person becomes a dual being while still existing in their original life. Most people only have one death experience in their original life and that is the real thing – a Real-Death Experience (RDE). As such the Daemon is never immanent in that first life. Clearly, in terms of an NDE experience the younger a person is at the time of the NDE the longer the life they will enjoy as a Dyad.

* Shor, R.E., Hypnosis and the concept of the generalised reality orientation, Amer. J. Psychother, 13. 582-602 (1959)

[1] Ring, K. & Elsaesser-Valarino, E., *Lessons from the Light*, Moment Point Press, p.77 (2006)

[2] Ibid., pp.73–97

[3] Clark, Kimberley, 'Clinical interventions with near-death experiencers' in B. Greyson & C.P. Flynn (eds), *The near-death experience; problems, prospects, perspectives*, Charles C. Thomas, Springfield, Ill. pp.242–5 (1984)

[4] Jansen, K.L.R., 'Neuroscience and the near-death experience: roles for the NMDA-PCP receptor, the sigma receptor and endopsychosins', *Medical Hypotheses*, 31, 25–9 (1990)

[5] Jansen, K.L.R., 'Neuroscience, Ketamine and the Near-Death Experience' in L. Bailey and J. Yates (eds), *The Near Death Experience*, Routledge (1996)

[6] Jansen, K.L.R., *Ketamine: Dreams and realities*, Multidisciplinary Association for Psychedelic Studies, Sarasota, FL (2001)

[7] Grinspoon, L. & Bakalar S., *Psychedelic Drugs Reconsidered*, Basic Books, New York (1981)

[8] Quirion et al., 'Evidence for an endogenous peptide ligand for the phencyclidine receptor', *Peptides*, 5, 967–77 (1984)

[9] Carr, D.B., 'Endorphins at the approach of death', *Lancet*, 1, 390 (1981)

[10] Carr, D.B., 'On the evolving neurolobiology of the near death experience', *Journal of Near Death Studies*, 7, 251–4 (1989)

[11] Ebbern, H., Mulligan, S., Beverstein, B.L., 'Marie's Near-Death Experience – Waiting For the Shoe to Drop', *Skeptical Enquirer*, p.32, Jul/Aug (1996)

[12] Ibid.

[13] Fox, Mark, *Religion, Spirituality and the Near-Death Experience*, Routledge, p.232 (2003)

[14] Moody, Raymond A. (jun.), *The Light Beyond*, Macmillan, London, pp.22–3 (1989)

[15] Heim, A., 'Notizen über den Tod durch Absturz', trans. in *Omega* 3: 45–52 (1972)

CHAPTER 9

The Protector

The god to whom man proves devout,
That is his own soul turned inside out
Johann Wolfgang von Goethe
(from a conversation with
Friedrich Wilhelm Riemer)

The voice of reason

The woman had settled down to a quiet evening in, curled up with a book. She was engrossed in the story and at first was not sure what she had heard. It then repeated itself. It was a voice that was somehow inside her head and yet not part of her thought processes. The voice was absolutely insistent. It had arrived from nowhere and was quite clear about its purpose. It told her that she had a medical problem but that she was not to worry because it was there 'to help her'.

After a few weeks of these strange communications, some of which were precognitive, the woman, known as AB, decided that her only course of action was to go and see her doctor. The local doctor simply could not understand what was happening but assumed that the problem was psychological and referred her to Dr Ikechukwu Azuonye of the Mental Health Unit at London's Royal Free Hospital. In the winter of 1984 Dr Azuonye diagnosed a straightforward case of hallucinatory psychosis. He prescribed a course of the antipsychotic drug thioridazine and expected that would be the end of it. How wrong he was.

Initially the thioridazine seemed to work. Thinking that the voice was simply a peculiar psychological interlude, AB and her husband went off on holiday. However, while out of the country the voice had found its way through the drug barrier and was more insistent than before. It pleaded with her to return to England as soon as possible, saying that she needed urgent medical treatment. Indeed, it even told her an address that she should go to for help.

The voice was now becoming quite precise as regards AB's medical problem. It told her that it had two reasons for wanting her to have a scan – firstly, that she had a tumour in her brain and secondly that her brain stem was badly inflamed. She convinced her husband that they had to go and find the address the voice had told her about. Much to her surprise and concern, the address turned out to be the computerized tomography unit of a large London hospital.

This scared her so much that she went back to see Dr Azuonye. The psychiatrist was, not surprisingly, reluctant at first to do as the voice requested. He knew that the woman had none of the symptoms associated with a brain tumour and for him to force the issue would reflect badly on his professional reputation – particularly if he divulged the source of the diagnosis. Against his better judgment he agreed that he would write to the clinic and see what they said. AB agreed and Dr Azuonye took her home.

A few months later, and after many letters, the clinic agreed to carry out the scan. Much to the surprise of all concerned – with the clear exception of 'the voice' – the scan clearly showed an unusual mass in the brain.

AB was called in to meet with a neurological consultant. The consultant explained that the mass was probably a 'meningioma tumour'. As he said this, AB heard the voice agree with this diagnosis. However, the voice was concerned that there had already been too much delay. It demanded that she be operated on straight away. Not only this but the voice wanted the operation done at Queen's Square Hospital. This was because it knew that that particular hospital specialized in neurological diseases.

This time the hospital authorities agreed, but the operation was to take place at the Royal Free Hospital. The voice considered this and decided that it was acceptable. A few days later AB, and presumably the voice itself, was under full anaesthetic and being wheeled into an operating theatre. As she came to after the operation the first thing she was aware of was the voice. All the insistence had gone. It said these words: 'I am pleased to have helped you. Goodbye.'

When the surgeon came round to see her she already knew that her life had been saved. He explained to her that he had removed a 6.4 cm (2.5 inch) tumour from her brain. He added that he was sure that had it not been removed she would almost certainly have died.

Over the years this case continued to fascinate Dr Anzuonye. By 1997 he had moved to Lambeth NHS Trust and had mentioned the AB case many times to his associates. He found that the response was always either extremely positive or extremely negative and with this in mind he decided to submit an article describing the event to the *British Medical Journal*. He was pleased when he received a positive response and the article appeared in the December edition.[1]

Many hypothetical suggestions were made as to what had taken

'My father was a manufacturer of washing machines and twice a year he would make a trip to the wholesalers and sell them a carload or two of washing machines. He saw dealers in Koekuk and was to take the 10 pm train for Davenport. He went to the depot, bought his ticket and then had a feeling that he should not go. It was so strong that he went back to the hotel and stayed in Koekuk overnight. In the morning when eating his breakfast he looked over the paper and found that the train he was supposed to have taken had been wrecked and nearly all the passengers in the smoker had been killed. Dad was an inveterate smoker.'

RESPONDENT TO A QUESTIONNAIRE SENT OUT BY DR LOUISA RHINE

place in 1984 but none have been considered satisfactory. However, there is now a possible answer to the question of what was happening to AB and what the source of 'the voice' was.

If we apply the 'Cheating the Ferryman' theory to this story then it is clear that last time round AB died of the tumour. By bringing about a temporal mutation the Daemon moved them both into another Everett Multiverse (see Chapter 4) where they both survived. The Daemon and its voice would then cease to have any precognitive powers because in this new version of 'reality' everything that subsequently happened to AB was totally new. In effect the Daemon and the Eidolon go back to being a unitary being travelling life's path for the first time. Although I have no hard evidence for such a belief I would argue that it was the tumour itself that brought about the opening of the communication channels between AB and her Daemon. In other words the cause of the illness also facilitated the cure.

This case is one of many that imply that the Daemon is not only active in the life of certain select individuals. As we have already seen, my 'Scale of Transcendence' allows ever more effective daemonic communication, but sometimes illness or extreme stress can bring about a short opening of the 'Doors of Perception'. I would now like to review the evidence for such a belief.

Mind's a Guinness

As we have seen, the Daemon is very aware of what is about to happen next in the life of its Eidolon. It knows if last time they were both seriously injured or possibly killed. Its job is to avoid this incident this time round and thus bring about a switch into another Everett Multiverse for the person in question. This can be done in a variety of ways depending upon the channels of communication available to the Daemon. So far we have seen communications through dreams, voices and, in exceptional

CHAPTER 9 The Protector

circumstances, a vision of one's own double. These events can be found in many autobiographies and anecdotal stories of the famous and not-so-famous. For example what can we make of the incident that was experienced by Sir Alec Guinness and which is reported in full in Arthur Koestler's *The Challenge of Chance*?

Guinness was a very devout Catholic and would never miss Sunday Mass if he could help it. When working in London he particularly enjoyed Mass at Westminster Cathedral. He would get up at 7.20 am and by doing so he could go to the service at the Cathedral and then catch the 9.50 am train at Waterloo. So determined was he not to miss this that he had two alarm clocks by his bedside. As he explained it:

> *On this particular morning I woke, glanced in the half light*
> *at the clock and thought: 'My God, I've overslept!' It*
> *appeared to me the clock said 0740 (I didn't refer to the*
> *second clock). I rushed through washing and so on, and*
> *hurried to the Cathedral. Very unexpectedly – in fact it had*
> *never happened before – I found a taxi at that early hour, so*
> *I thought I was at the Cathedral at 0755. With time to spare*
> *I went to confession.*

He became involved in the service and never bothered to look at his watch until the sermon. To his surprise, and annoyance, he found that he was at the 9.00 am, not the 8.00 am, Mass. His plans were totally thrown. He quickly realized that he would miss the 9.50 am train and would have to catch the next one, an hour later at 10.50 am. When Mass had ended he rushed across London to find that all the trains on the Portsmouth line were delayed. To his horror he discovered that the reason for these delays was that the 9.50, the train he had planned to catch, had been derailed a few miles outside London. What disturbed him even more was that the front coach of the train had toppled on to its side and many of the occupants had been taken to hospital. This was the very coach he always travelled in. What needs to be noted here is that had Guinness not overslept he would have been on the train. But it becomes more Daemonic when one realizes that his 'hidden companion' made him misread the time on one clock and not bother to look at the other.

Sometimes the Daemon will change a regular habit in order to save its companion. One of the most iconic figures of the 20th century was Winston Churchill. Without his steadfast and resolute personality it is possible that Britain may not have stood so firmly against the Nazis. Churchill embodied the 'bulldog spirit' so admired by the Americans and so feared by the Germans. If he had not survived for the duration of the Second World War European history might have been quite different. Indeed, it is probable that in another Everett Multiverse Churchill didn't survive and the outcome of that war might have been different. Fortunately, in the universe that you and I inhabit this did not take place. However, we may have a Daemon to thank for this.

In the autumn and winter of 1941 the war was not going that well. Britain stood alone against a Europe dominated by Nazi power and British cities had become the front line. Night after night the Luftwaffe bombed London. Churchill was playing his part in boosting morale. He would frequently go out at night and personally visit the anti-aircraft gun sites dotted around the capital. This concerned his wife Clementine so much that she arranged, unbeknown to Winston, for a car with special reinforced armour plating to be supplied. One night the prime minister decided to make one of his visits and Clementine requested that the new reinforced car be used.

'Mr Churchill won't ride in it,' said his chauffeur.

'He will,' answered Clementine. 'There won't be any other car waiting for him when he goes out.'

As he stepped out of No. 10 Churchill saw the new car.

'What's this for?'

'Well, sir,' answered his bodyguard, detective Thompson, 'You're going round the gun sites, the bombs are coming down and, what with all the firing and shrapnel, we've got to keep you reasonably safe from bits of metal in the air.'

'I won't ride in it,' answered Churchill determinedly. 'I'll ride in the police car.'

'I'm sorry, it's not available,' he was informed.

Clementine had taken the precaution of making certain that no alternative transport would be available. Churchill was furious.

As he approached his car the nearside door was opened for him to get in. However, his Daemon knew that a bomb was about to damage that side of the car. Being doubly aware of how important Winston was to become it had decided, on this occasion, to ensure that he was not killed or maimed. The Daemon therefore willed its Eidolon to do something he had never done before: he ignored the door that was being held open for him on the nearside, walked round to the other side and opened the door for himself.

Feeling just a little confused, the Eidolon sat down wondering why on earth it had done such a thing. On the way home the car was travelling at over 60 miles an hour along the Kingston Bypass. As it did so a bomb landed nearby and lifted the car up on to its two offside wheels. For a second or two it looked as if the car was about to somersault over. It teetered on the edge of disaster and then righted itself.

'That was a near one,' joked the Prime Minister. 'It must have been my beef on this side that pulled it down.' Clearly, only Churchill's extra weight had prevented his serious injury or even his death. Had he sat on his usual side of the car his weight would have added to, not counteracted, the ability of the blast to flick the speeding car over. After the event he did not mention it to Clementine but she heard about it from

somebody else. She asked him why he had done such a
strange thing. His initial reaction was 'I don't know, I don't
know', but then he stopped himself and said: 'Of course I
know. Something said to me: "Stop!" before I reached the car
door held open for me. It then appeared to me that I was
told I was meant to open the door on the other side and get
in and sit there.' [2]

However, Churchill's Daemon had been active in his life for years before this incident. It is clear to me that Churchill's survival was crucial and that his 'hidden companion' was well aware of this. He once wrote about this protector, 'I sometimes have a feeling – in fact I have it very strongly . . . a feeling that some guiding hand has interfered.'

He was keen to show that this was the case and in his book *My Early Life* he tells of an incident that took place during the Boer War. At this time he was employed to cover the war for the *London Morning Post*. Due to an unfortunate set of circumstances he found himself in a very precarious position in that he was alone and had no way of telling if the settlement nearby was a Boer village or a 'Kaffir' settlement. The Kaffirs were known to dislike the Boers and as such might have been helpful to a lone Englishman. This would clearly not have been the case if the inhabitants had been Boers. Churchill pondered his predicament as he stared through the darkness at the distant fires and possible safety. Then . . .

Suddenly, without the slightest reason, all my doubts
disappeared. It was certainly by no process of logic that they
were dispelled. It just felt quite clear that I would go to the
Kaffir kraal. I had sometimes in former years held a
'Planchette' pencil and written while others had touched my
wrist or hand. I acted in exactly the same unconscious or
subconscious manner now. [3]

With new-found vigour he walked towards the fires. As he got closer he realized that these were actually furnaces situated around a coalmine. Before him he saw a group of houses, all of which could offer either shelter or, possibly, death. He had no choice but to guess which house to enter. He knocked on a door to be greeted by a very nervous-looking man holding a revolver. Something within him instructed him to tell the truth, a potentially fatal tactic under the circumstances. He explained that he was British and needed help. The man approached him with a threatening look and, while keeping the revolver pointing at Churchill, locked the door. Churchill then describes what happened next:

> After this act, which struck me as unpromising, and was certainly ambiguous, he advanced upon me and suddenly held out his hand. 'Thank God, you have come here! It is the only house for twenty miles where you would not have been handed over. But we are all British here and we will see you through.'

Churchill (or his Daemon) had chosen the one house in which he would be safe. The future prime minister was then hidden in the mine before being smuggled out to safety. Had he knocked on any of the other doors, and been captured, who knows what fate may have awaited him. It might have changed the course of his life forever – or at least in that universe.

The early warning system

Churchill's Daemon communicated in a very subtle way that things were right or wrong, using 'hunches' and instinctive feelings. This is not unusual and there are many cases where a hunch has proved to be a life-saver.

One much-quoted incident took place on 28 February 1844

when the governor of Wisconsin, Nathaniel Tallmadge, was invited to view a demonstration on board the new steam frigate the *Princeton*, together with a group of other illustrious guests including the president, John Tyler. Two huge guns called 'the Oregon' and 'the Peacemaker' were the pride of this ship. Indeed, the Peacemaker was the biggest gun in the United States Navy, weighing in at more than 27,000 pounds.

As the warship sailed down the Potomac River the gunners rammed 40 pounds of powder and rolled a 12-inch iron cannonball down the breech of 'the Peacemaker'. Tallmadge was standing right next to the breech when the cannon was fired. He and all the guests were startled, then delighted, as the 228-lb ball hit the water two miles away. At this stage Tallmadge was perfectly happy and was at ease when the gun demonstrated its powerful abilities twice more. Feeling elated, if a little deaf, he went below deck for lunch, together with 200 others. During the meal Secretary of State Abel Upshur stood up to give the customary toast to the president. Upshur accidentally picked up an empty bottle of champagne. He remarked that the 'dead bodies' must be cleared away before he could start. The ship's captain, Robert F. Stockton, seemed surprised when he found himself adding the comment: 'There are plenty of living bodies to replace the dead ones', as he handed Upshur a full bottle.

At this time Stockton had no intention of firing the gun a fourth time but relented when a request came from the Secretary of the Navy, Thomas Gilmer. He announced that 'the Peacemaker' would be fired one more time and would the guests please return to their previous positions round the gun. William Wilkins, Secretary of State for War was to announce that he would not go on deck. 'Though secretary of war, I do not like this firing and believe I shall move out of the way.'

The president started on his way then, inexplicably, Tyler's son-in-law, William Waller, started singing a patriotic ditty about 1776. As he was not known for his sense of fun many of the guests were surprised to see Tyler stop, then walk back below deck to join in the singing.

By now Tallmadge had taken up his customary position right next to the gun. However, a delay in the firing was announced because the president had not yet made it on to the deck. Suddenly, Tallmadge was overcome by a powerful and mysterious feeling of apprehension and dread. It was so strong that he immediately acted upon it and hastily made his way below deck.

As he reached the cabin he heard Waller sing the word 'Washington', then the sound of an almighty explosion came from outside. The ship trembled and a dense cloud of white smoke smothered the deck. When the smoke had cleared a horrible sight confronted Tallmadge.

> *I rushed on deck, saw the lifeless and mangled bodies, and found that the gun had burst at the very spot where I had stood at the three former fires, and where – if I had remained at the fourth fire – I should have been perfectly demolished.*[4]

The blast had killed six people, including Secretary of State Upshur and Secretary of the Navy Gilmer, and seriously injured many others. Captain Stockton, who was standing at the base of the gun, received severe powder burns to his face and all the hair on his head was burned off.

As he was carried away from the scene he was heard to cry: 'My God! Would that I be dead too.' This is a terrifying, and probably significant, echo of his flippant remark of less than an hour before when he said: 'There are plenty of living bodies to replace the dead ones.'

If one evaluates 'the Peacemaker' incident in the light of my theory one can only conclude that many Daemons were active that day. William Wilkins announced that he would not go, even though such a decision was against all the protocol of such an event. As secretary for war he would have been expected to join the president, the secretary of state and the secretary of the Navy at the fourth firing of the gun. The president acted out of character by going back to listen to the singing. Why did he do such a thing? Yet again protocol was broken. Could it be that Tyler's Daemon was keen for him to avoid death this time?

But it is Tallmadge's behaviour that is particularly fascinating. He would most definitely have been killed had his Daemon not brought about a feeling of apprehension and dread. As he was later to write he was amazed at how such a precognitive feeling had saved his life.

At least two other Daemons might have attempted to save their Eidolons. Could this be why both Upshur and Stockton made such strange comments about the living making way for the dead? Indeed, was the comment made by Stockton as he was carried away a subtle echo produced by the Daemon?

Here, we have an example of how a major disaster is somehow sensed by those involved before it actually takes place. This is not that unusual. In 1956 a fascinating study by W.E. Cox indicated that precognition can operate on the level of mass-awareness.[5] Cox accumulated data involving 28 railway accidents. He obtained statistics from the railway companies on the number of passengers that travelled on the day of the accident and similar statistics for

'During a migraine "aura" I suddenly had an overpowering urge to visit an old friend. I had not seen this person for several months, and had no particular reason to think of her. The thoughts became so strong that I decided to cycle up to her home (some three miles away) despite a throbbing, painful head. When I arrived I found that she had taken an overdose of pills in a suicide attempt. I called the ambulance; her life was saved and I was there to care for her three small children.'

MARY FARQUHAR (MIGRAINE-SUFFERER)

each of the six days preceding the crash and for the corresponding days in each of the four preceding weeks. He was surprised to discover that significantly fewer people travelled on the day of the accident than usual. He also found that there were always fewer than normal passengers in the damaged and derailed coaches in these accidents.

For example, on 15 June 1952 a Chicago and Eastern Illinois train had an accident. On that day only nine passengers were on board. For the six days running up to the 15th the numbers were 68, 60, 53, 48, 42 and 70. As regards the same day a week earlier the number had been 35. Over the full period examined the average daily number of passengers was 55.8. On the day of the accident the numbers dropped by a startling 84 per cent!

This pattern was repeated on all trains that had accidents. Clearly there is something statistically significant going on here. It seems that a significant number of people seem to have some form of subliminal 'early-warning system' when it comes to disasters. Of course I will argue that this is exactly what I would expect. Those individuals who are living their lives again have a Daemon that will try very hard to change this life so that it goes in a positive direction – and what can be more positive than avoiding injury or death? Although it is not possible now, it would have been interesting to have made an analysis of the non-travellers on these trains with respect to whether they did or did not experience *déjà vu*. If my theory is right then there should be a significantly higher number of *déjà vu* experiencers in the non-travelling group.

Each passenger would have a personal reason for not travelling on that day. These reasons might range from accidental circumstances to full-blown precognitions, but all would ensure the Eidolon's survival. Before the horrors of 11 September 2001 the most cited disaster in modern history was that of the *Titanic* in 1912. If my theory is correct then this disaster should involve many cases of Daemonic warnings. It is to this I now turn.

It wasn't over until the thin lady sang

The *Titanic* disaster has passed into history. Hundreds of articles and books have been written and many films have been made with that tragic night as the theme. However, what is interesting is the number of stories that circulated soon after April 1912. These all evaluated the significance of precognition in relation to this disaster. It was as if this, of all events, sent waves backwards and forwards in time.

An example of how these waves rippled through time can be seen in the often quoted, but still uncanny, prediction of the disaster outlined in the novel *Futility*. This book, written by Morgan Robinson, was published 14 years before that fateful April night. The book tells of a huge unsinkable liner that struck an iceberg and sank. The displacement of the *Titan* was 70,000 tons; that of the *Titanic* 66,000. Both were triple-screw vessels capable of 25 knots. The *Titan* had 24 lifeboats, *Titanic* had 20. Both ships set off on their maiden voyage from Southampton and planned to arrive in New York. That this book was published and read years before the real disaster is objective evidence that if nothing else an amazing coincidence took place.[6] However, research by George Behe published in his book *Titanic: Psychic Forewarnings of a Tragedy* shows that Robinson was not alone in sensing the catastrophe. Each of the following examples can be found in this fascinating book.

At the end of March 1912 Helen E. Bell had just finished her morning breakfast. She turned from the breakfast table to read her copy of the *Daily Mail*. She noticed an article by Hamilton Fyfe describing the *Titanic* as she was due to leave the docks at Belfast for Southampton in preparation for her maiden voyage. She later recalled:

> As I read, a picture suddenly formed between myself and the paper, showing a night scene with what I took to be jagged and pointed rocks, with the hull of a boat standing out of the

water. With the picture came a voice, clear and distinct,
which said, 'This will be on its first voyage.' I instantly asked,
'Why? What is the matter with the boat?' The reply came,
'Nothing; that is all right, but it will be on its first voyage.'

Mrs Bell said that she felt a 'thrill of dismay' and tried to learn something further, but 'no other answer came'. In describing her vision Mrs Bell said:

The picture appeared to be about four or five inches in size,
and resembled in its various gradations of light and shade an
old steel engraving. I should have called it a gem had I seen
it at an exhibition.

This example is a classic precognition of a major event in which the person can do nothing. Indeed, it seems that her Daemon had managed not only to break through into her consciousness but also to actually speak as well. This has similarities with Dr Azuonye's patient and the voice that told her of her tumour.

As we saw earlier in the case of Nathaniel Tallmadge, sometimes the daemonic guidance is simply a feeling of disquiet. In these cases the Daemon cannot exert any form of direct influence on the actions of its Eidolon so it has to be subtle. The fear is buried deep in the subconscious and seems to stay there. Here are a few examples.

Colonel John Weir, a world-famous mining engineer, was due to sail on the *Titanic*. On the night of 9 April he was in the smoking room of the Waldorf Hotel. He told the manager that he really did not wish to sail the next day because he had a 'funny feeling'. Weir went down with the ship.

Henry B. Harris was one of the leading theatrical producers in America. He was on holiday in Europe and had booked himself and his wife to return on the *Titanic*. However, a friend of his, William Klein, a Broadway lawyer, was filled with an inexplicable sense of doom and he asked Harris to cancel. Harris sent an answer to Klein that his plans had already been set. On receiving this reply Klein became even more concerned. He sought out Max D. Steuer, another lawyer friend of Harris, and urged him to also cable Harris and ask him not to travel. It is not recorded if Steuer sent the cable, but if he did it was to no avail. Harris and his wife boarded the ill-fated ship. After putting his wife into the lifeboat, Harris went down with the ship.

Major Archibald Butt was the military aide to President Taft. Butt was due to sail to Europe to visit Rome. On his return trip he was to sail on the *Titanic*. However, he had ongoing and very strong premonitions of disaster. He made sure that all his papers were in order before sailing as if he knew he was not going to return. Although he had tried to cancel his sailing orders the President insisted that he went on the ship. One of Butt's friends said:

> *I took a walk through the White House grounds with Major Butt a day or two before he left Washington, and he told me that he had the strangest feeling that he had had in his life that he was to be at the centre of some awful calamity. He said that he had had it for several weeks and could not shake it off.*

Butt chose to return on the *Titanic* and he died with her.

A second group of warnings regarding the *Titanic* was made by daemons whose communication skills were channelled through dream manipulation. Some of these are very precise in their imagery and others more symbolic.

Isaac C. Frauenthal was a lawyer living in New York. In March of 1912 he travelled to Europe to attend the wedding of his brother Henry in Nice. They planned to return to New York on the *Titanic* on the 10th of April. After the *Titanic* had set sail Isaac Frauenthal told his brother and new sister-in-law that before boarding he had had a dream. He described it as follows:

> *It seemed to me that I was on a big steamship which*
> *suddenly crashed into something and began to go down.*
> *I saw in the dream as vividly as I could see with open eyes*
> *the gradual settling of the ship, and I heard the cries and*
> *shouts of frightened passengers.*

Frauenthal's Daemon felt that the message had not been fully understood by its Eidolon and it resorted to the daemonic equivalent of shouting – repeating the dream. This second occurrence was still not sufficient to make Frauenthal cancel his ticket, but fortunately he survived and so did his family.

Patrick O'Keefe, a young Irishman, had made his way to Queenstown, the *Titanic*'s last port of call, planning to board the ship there. The night before he was to join the ship he had a vivid dream in which he saw the ship sink in mid-ocean. I can only imagine the dismay of his Daemon when O'Keefe decided that he would still travel. Fortunately, the warning had not gone unnoticed by the Eidolon. Although travelling in steerage O'Keefe managed to get himself into such a position on the fateful night that he was one of the few to survive from that part of the liner.

The Daemon of another Irishman, Eugene Ryan, failed to save its Eidolon even though its message was graphically detailed. He and his friends had already set sail when the Daemon presumably woke up to the fact that last time round Eugene's life ended as the ship sank. Why it left the warning so late is puzzling, but it is possible that it had tried earlier but had not broken into a dream that was recalled by its Eidolon. According to his friend Bertha Mulvihill, Ryan had a really vivid dream in which the *Titanic* sank and many people died. In this dream Ryan even saw the ship hit the iceberg. Unlike what we have seen so far this dream is quite precise and specific. Not only that but the dream was repeated each night they were on board. Clearly, Eugene's Daemon, realizing that the danger was getting closer, wished to drive home its Eidolon's predicament. The tragedy was that Bertha survived to tell the tale of her friend's precognitive dream whereas Ryan did not. I would like to believe that on his next life-run the Daemon manages to have the dream take place in a similar way to O'Keefe's – on dry land.

Sometimes it is the Daemon of a loved one that tries hard to save the potential victim of fate. Clearly, a Daemon will know of the future life-events of all its associates so it is not really surprising that an active Higher Self will be altruistic.

In late March 1912 a young farmer in Athenry, Ireland was determined to emigrate to America and booked his passage in the same steerage section as O'Keefe and Ryan. It is possible that he was living his life for the first time because there was no evidence of daemonic warning. Fortunately his mother had been here before. Her Daemon was determined that this time round she would save her son. For three nights in succession she saw the *Titanic* sink. This made so deep an impression on her that she pleaded with her son to stay at home. In the end he relented.

A month earlier Mr O.B. Shepherd of Hemingford, Nebraska was in England on business. He intended to return in mid-April on the *Titanic*. Back home in Nebraska his wife had a frightening dream in which she saw the *Titanic* sinking. So shaken was she that she wrote to her husband asking him not to take the *Titanic* home. Deciding that her letter was not enough she then sent him a telegram repeating her plea. Mr Shepherd was so impressed that he cancelled his ticket on the *Titanic* and came home on another ship.

So far I have reviewed evidence involving famous people or famous events. However, the Daemon works quietly all the time warning its Eidolon or actively saving its life. I would now like to finish this chapter with a series of more mundane, but nevertheless fascinating, daemonic interventions.

Saving the little guy

All through our lives we live in danger. In a second a situation can change from being ordinary to life-threatening. If we have an effective Daemon we never perceive these hazards because it ensures that we are well away from the source of danger. This can be brought about by keeping the Eidolon be a safe distance away in terms of time and space. For example, it only takes a split second to be hit by a car, even less to be felled by a bullet.

In these circumstances the Daemon has to recognize the circumstances around it and remember that last time this situation was fatal to both it and its Eidolon. This could simply have been because the Daemon recognizes everything too late and the opportunity for medium-term evasive action had been lost. Action has to be decisive and quick.

Here are a few examples of daemonic intervention. In order to convey the power of these narratives I quote them in their entirety. The first incident involves a Kansas coal miner.

> One day before noon I pushed out to the entry a loaded car. A man driving a mule would hook the mule to the car and drive it away. As I had crawled back to work the driver yelled, 'Kid – here's an empty for you.' As I started out for the car I heard a voice, 'Stop.' I sat there, I did not move, then I heard, 'Quick, go, go.' I was scared. I crawled as fast as I could to the face of the room (the passage was three foot high) then through the cross cut (this is an opening between the rooms allowing air to circulate). I cannot describe the noises the falling rocks made. The falling roof pushed the air with great force – my miner's lamp was put out, I could see

*nothing. The room next to mine being worked out, the rails
had been removed so I had no way of knowing which way to
go. The men who had heard the rockfall came then, and I
could see by the light of their lamps the way out. If it had
not been for that voice saying 'Stop' and a few seconds later
'Quick, go, go,' I would have been covered by that rockfall.*[7]

The second event takes place in a totally different environment
but the dangers were just as intense, as was the Daemon's response.

*One afternoon in August 1988, at Fremont in the heart of
Silicon Valley, I had just ended a visit to the assembly plant
of Grid laptops. My lady friend and I hopped into our rental
car, and after hunting for ten minutes or so we finally found
Highway 880, to take us back to San Francisco. On the
highway everything seemed normal and calm. It was a sunny
day, and not being the driver I looked at the big rigs we were
passing, so American with all their shiny chrome, and
suddenly, without thinking, I flung myself to the left. One
second later a bullet pierced the windshield, smack in the
middle of the passenger side. My side. An hour later, with a
statement (obligatory for the insurance) from the Highway
Police, who assured us that it was a relatively common (sic)
incident of sniper fire, I was wondering why I had flung
myself to the left before the bullet hit the windshield. Later,
while talking with other journalists, I discovered that I wasn't
the only one to experience this sort of phenomenon. Other
colleagues – reporters or press photographers – told me how
at the very moment of inevitable death something inexplicable
had saved their lives, some million-to-one shot. And most of
them explained to me that time had suddenly stood still, and
they had begun to see their whole lives unfold, as if 'outside
of time'. An inexplicable phenomenon, so they tuck it away in
a corner of memory. But the memory pops up again when*

some other person talks about such matters: 'Listen,
something just like that happened to me in Lebanon', or Iraq,
or wherever.[8]

This set of circumstances was experienced by the writer Pierre Jovanovic. He was so shocked by what had happened that he began researching into the existence of guardian angels. His subsequent book, *An Inquiry into the Existence of Guardian Angels*, is a fascinating read, particularly if you apply the 'Cheating the Ferryman' theory. Indeed, one can easily substitute my Daemon concept for the angels and you will find a good deal of supporting evidence for both interpretations.

The third example has elements of both of the previous incidents. In this report the lady in question, Allison M., was driving to her job. As she worked weekends the traffic was light, particularly this Sunday afternoon. She stopped at a set of traffic lights and waited. She describes what happened next:

When the light turned green, for some illogical, inexplicable,
reason instead of putting my foot on the accelerator, I waited.
I saw nothing, yet still I sat there, not moving. Just then,
from my left a large pickup truck came careening through its
red light. Had I proceeded, I would have been broadsided by
that speeding truck, and surely killed.[9]

Using a similar line of logic as Pierre Jovanovic, Allison decides that this was an intervention by a guardian angel. Why she makes this link puzzles me. In both cases it was something inside that brought about a sensory-motor change in the body – to make Pierre fling himself down and for Allison to not press the accelerator. These are, ultimately, brain functions and clearly have nothing to do with an external source, angelic or otherwise.

As we have seen, dreams are another form of daemonic

communication. In her book *The Invisible Picture*, Dr Louisa Rhine collected a great deal of anecdotal evidence to support the idea that time itself is not as it seems. She cites many examples of precognitive events that saved lives.

In one she tells of a woman in New York who dreamed that she heard a scream, turned round, and saw her two-year-old son falling from an open window. She then heard the siren of an ambulance. Indeed, it was this sound that woke her up. In a panic she checked her son and the window and both were in order. A couple of days later, she put the child's mattress on the windowsill for airing. To maximize this she opened the window slightly. She then started doing her housework in the next room. In a flash she recalled her dream and dashed back into the baby's room. He had managed to push the window up and had climbed on to the windowsill. She grabbed her son just as the mattress fell out of the window. She watched in horror as the mattress crashed to the ground far below. Her son would have fallen with it had she not realized the danger.[10]

Dr Rhine seemed to collect stories such as this. Another tells of a mother who had a particularly vivid dream. In this dream she found herself on a camping holiday with friends. They had decided to pitch their tent next to a river creek. Her dream had her deciding to go and wash some clothes in the water. Taking her baby with her she made her way down to the water's edge. On arrival she realized that she had left the soap back in the tent. Without thinking she made her way back to the camp, leaving the child throwing stones into the water. On her return she found her baby floating face down in the waters of the creek. When she pulled him to the shore she found that he was dead. The dream was commented on at the time but was then forgotten. The following summer she went camping with friends. She decided to do some washing so took her baby down to the nearby creek. She realized that she had forgotten her soap. As she began to walk back she saw the child throwing stones into the water. But then the dream crashed through into her consciousness. Suddenly she could recall the dream in vivid clarity, even to the clothes that her son was wearing. With a shudder she picked up the child and took him back to the tent with her.

My last book brought about an avalanche of emails from people around the world who related strongly to the theory of 'Cheating the Ferryman'. One unsolicited response was particularly fascinating. It was sent to me by a gentleman called Allan Rumney who lives in South Africa. In 1979 Allan was serving in the Rhodesian army and was involved in 'Operation Hurricane' in Rushinga, east of Mount Darwin. It was a Saturday morning and Allan was involved in a routine vehicle convoy into Mount Darwin for supplies.

Things went smoothly on the outbound part of our journey, I was stationed on top of an armoured personnel carrier, manning a twin-Browning machinegun, mounted behind a movable V-shield, in case of an ambush. It was patently obvious that a lot had happened that night, there were burnt-out vehicles and gutted shops on the side of the road. After collecting supplies, we started the journey back, and that is when something very weird happened. The stretch of road between Mount Darwin and Rushinga was notoriously known as 'ambush alley', but I had somehow been most fortunate not to have seen such action, it always seemed to have happened to somebody else. However, on that day, I had a very prickly and ominous feeling about our trip back, as I stood behind the V-shield, with the machinegun pointed directly ahead. We rounded a bend, and then it happened. A 'voice', which seemed to come from inside my head said to the effect, and very clearly, 'This is an ambush,' which put me on high-alert, and almost immediately, I spotted the tell-tale puffs of grey smoke on the left-hand verge of the road ahead, before I heard the rifle-fire, and the vehicles ahead

started taking evasive action. Immediately, I swung the
machinegun to the left, and as I did so, I suddenly found
myself pulled quite violently and explicably forward, and
found myself hanging sideways in the V-shield webbing, and
a strange sensation in my left arm and hand. Looking
around, I first noticed my bloody hand, and the rather awful
sight of my left thumb hanging on by a thread of flesh. There
was blood oozing out of my elbow and upper arm, and then
it struck me, I had been shot several times.

Allan survived and his injured thumb was re-attached later. He remains convinced that the 'voice' saved his life. He was unaware that his location was right in the middle of a known 'killing ground' and as such was not in any state of alertness. The voice made him jump to action. If he had not done so the bullets that hit the personnel carrier and came to rest against the inside of the shield would have hit him full in the torso, probably his spine. In his email he commented with no irony about the strong possibility that he would have taken . . .

. . . three shots, from the base of my neck to the middle of
my back, death would have been a certainty. I was meant not
to die that day, and indeed, that was potentially the most
life-threatening day of my life.

Had the voice not warned him about the ambush at exactly the moment it did he would have been badly injured or even killed. The voice saved him to live the future life that he may not have had the last time round.

Sometimes the Daemon acts to save others. In 1971 a terminally depressed architect decided to kill himself. He took himself down to a London underground station and stood at the edge of the platform. He waited until he could hear the sound of an approaching train. As the draught of displaced air hit the platform the young man knew that this was the moment. To the horror of bystanders he launched himself off the platform and on to the rails below. Everybody waited in horror as the train entered the station. Inexplicably, the train screeched to a halt, its wheels only a few feet away from the young man. The onlookers couldn't understand what had happened. There was no way that the driver could have possibly seen somebody on the rail and, even if he had done so, there would simply not have been enough braking distance. Clearly, the train had started to brake while it was still in the tunnel, a good 100 yards away from the station.

Apparently, the young man's life had not been saved because the train driver had seen him and applied the brakes in time. Quite independently, a passenger, for no apparent reason, had chosen to pull the 'emergency' handle. He said later that he had just had an overwhelming urge to do so.

I have argued that under most circumstances the Daemon needs unusual mental states in order to manifest itself successfully within the consciousness of its Eidolon. This can be brought about by epilepsy, migraine, bipolar episodes or schizophrenia. However, I consider that extreme stress or tiredness also seem to open up the 'Doors of Perception'. In my opinion this is what happened to Sir Alec Guinness on the night of 2 September 1955.

Guinness had flown from London to Los Angeles on the overnight flight. Because of difficulties in getting a ticket on a major airline he had flown with Scandinavian Airways. This had involved a fuel stop in Iceland which disturbed his sleep but worse was to come. Just as the second leg of his journey began, his sleeping berth collapsed, leaving him hanging head down with his feet suspended in the air.

Not wishing to disturb the lady below him he spent hours in this precarious situation. Despite discomfort, he stayed in this position for the whole flight. Could his lack of sleep have allowed Daemonic access to his Eidolon? On his first night in Hollywood he describes his meeting with James Dean:

> I had arrived off the plane, and I had been met by Grace
> Kelly and various people, but I found that I was alone for the
> evening, and a woman I knew telephoned and asked me out
> to dinner . . . We finally went into a little Italian dive and
> that was full, so we were turned away. Then I heard feet
> running down the street, and it was James Dean. He said,
> 'I was in that restaurant when you couldn't get a table and
> my name is James Dean.' He asked us to join him and then
> going back into the restaurant he said, 'Oh, before we go in I
> must show you something – I've got a new car', and there it
> was in the courtyard of this little restaurant, some little silver
> car, very smart, all done up in cellophane and a bunch of
> roses tied to its bonnet, and I said, 'How fast can you drive
> this?' and he said, 'Oh, I can only do 150 mph in it.'
> I asked if he had driven it, and he replied that he had never
> been in it at all. Some strange thing came over me, some
> almost different voice and I said, 'Look, I won't join your
> table unless you want me to, but I must say something,
> please do not get into that car because if you do (and I
> looked at my watch), it's now Thursday (whatever the date
> was) ten o'clock at night, and by 10 o'clock at night
> next Thursday you will be dead if you get into that car.'
> I don't know what it was – nonsense, so we had dinner.
> We had a charming dinner, and he was dead the following
> Thursday afternoon in that car.[11]

Dean brushed this warning off with a smile and the three of them walked back into the bistro. As predicted by Guinness's Daemon, on the afternoon of the following Thursday the dead body of James Dean was found in the smashed remains of the car he had so proudly taken possession of less than seven days before. Alec claimed never to have experienced anything like this before and he had no idea how it had happened. My feeling is it was to do with his state of mind in that his tiredness opened up the channels of Daemonic communication.

With the exception of the failed James Dean warning, in all the cases cited above a daemonic intervention brought about a massive change in the Bohmian IMAX life review of each of the people involved. I argue that had not the Daemon acted then deaths would have taken place – deaths that did take place in a previous life. Sometimes the Daemon does not act to save a life but to ensure that a new life-course is taken in a different Everett Multiverse.

One of the best examples of this concerns a lady by the name of Joyce Donoghue. In early 1961 she was prescribed a sedative for her rather hyperactive three-year-old son. Up until the late 1950s barbiturates were widely prescribed for adults, but it was all too easy to give a child a fatal overdose. In April 1958 the company Distillers launched a new sedative called Distaval in the UK. This was said to be much safer and Distillers actively marketed the new wonder drug with the advertising strapline, 'This child's life may depend on Distaval'.

By 1961 Distaval was the best-selling sleeping pill in the UK. As well as being safe for children it was advertised as being completely safe even for pregnant and nursing mothers. Clearly, both Mrs Donoghue and her doctor had nothing to worry about. She took the drugs home and started to give her son the pills. Unfortunately, they did not seem to work for him so Joyce left them in a cupboard in her bathroom.

A short time later she discovered she was pregnant. As with most early pregnancies Joyce found that she was not sleeping well. One particularly sleepless night saw her seek out the Distaval. She knew that it was safe for her son and was aware of how Distillers had said that it was even safe for pregnant mothers. What happened next is inexplicable unless it is viewed in the light of my 'Cheating

'One day I dreamt in a most vivid manner that I saw an exact picture of a certain small bridge. All the surroundings were complete, and left no doubt as to which bridge it was. A voice at the same moment said to me, "Go and look at that bridge." This was said distinctly three times. In the morning the dream still persisted in my mind, and so impressed me that I rode off at once about six miles to the bridge. Nothing was to be seen out of the ordinary. The small stream was, however, coming down a flood. On walking to the water, I found to my astonishment that the foundations of the bridge had been entirely undermined and washed away. It was a marvel that it was still standing. Of course, the work necessary for preserving the bridge was done. I have no doubt that a special warning was given to me by a higher intelligence.'

FRIEND OF HORACE HUTCHINSON (GOLF WRITER)

The Ferryman' theory. As she filled the glass of water and was about to swallow the pills, she heard a voice – from within – say this, quite clearly: 'They were not prescribed for you so don't take them.'

The voice had such authority that the young woman threw the tablets away and made herself a hot drink instead.

Here we have a classic Daemon communication. However, what is particularly interesting about this case is that Joyce's Daemon had prior knowledge of information that would not be known for over three months. Distaval was the trade name that Distillers used for the drug that was usually called thalidomide.

In 1960 an extremely rare type of birth defect started appearing across Germany. Babies were being born with hands and feet attached directly to the body. This condition is known as 'phocomelia'. Almost every clinic in Germany had seen similar cases, but each one thought they were isolated instances. In June 1961 an Australian doctor called William McBride delivered three babies who had this defect. He was naturally curious and found that the only common factor was that all three mothers had taken Distaval. In November 1961 McBride delivered another two babies with phocomelia. That was enough for him. He met with Distillers to voice his concern and wrote a letter to *The Lancet*.

On 2 December 1961 *The Lancet* and the *British Medical Journal* both published a letter from Distillers stating that thalidomide had been withdrawn from the UK. In a subsequent article McBride disclosed the fact that the danger to the foetus was in a very short window – between the 20th and the 36th day after conception.

How did the Daemon know these things? In early 1961 nobody had made the link between thalidomide and phocomelia. Indeed this would be not be known to the general public until December of that year – months after Joyce's daemonic interruption. Clearly, Joyce could not have subliminally read about this anywhere so only one conclusion is possible: the voice knew the future. But there is more. How did the Daemon know about the short window in which the drug would be dangerous? It clearly did and in desperation it decided that no other form of communication was possible. It had to stop Joyce taking the tablets when she had them in her hand.

The 'Cheating The Ferryman' theory proposes that the Daemon remembers everything that took place in the previous life of its Eidolon. This is because it lived that life as a unitary being. However, these memories might be similar to our everyday recall. It takes a set of circumstances to stimulate the recollection process. Is this what happened back in 1961? Did Joyce's Daemon suddenly recognize the circumstances – her standing with a glass of water in one hand and the tablets in the other – and realize that it had to do something drastic?

There is an interesting final bit of information regarding this story that I have withheld until the end. Joyce subsequently had a perfect baby boy. This child had one particularly powerful talent.

He grew up to be an artist. Could it be that the last time round Joyce did take the drug and in doing so probably destroyed his chances of becoming a painter? Could it be that within the Bohmian IMAX rerun, the Daemon was keen to have things work out right?

The interesting thing about all the cases I have cited so far in this chapter is that the events were experienced by individuals that showed no obvious signs of migraine, epilepsy or schizophrenia. As such the Daemon had to communicate quickly and effectively without the aid of my 'Scale of Transcendence'. If my theory is correct, there should be evidence that those higher on the scale should have more immediate assistance with regard to eidolonic survival. I would like to finish the chapter with an astonishing example of how this process can work for an epileptic.

My quotation comes from the journal of Dr Alfred Thomas Meyers, or 'Quaerens' as he was known. It will be recalled (see Chapter 7) that this patient was diagnosed with temporal lobe epilepsy after a post-mortem examination of his brain by the great surgeon, and nascent neurologist, John Hughlings Jackson.

Fortunately, many of the journal entries written by 'Quaerens' are now available to the general reader and they add even more weight to my theory. Indeed, virtually all the elements of the Daemon-Eidolon Dyad can be found. However, it was one particular entry that caught my eye. In this 'Quaerens' describes how during his aura state he was able to do the seemingly impossible.

> I well recollect running across a Swiss glacier, and jumping
> across many small crevasses when the initial stage of 'aura'
> came on, and a reflection shot through my mind, that if ever
> I was likely to pay dearly for the imprudence of going on, it
> would be then. But I had insufficient control to stop myself
> and felt no fear, but only a slight interest in what would
> happen. I went through the familiar sensations of petit mal

CHAPTER 9 The Protector

*with such attention as I had to give concentrated on them,
and not on the ice, and after a few minutes regained my
normal condition without any injury. I looked back with
surprise at the long slope of broken ice I had run over
unhurt, picking my way I know not how, over ground that
would normally have been difficult to me.*[12]

Here we have a very active Daemon who protects its Eidolon
whilst the lower self was preoccupied with experiencing a *petit
mal* seizure. A moment's reflection will show just how strange
this whole event is. 'Quaerens' is running across a glacier when
the seizure hits him. Even a person with all their faculties fully
functioning would struggle to avoid being injured under such
circumstances. However, 'Quaerens' is also having a *petit mal*
seizure that involves temporary loss of consciousness. How on
earth did he not fall over? For me the answer is clear. During such
a TLE event the Daemon literally takes over the motor cortex of
the brain and with its super-perceptions can easily negotiate such
a minor hazard as crevasses and ice. Under normal circumstances
'Quaerens' could have been seriously injured or even killed at this
time, but the Daemon was, as always, at hand.

At the end of the chapter on precognition (Chapter 6) I discussed
the incident with the coffee cup reported by my reader Tom Jones.
You will recall that his Daemon stopped his cup of coffee being
ruined by a glob of oil that had fallen from a ceiling pipe. Clearly,
this is a Daemonic encounter of a very minor nature. However,
Tom's Daemon was to prove considerably more effective a few
weeks later when, in the same steel mill, Tom was involved in a
customer acceptance exercise with members of his senior manage-
ment in attendance. It was crucial for all concerned that things
went well. Tom explained to me what happened next.

*We were all in the operator pulpit when the computer screens
went blank! We had had this happening on and off for a*

while and didn't know what the problem was. Our only recourse had been to reboot the offending PC, resulting in the loss of the tell in the Mill.

The GE manager turned to me and said, 'Tom, go and fix it.' So off I went to the computer room, already knowing that I hadn't the faintest idea what to do! As I stood looking at the wall-mounted processor with its hundreds of I/O connections, suddenly a voice in my head very clearly declared, 'It's that yellow wire there.'

I touched the yellow wire and it fell out of the terminal strip where it should have been securely screwed in! I stripped the wire and re-connected it and the system started working again!!!!!!!!!! On returning to the pulpit my manager was jubilant and asked me excitedly, 'How did you fix it?' 'Oh,' I replied casually, 'a little voice told me what to do.'

Yet again we have clear evidence that the Daemon can, if the channels are opened, communicate directly with its lower self. I would now like to turn to the life story of one man, a man who encapsulates every single element of my Daemon-Eidolon Dyad and my 'Cheating the Ferryman' thesis. That one man may yet become one of the most influential writers of the 20th century. His name was Philip Kindred Dick.

Summary

With the exception of the final chapter on Philip K. Dick the case for the Daemon has now been completed. Evidence has been presented from across the worlds of science, theology and personal experience. I would like to believe that the case speaks for itself. However, like my first book and its 'Cheating the Ferryman' thesis, the 'Daemon-Eidolon Dyad' is only a theory. In the final analysis you, dear reader, are the person who will make the final judgment as to whether I have made my case or not. Ultimately, your Daemon may or may not assist you in this decision. My only assumption is that if it has made you read this far then it is keen for you to understand why it is with you and what plans it has for you.

[1] Azuonye, I.O., 'A Difficult Case: Diagnosis Made By Hallucinatory Voices', *British Medical Journal*, vol. 315, pp.685-6 (1997)

[2] Fishman, Jack, *My Darling Clementine: The Story of Lady Churchill*, D. McKay, New York, pp.124-5 (1963)

[3] Churchill, W., *My Early Life*, p.294 (1944)

[4] Inglis, Brian, *The Unknown Guest*, Coronet Books, p.111 (1989)

[5] Cox, W.A., 'Precognition: An Analysis II', *Journal of the American Society for Psychical Research*, 50: pp.99-109 (1956)

[6] Hannah, J.W., *The Futility God*, privately printed (1975)

[7] Hardy, A., Harvie, R., Koestler, A., *The Challenge of Chance*, Random House, New York, pp.173-4 (1974)

[8] Jovanovic, Pierre, *An Inquiry into the Existence of Guardian Angels*, pierre@jovaovic.com

[9] http://globalpsychics.com/amusing-you/ghost-stories/angel-miracle.shtml

[10] Rhine, Louisa E., *The Invisible Picture*, McFarland, New York (1981)

[11] O'Connor, Gary, *Alec Guinness. The Unknown. A Life*, Sidgwick & Jackson, London, pp.244-5, (2002)

[12] Hughlings Jackson, J., 'Case of epilepsy with tasting movements and "dreamy state"' from *The Selected Writings of John Hughlings Jackson*, vol. 1, ed. J. Taylor, Basic Books, New York, pp.458-63 (1958)

CHAPTER 10

Summary:
One Man's Experience

God Appears & God is Light
To those poor Souls who dwell in Night,
But does a Human Form Display
To those who dwell in Realms of day.

William Blake, 'Auguries of Innocence'

The all-seeing I?

In this final chapter I would like to summarize the evidence
I have presented in this book by discussing the life of one man
– Philip K. Dick. This is because every single element of my
Daemon-Eidolon Dyad and my 'Cheating the Ferryman' thesis is
encapsulated in his experiences.

Philip K. Dick is probably the best example of a person that
has experienced many, if not all, of the elements of my 'Ferryman'
thesis. As we have already seen, central to this new theory of
human consciousness is the premise that all sentient beings consist
of not one, but two, centres of conscious awareness. The lower,
everyday self – the 'I' as we call it – lives its life in a linear fashion
and perceives via stimuli presented by the senses. It exists within
a self-created illusion that it assumes to be solid evidence of an
objective 'reality' that exists 'out there'. The vast majority of beings
processing these black marks on a white background exist in this
state of blissful ignorance.

This inwardly generated illusion I term 'The Bohmian IMAX' in
recognition of Daniel Dennett's Cartesian Theatre (see Chapter 2)
while at the same time acknowledging the holographic nature of the
illusion as suggested by the physicist David Bohm (see Chapter 2).

I argue that most of us exist within this Bohmian IMAX – a complex and ever-changing hologram generated by the brain. Indeed, if the ideas of Karl Pribram are to be accepted then the brain itself, and the memories and thoughts it processes, are themselves holograms (see Chapter 2). Most of us do not realize that this is the case. Occasional errors of processing such as *déjà vu* experiences are glibly ignored as being just weird psychological anomalies.

But there is another part of us, the part of us that knows all about the illusion and sees reality as it really is. This element of our nature perceives the buzz and swirl of the world-behind-the-world – a place known to mystics and other adepts as the Pleorama. The element of us that knows only the Bohmian IMAX I term the 'Eidolon' and this other, all-knowing element, I call the 'Daemon'. As we know, each of us has a personal Daemon and this being can, and does, communicate with some of us – but with some more than others.

Some of these more attuned individuals have a vague sense that something is not quite right. These people have migraines. Some have a much stronger exposure to the ultimate. These are temporal lobe epileptics. For another, surprisingly large, group the underlying nature of reality is presented to them on a regular basis. As they are not intellectually or emotionally prepared for such a truth they cannot cope. These unfortunates can sometimes access the perceptions of their Daemon – this is similar to receiving a High Definition TV signal on a 1950s analogue television. This onslaught of reality as it really is literally drives some of these people insane – or at least drives them to response-actions that seem insane to those onlookers who do not perceive what the super-sensitive person perceives. These people are usually diagnosed as suffering from the mysterious mental illness termed schizophrenia.

The scanner brightens
The bearded and slightly portly middle-aged man sat back feeling the late summer Californian sun play over his face. He needed

this relaxation. The pain in his shoulder still ached away quietly and the worries of the last few months continued to push their way into his consciousness. However, today felt good. He was doing what he enjoyed most, quietly listening to music. This afternoon his choice was The Beatles but with his wide-ranging tastes it could easily have been Robert Schumann or Gustav Mahler. The first few bars of 'Strawberry Fields Forever' drifted through the motes dancing in the sunlight. As the lyrics chimed away he found himself being drawn to what they were saying. He heard the words 'living is easy with eyes closed, misunderstanding all you see'. He found this curiously apposite as he lay back with his eyelids tightly shut.

Then he found himself opening them as if under lyrical instruction. The sunlight from the window, so pleasant a moment before, became harsh and stark, causing his head to ache. He closed his eyes quickly and suddenly became aware of a colour, strawberry ice cream pink. As this strange light suffused the room the Beatles began to sing again, but the lyrics had changed.

Much to his surprise his brain distinctly heard the nasal voices of Paul McCartney and John Lennon harmonize: 'Your son has an undiagnosed right inguinal hernia. The hydrocele has burst, and it has descended into the scrotal sac. He requires immediate attention, or will soon die.'

Confused and, quite naturally, surprised the man was unsure of what to do. However, this indecision was to last only a few seconds. He found himself rushing upstairs, bundling his four-year-old son into his arms and carrying him to the car. A few hours later he was to be informed by a doctor that had he not taken the little boy straight to hospital the child would have certainly died of an undiagnosed birth defect. Something inside the man had shown not only precognitive abilities but also knowledge of medicine far beyond his own. These events, although strange, were simply the culmination of a series of curious incidents that had been taking place all his life but had become weirder and more focused since March that year. They were going to lead the man to some very strange conclusions about himself, his consciousness and the nature of reality itself.

The man in question was the science-fiction writer Philip K. Dick and the year was 1974. Although they are still not that well known outside his fan-base, Dick's stories and novels have proved to be immensely popular over the last 25 years or so. Indeed, his ideas on the nature of memory, reality and what it is to be human have directly influenced many other writers and film-makers. A list of film adaptations of his writings includes *Blade Runner, Paycheck, Minority Report, A Scanner Darkly, Screamers, Total Recall* and *Impostor*. Some of these are better known than others. However, it is also the films whose writers readily acknowledge their debt to 'Dickian' philosophy that show just how influential this writer has been. These include *The Matrix* series, *The Truman Show* and *Vanilla Sky*.

Philip K. Dick's experience that afternoon in 1974 was a direct encounter with his own Daemon. For some reason this being had decided to make a precise and crucial intervention into the life of its Eidolon. But this was not the first, nor indeed the last, time that this being was to be involved in Dick's life. For Dick his Daemon – or 'Valis' as he came to call it – had been with him since his childhood. Facilitated by his self-diagnosed schizophrenia, subsequently considered temporal lobe epilepsy, and ongoing migraine attacks, Dick's Daemon found the channels of communication well and truly open – and at times would shout out its presence for all to hear.

The glade runner

Philip Kindred Dick was born on 16 December 1928. His father, Edgar, was a livestock inspector for the US Department of Agriculture and his mother, Dorothy, was a housewife. The events of his birth were to play a major part in Dick's complex psychology because he was born a twin. Unfortunately, his twin sister, Jane, was to die a few weeks later. In the following year Edgar was transferred to San Francisco. Dorothy found the atmosphere of their new hometown of Berkeley to be very much in keeping with her quietly radical ideals. Indeed, when Edgar announced in 1933 that he was to be moved again Dorothy divorced him and set up home with Philip. From then on the young Philip saw very little of his father and was brought up exclusively by his mother.

However, this lonely little boy was going to have some very strange things happen to him, things that may be clues to the nature of human consciousness and ultimately to the nature of reality itself. The curious thing is that it took a much older Philip K. Dick to realize how strange this world can be. An incident that took place in 1951 was to convince Dick that both duality and the illusory nature of time and reality were central clues to a deeper, more profound universe. The writer was to discuss this many years later in an interview with Richard Lupoff in 1987. He explained:

> Back at the time I was starting to write science fiction, I was
> asleep one night and I woke up and there was a figure
> standing at the edge of the bed, looking down at me. I
> grunted in amazement and all of a sudden my wife woke up
> and started screaming because she could see it too. She
> started screaming, but I recognized it and I started reassuring
> her, saying that it was me that was there and not to be
> afraid. Within the last two years – let's say that was in 1951
> – I've dreamed almost every night that I was back in that
> house, and I have a strong feeling that back then in 1951 or
> '52 that I saw my future self, who had somehow, in some
> way we don't understand – I wouldn't call it occult – passed
> backward during one of my dreams now of that house, going
> back there and seeing myself again. So there really are some
> strange things . . .[1]

You may recall that in my earlier chapter on *doppelgängers* (Chapter 7), I discussed the case of the young student who, in a hypnotic trance, followed the life of his younger self for many years. The psychologist involved, Milton Erickson, on describing the event, wrote that his subject:

> . . . *explained that the experience was literally a moment by moment reliving of his life with only the same awareness he had then and that the highly limited, restricted awareness of himself at 26 was that of being an invisible man watching his own growth and development from childhood on, with no more knowledge of the child's future than the child possessed at any particular age.*[2]

If this is then the case it is reasonable to conclude that two independent – but literally and metaphorically related – centres of conscious awareness coexisted in the same brain. Posit for a moment the idea that the younger version of the student could have been in some way 'aware' that he was not 'alone' in his head then would this not be diagnosed as schizophrenia? Could this be what happened to the young Philip Dick? Is it possible that he 'sensed' the presence of his own future self watching over him?

This younger version of Philip Dick was an unhappy, lonely child. He was overweight and suffered from eczema. His self-image was such that he became a loner who preferred to stay at home and lose himself in the pulp science fiction novels popular at the time. He developed an interest in classical music and would occasionally attend concerts in Berkeley. It was while attending one of these concerts that Dick was to experience a curious mental state that we have already seen in other creative temporal lobe epileptics such as Lewis Carroll – micropsia. As the music played on Dick felt as if he was shrinking away from the world around him. He described it as if he was looking at reality from the end of a submarine periscope. This is reminiscent of Carroll's famous indirect description of his micropsia as he has Alice swallow the shrinking potion contained in the enticing 'Drink me' bottle. Indeed, this curious mental state is now termed 'Alice In Wonderland Syndrome' and it is also linked to migraine.

However, it was an event that took place shortly afterwards that supports the suspicion that it was TLE, not migraine, that was central to Dick's creativity. Like many of his schoolmates, he was expected to attend the University of California in his hometown of Berkeley. But in order to do so he needed to reach the entrance grades required. However, this possibility started to fade rapidly when, during a crucial physics test, Dick couldn't remember the key principle behind the displacement of water. As eight of the ten questions were to involve this principle he was clearly in trouble. And then it happened – an entity decided, for the first time, to manifest itself in Dick's life – and Dick's life changed forever. A voice clearly and precisely explained to the surprised young man the scientific principles he so desperately needed to understand. All Dick had to do was write down the words in his head. Dick received an 'A' grade.

Now could it be that this 'voice' was, in fact, an older Dick manifesting himself into the mind of his younger self? It is interesting to extrapolate the evidence from the Erickson incident and assume for a moment that we can all, in some yet unknown way, communicate with our younger selves from our position of greater knowledge and experience. Is it possible that there is another part of our subconscious that can communicate across time?

For Dick the exam incident was the starting point of his spiritual journey. From now on this presence was to be continually active in his life. Many years later Dick was to reflect on this incident:

> This shows the hauntingly eerie paradoxical (almost
> seemingly whimsical or playful) nature of enlightenment: it
> comes to you only when you cease to pursue it. When you
> totally and finally give up . . .[3]

CHAPTER 10 Summary: One Man's Experience

Possibly stimulated by his 'voice' he became interested in psychoanalysis, particularly the works of Carl Gustav Jung. One work fascinated Dick; this was the *Seven Sermons To The Dead*, which Jung had published in 1916. It is possible that the young Dick was searching for an answer to the mystery of the 'voice' because Jung claimed that this article was not written by him, but dictated to him by a disembodied voice that claimed itself to be Basilides, a 2nd-century Gnostic. We will return later to the significance of Gnostic philosophy to Dick, but for the moment we need to focus on the implications of 'the voice'.

As well as the dictation from Basilides, Jung also describes in some detail the mystical companion he called 'Philemon'. He wrote:

> *Philemon and other figures of my fantasies brought home to me the crucial insight that there are things in the psyche which I do not produce, but which produce themselves and have their own life. Philemon represented a force which was not myself. In my fantasies I held conversations with him, and he said things which I had not consciously thought. For I observed clearly that it was he who spoke, not I . . . Psychologically, Philemon represented superior insight. He was a mysterious figure to me. At times he seemed to me quite real, as if he were a living personality. I went walking up and down the garden with him, and to me he was what the Indians call a guru.*[4]

Jung thought Philemon was a consciousness outside his own that coexisted in his mind with his day-to-day self. He considered this to be the case simply because Philemon knew things that Jung did not. It is reasonable to conclude that the young Philip K. Dick found solace in finding such an important figure who also had a verbally active companion.

Seeing echoes of his own duality in this strange work Dick became obsessed with the whole concept. Indeed, he did consider writing a tale woven round this idea – similar to the then recently published *Dr Faustus* by Thomas Mann.

Dick was to find evidence of personal duality from the writings of other intensely creative individuals. His favourite composer was Robert Schumann, who wrote his music from two separate creative sources. According to Schumann's journal these sources were regularly in philosophical and musical conflict. Schumann called them Florestan and Eusebius. Indeed, in his work for the piano, *Carnaval*, Schumann names two of the sections after these elements of his personality.

All this convinced Dick that his writing was generated not by him but by something outside his conscious control. He once commented to his then wife Anne: 'The words come out of my hands not my brain. I write with my hands.' As regards this creativity he was later to write:

> The intuitive – I might say, gestalting – method by which I operate has a tendency to cause me to 'see' the whole thing at once. Evidently, there is a certain historical validation to this method; Mozart, to name one particular craftsman, operated this way.[5]

In 1960 Dick, or whoever guided his pen, showed a curious ability to foretell the future in his writing. In his novel *The Man Whose Teeth Were All Exactly Alike*, the central character forces himself on his wife in the hope that she will become pregnant and will have to give up her job. Although he succeeds in the first part of his plan – she does become pregnant – she decides that she will have the baby aborted and against all the objections of her husband goes ahead with this act. In the autumn of that year Dick's new wife Anne also became pregnant. In a weird rerun of *Teeth* Dick found himself living a real-life equivalent to the situation in his novel. And, as predicted by his muse, Anne did, against violent opposition from Dick, go ahead with a termination.

This ability to see the future was a theme that Dick was to visit on a regular basis throughout his career. Indeed, in a few of his books he used the term 'precog' to describe individuals – possibly suffering from a form of autism – who had short-term precognitive abilities. Evidently, an element of his own psyche also had this ability. He first used the term in his 1954 short story *A World Of Talent*, but it was to reach its twin apotheosis in the novels *Minority Report* and *Ubik*.

In order to be able to predict the future the future has to be out there – already perceived. This is the literal meaning of the word precognition. If this is the case then it is reasonable to conclude that if an event is perceived in this way it must be, in some strange way, already in the memory of the perceiver. A precognition is a memory of an event that has already been experienced in the past.

Dick became fascinated with the idea of memory as some form of recording that can be placed in fast-forward. He had always insisted that after the curious micropsia incident he had been diagnosed as a schizophrenic. Although this was never confirmed many psychologists have argued that much of his writing and later behaviour implies that this may have indeed been the case. As such this mysterious 'illness' – if indeed illness is the correct description – became an area of great fascination to him. However, he believed that schizophrenia was not an illness but a particular catalyst that brings about the opening up of perceptions to the universe behind the prison of the senses. In later years Dick was to call this charade the 'Black Iron Prison'.

He had come across the philosophical concepts known as the *idios kosmos* and the *koinos kosmos* whilst researching background material for his stories. He was of the opinion that these fascinating ideas could be applied to both the ephemeral nature of reality and to schizophrenia itself. In 1975 he attempted to explain the origin of these concepts:

*I have been very much influenced by the thinking of the
European existential psychologists, who posit this: for each
person there are two worlds, the* idios kosmos, *which is a
unique private world, and the* koinos kosmos, *which
literally means shared world (just as* idios *means private).
No person can tell which part of his total worldview is* idios
kosmos *and which is* koinos kosmos, *except by the
achievement of a strong empathetic rapport with
other people.*[6]

As far as Dick was concerned we all exist in our own private *idios kosmos*. However, and this is the important point as far as Dick was concerned, unless something drastic happens to the chemical balance in our brains then we labour under the illusion that the *idios kosmos* is a true reflection of the *koinos kosmos*. If this breakdown takes place, then the person is freed from the confines of the Black Iron Prison and is exposed to the archetypal or transcendental forces of the *koinos kosmos*.

The problem with this is that our senses simply cannot cope with this 'reality behind reality'. A person exposed to such an experience may find that they are in a state of sensory overload and in this frenzy of data can lose all grip on sanity. For Dick this was what is interpreted as the schizophrenic state.

This state of overload is exactly how schizophrenics describe their illness. Physicist and mystic Raynor Johnson suggested a wonderful analogy that can be applied to schizophrenia. He said that a non-schizophrenic is like . . .

*. . . a prisoner in a round tower permitted to look out
through five slits in the wall at the landscape outside. It is
presumptuous to suppose that we can perceive the whole of
the landscape through these slits – although I think there is
good evidence that the prisoner can sometimes have a glimpse
out the top!*[7]

CHAPTER 10 Summary: One Man's Experience

Could it be that Dick was, yet again, correct in stating that schizophrenia opens up a window to the world as it really is, a window that gives a view out of The Black Iron Prison and into the *koinos kosmos*? You will recall that Aldous Huxley, the English writer and philosopher, certainly thought so. He was convinced that man was living his life as a sleepwalker, unaware of the potential knowledge that was available to him. Huxley, in his book *The Doors of Perception* quotes the Cambridge philosopher Dr C.D. Broad as follows:

> *We should do well to consider much more seriously than we have hitherto been inclined to do the type of theory which Bergson put forward in connection with memory and sense perception. The suggestion is that the function of the brain and nervous system and sense organs is in the main eliminative and not productive. . . .*
> *The function of the brain and nervous system is to protect us from being overwhelmed and confused by this mass of largely useless and irrelevant knowledge, by shutting out most of what we should otherwise perceive or remember at any moment, and leaving only that very small and special selection which is likely to be practical and useful.*[8]

Huxley was clear that this opening up of awareness is not at all pleasant. In the *Journal d'une Schizophrène*[9], the autobiographical record of a young girl called Renée discusses in great detail her passage through madness. She describes the awful world of the schizophrenic. She calls it 'le Pays d'éclairment' – the country of lit-upness. For Renée, this illumination is not wonderful as it would be to a mystic, but infernal – an intense glare without a shadow, ubiquitous and implacable. Later Huxley makes the following very interesting observation.

> *The shadow world inhabited by some schizophrenics and neurotics closely resembles the world of the dead as described*

in some of the earlier religious traditions. Like the wraiths
in Sheol and in Homer's Hades, these mentally disturbed
persons have lost touch with matter, language and
their fellow beings. [10]

I argue that this world of the extreme schizophrenic is, in fact, the 'real' world behind the Bohmian IMAX. In deference to the Gnostics I have called this holographic reality the 'Pleorama'. In effect schizophrenia is brought about by a cocktail of neurotransmitters opening up the Eidolon to the full sensory perceptions of the Daemon. The schizophrenic Eidolon literally sees through the eyes and hears through the ears of the Daemon and is presented with the swirling nature of David Bohm's Holomovement, my Pleorama.

In my opinion certain artists have, by accident, perceived this world and painted what they saw. For example it has long been suspected that Vincent Van Gogh was a schizophrenic. His more tortured paintings demonstrate an unusual perception of the world around him. His painting 'Wheatfield With Crows' certainly shows a very threatening and unreal environment and his famous 'Starry Night' painting has recently been analyzed using a computer and the implication is that he was actually seeing 'cosmic radiation'.

In 1955 Dick applied these ideas for the first time in a novel entitled *Eye In The Sky*. He was keen to show that the universe of his characters was an illusion. An accidental exposure to a proton beam breaks down the private world (*idios kosmos*) of four of the central characters and in doing so exposes them to all the archetypal forces of a shared world (*koinos kosmos*). Seven years later he explored the inner and outer natures of reality in regard to schizophrenia. *Martian Time-Slip* is a novel that explores many themes but centres on an attempt to understand the nature of schizophrenia itself. The main character, Jack Bohlen, is what Dick terms 'an ex-schizophrenic'. The book describes the theories of a Dr Milton Glaub. Glaub believes that mental illnesses, particularly schizophrenia, may be brought about by altered states of time perception.

Glaub considers that what differentiates schizophrenics from other people is that they exist outside time. The schizophrenic receives the whole picture at once. For non-schizophrenics experience, embedded in time, passes in front of consciousness like a reel of film. When the observer has schizophrenia the whole reel unravels at once. However, this can be advantageous because the schizophrenic is already aware of the future because he or she has already experienced it. There are many examples of schizophrenics who seem to exist outside time in a way similar to Dick's precogs. They do not experience everything at once, but they do seem to be able to see a few seconds or so into the future.

An example of this, one I have used earlier, was cited by Eugen Bleuler, the psychiatrist who first coined the term schizophrenia. Bleuler tells of a patient whose voices showed an ability to foretell events about to happen.

A janitor coming down the hall makes a slight noise of which the patient is not conscious. But the patient hears his hallucinated voice cry out, 'Now someone is coming down the hall with a bucket of water.' The door opens and the prophecy is fulfilled. [11]

Clearly, if this report can be believed then we have evidence from orthodox psychiatry that precognition, albeit for just a few seconds, has been observed and reported.

Later in his life Dick was to come up with a fascinating theory as to how this might happen. In his 1975 essay, 'Man, Android & Machine', he considered that there was another form of time that ran perpendicularly to 'linear time'. This form of time he called 'orthogonal'. He suggested that orthogonal time contains:

. . . as a simultaneous plane or extension everything which was, just as the grooves on an LP contain the part of the music which has already been played; they don't disappear after the stylus tracks them.[12]

In a letter to student Claudia Krenz he expanded on this idea and thought that orthogonal time was real whereas what we perceive as time is an illusion. And as everything we perceive exists within linear time, then reality as it is perceived by us is also an illusion. Interestingly enough, he went on to say that perceived time may be circular in nature. As such it is not at all surprising that he was later to consider that future events can be perceived as a memory.

Clearly, Dick's philosophy regarding the nature of reality had been brought about by the way the world presented itself to his senses. However, he needed validation that such a peculiar world-view was intellectually, or at least theologically, valid.

It was not at all surprising that Dick would eventually find his interests turning to the fascinating philosophy-cum-religion that we encountered earlier, Gnosticism. All of the events in his life could be explained by this secretive and curiously neglected branch of Christianity. Indeed, many of those whose works Dick had read in an attempt to find answers were either interested in, or actual members of, the fraternity. The philosophy of the *idios kosmos* and the *koinos kosmos* came originally from Pythagoras, but found its Western apogee in the writings of two German mystics, Meister Eckhart and Jakob Boehme. Both these men had strong Gnostic beliefs.

I think that it is important for us to go back to review exactly what the Gnostics believed in the light of Dick's experiences and writings.

Counter-clock theology

The beginnings of Gnosticism have long been a matter of controversy and are still largely a subject of research. The more these origins are studied, the further they seem to recede into the past. Whereas Gnosticism was formerly considered to be mostly a corruption of Christianity it now seems clear that the first traces of Gnostic systems can be discerned some centuries before the Christian Era. However it was during the first few centuries after the death of Christ that this most rational of all religions was to fight a long, drawn-out battle with orthodox Christianity. Initially, this confrontation was simply doctrinal but it rapidly turned into something far nastier.

So why did orthodox Christians dislike their Gnostic brothers-in-Christ so much? Well, it was to do with the age-old theological problem of the existence of evil. If the universe was created by an omnipotent, all-loving God, why did he allow evil to take place? Indeed, why did he feel the need to create evil in the first place? Gnosticism solves this problem by suggesting that the universe is under the influence of two conflicting forces: Light and Darkness.

Human beings are in turn a reflection of this duality. Our soul is a spark that comes from the Light. It is therefore part of the positive side. However, our bodies are made up of matter. Matter is part of the Darkness. As such there is this ongoing conflict within the human condition. The soul is imprisoned in this body of darkness but it retains memories of its divine origin. God, the source of the Light, sends out his angels, who have the power to lead the soul back to its real home, the abode of Light or Paradise. However, things are not that simple. Gnostics believed that the true God did not make the world. They came to this conclusion by observing one simple fact: why, if God is good, does he allow evil to exist in a world that he himself created? Indeed, how can a good God not only tolerate but also create evil as part of his universe? This is a contradiction. Christians and Jews rationalize this by saying that man causes evil.

For the Gnostics this was simply not good enough. God created man therefore he cannot avoid the ultimate responsibility. For this reason the Gnostics concluded that the God who created the world in the Old Testament believes himself to be the ultimate God. However in the opinion of the Gnostics, he is not. There is a supreme God, a creature of pure Goodness and Light. This supreme God has no human features and men can only reach him through the divine spark in themselves. It is therefore logical to conclude that the God Yahweh is not this ultimate being. Yahweh is simply too human. He has temper tantrums and fits of jealousy.

In the Old Testament (Exodus 20:5) Yahweh proclaims, 'I the Lord thy God am a jealous God.'[13] In response to this the Gnostic *Secret Book of John* calls this 'madness' and comments:

> *By announcing this he indicated to the angels that another God does exist; for if there were no other one, of whom is he jealous?*[14]

This is a God that is all too human. He also has a physical side. Moses sees him and his voice is heard many times. To the Gnostics this is simply impossible unless this God is not all he believes himself to be.

For the Gnostics there is only one God and he exists outside space and time. This being is completely incomprehensible to human intellect. However, the creator of our universe is not this God but a lesser being, termed the 'Demiurge' by the Gnostic writer Valentinus. This entity is, by all human standards, a god, but not *the* God. The term Demiurge was first used by Plato in *Timaeus* and literally means 'half-maker'. This term is quite specific because this lesser god is flawed and in creating our universe out of the 'divine essence' of the ultimate God wove that flaw into the very fabric of the reality we perceive.

As far as the Gnostics were concerned the whole of the physical world, the creation of the Demiurge, was part of the Darkness. However, the only way that the inner soul of man could reach the True Light was by avoiding the powers of evil. He could only do this by inner knowledge gained by study and the understanding of closely guarded secrets, the 'mysteries' conveyed by angels to the select few, those who had the Knowledge or *gnosis*.

This idea of a shared reality being an elaborate illusion is not just a Western Gnostic belief. Eastern philosophy has long accepted the concept of *Maya*, this being central to both Buddhism and Vedic Hinduism and it was in these areas of intellectual enquiry that Dick was to immerse himself. The realization of this illusion was hinted at in his original title for *Eye In The Sky* which was *With Opened Mind*.

Taking these ideas literally, Dick suspected that the world that we perceive with our senses is simply a fake, a creation of our own mind, possibly controlled by a sinister organization with motivations of its own. He saw parallels with the Gnostic belief that this universe is the creation of the Demiurge. We shall see later that this belief was to be woven into many of his later novels and short stories, particularly *Ubik* (1969).

However, the illusory nature of reality was only one of two main strands of Gnosticism that, after personal experience, Dick became fascinated by. This second strand suggested that all human beings consist of not one but two separate, coexisting, consciousnesses. As we have already seen with Dick, this 'other' was an essential element of his life. He eventually decided to call this being Valis, but he had many names for it, including 'AI' (Artificial Intelligence). He was to encounter this entity in many guises, both male and female. Indeed, it has been argued that the female aspect of his presence, sometimes called *Sophia* (wisdom), was a projection of his dead twin sister.

As we have already seen, the Gnostics had another word for this being – they called it the 'Daemon', a term they took on permanent loan from the earlier Greek Mystery cults. You will recall that this entity was part of the Pagan duality, but it became easily incorporated into the philosophy of Gnosticism. The Daemon is the spark, that part of you and I that is also a component of the Pleorama, the Realm of Light.

However, the Daemon is only part of the duality within each person. There is a part of the human consciousness that is rooted in the world of Darkness. This takes the form of a being known as the 'Eidolon'. The word had been originally used to describe an image or a statue of a god and over time it became associated with a copy of something divine. This copy looked like the original but lacked all the qualities. For the Pagan sages this was a perfect description for the part of the human duality that was trapped in the Realm of Darkness; this entity thus became known as the 'Eidolon'. This is the embodied self, the physical body and the personality. Put simply, this is the person. This 'lower self' is mortal and is totally unaware, unless initiated into the mysteries, of its Higher Self. It is very much a part of this world of darkness. It is a slave to emotion and all the other ills that beset the physical being. The Daemon, on the other hand, is the immortal self. This Daemon is always with the Eidolon and, where possible, tries to assist and guide. However, it is dangerous for the Eidolon to know of the existence of its other self without *gnosis*.

Despite this, there are times when the Daemon has to make itself seen or heard. The Eidolon in these circumstances will perceive the Daemon to be some form of guardian angel or spirit guide. Indeed, Plato had his own way of putting it:

> *We should think of the most authoritative part of the soul as the Guardian Spirit given by God which lifts us to our heavenly home.*[15]

The Gnostic sages carried this belief forward in its entirety. Valentinus taught that a person receives *gnosis* from their guardian angel, but that in reality that being is simply that person's own

Higher Self.[16] This implies that the angels that communicate between the World of Light and The World of Darkness are in fact not independent beings at all: they are Daemons from this world. We are our own teachers!

What may have initially attracted Dick was the Gnostic fascination with duality and the concept of the twin – specifically the teachings of the mystic Gnostic known as Mani and his vision of his mystical twin, or *al-Tawm* (Arabic for twin). As we saw earlier in the theology chapter (Chapter 4), Mani considered that this 'twin' was an older version of himself that was communicating with his younger incarnation across the years. Mani gave this being many names – '*al-Tawm*', as we have already seen, *The Divine Adam* and his personal description *syzygos*. This last term is particularly interesting. It translates from the Greek as a 'yoke' and implies a linkage or bond.

Indeed, it may come as some surprise to discover that this experience is also central to Jewish mysticism as expounded in the teachings of the Kabbalah. In these esoteric writings it is believed that one can encounter a version of oneself, a *doppelgänger*, that can recount the future events it has experienced.

Mani's first encounter with his twin is similar to the events described earlier when the younger and older Dick experienced the presence of each other. There are certain texts that claim that this 'twin' was, in fact, an older version of Mani communicating with and guiding his younger self. If this is the case, we have a startling similarity between Dick and Mani.

Later we will see that Dick's Daemon was to reappear in his life when he was an adult. This version was to prove itself far more communicative and directing in its approach to its lower self. Exactly the same thing happened to Mani when, in CE240, his *syzygos* reappeared and urged him to preach what he had learned. This later visitation involved an interaction with a much more focused and knowing version of himself. Mani explained what this 'twin' taught him:

Who I am and what my body is, and how my arrival at this
world occurred . . . Who is my father on high and what
order and commission he gave me before I put on this
material body and before I was led astray in this abominable
flesh . . . Who is my inseparable twin . . . He revealed it to
me too, the boundless heights and the unfathomable depths.[17]

In keeping with these dualist beliefs Mani taught that there was a primeval conflict between the realms of Light and Darkness, in which the material world represents the invasion of the Realm of Light by the Realm of Darkness. For Mani the purpose of religion was to release the particles of light imprisoned in matter. However, it is how Mani describes his spirit guide that reinforces the concept of the Daemon. Mani said that his heavenly twin was 'the most beautiful and largest mirror image of his own person'. [18]

This use of the term 'mirror image' is an interesting echo of a section of the apocryphal *Acts of Thomas* called 'The Hymn of the Pearl'. This tells of a prince who is sent into Egypt to recover a lost pearl. However, while in this land, he falls under the spell of Egyptian magic and forgets who he really is, where he has come from and what his destiny is to be. Fortunately his double, or true self, has stayed at home and this being can send messages to his forgetful twin in the land of the Nile. Eventually these messages are perceived by the lower self and the prince awakens from the illusion and returns to his true home. On arrival his twin meets him and they meld into one. When the young man first receives a message regarding his true self he describes his feelings:

. . . [it] seemed to me to become like a mirror of myself. I
saw it all in all, and I received all in it, for we were two in
distinction and yet again one in one likeness. And the
treasurers too, who brought it to me, I saw in like manner to
be two (and yet) one likeness . . .

Clearly this story alludes to both the illusory nature of reality (as symbolized by Egypt) and the duality of human consciousness as evidenced by my 'Daemon-Eidolon Dyad'.

It is therefore no surprise that Dick felt such a personal affinity to Mani that he had seriously considered writing an alternative history novel (similar to his *The Man In The High Tower*) that assumed that the religion of Mani – Manicheaism – had become a world religion to replace Christianity. He was to call this book *The Acts Of Paul*. This would have been a fascinating insight into Philip K. Dick's philosophy and world-view.

While searching the web for material on Dick, I came across an article that had first been published in the *Schizophrenia Bulletin*, vol.18, no. 2. This fascinating description of what it is like to be a schizophrenic is both terrifying and enlightening.

'Julie' describes how her 'inner world' was more real than the world the rest of us inhabit. In her version of *'le Pays d'éclairment'* she existed in a passage of underground caves. These were torture chambers for the gods that also lived there. She was continually assaulted by voices telling her that she could only exist in this underground hell. In a fascinating description of her world she writes in pure Gnostic terms:

> *Another constant during these years was the belief that I was*
> *of evil substance, born of an evil realm and inserted into this*
> *world as an oversight. The justifications for this belief had to*
> *do with my being the second-born of a set of twins,*
> *being gay, and being mentally ill.*[19]

Here, we have the Gnostic idea that the world is the creation of the Demiurge, and that all matter is inherently evil. This includes the human body itself. The Gnostic theme of the twin also occurs but this time in a very negative way.

However, 'Julie' manages with help to recover from these terrors and later revisits the caves to discover that they had changed.

I recently revisited the caves, and they had changed. Inside there was immense space, a veiled light, and silence. It was misty, and I sensed a presence there. So I wandered through the mist in a sort of walk of discovery, and as I wandered, the sense of the presence increased. Eventually, I came upon this presence and this place inside me, formerly inhabited by evil and torturous gods, is now inhabited by a being of great creativity and goodness and peace.[20]

Could this 'presence' be none other than the Daemon?

That Philip K. Dick did not follow up this idea is unfortunate for anyone trying to understand his psychology, but there is more than enough evidence of Dick's 'Daemon' from his biographical and semi-autobiographical writings. Indeed, in his extensive and mostly unpublished autobiographical work *Exegesis*, there are specific descriptions of what took place early in 1974. At this time a series of events took place that he was to call 2-3-74. This was the date on which Dick was to realize that the whole Gnostic idea of Daemon-Eidolon duality was far from a theological myth.

Shaking off the mind-forged manacles

It all started quite innocently. A few weeks before the incident with his son's birth defect Dick was in considerable pain after having had a wisdom tooth pulled out. His then wife, Tessa, called the dentist who prescribed painkillers. As Tessa did not want to leave her husband alone in such a state of agitation she asked if somebody could deliver the prescription to their house in Fullerton.

Half an hour later the doorbell rang and Dick dashed to the door. On opening it he saw a young woman clutching the much-needed painkillers. However, Dick recoiled in astonishment when he saw what hung around the young woman's neck – a necklace with a fish pendant. Dick recognized this as a symbol of something deep within himself. He asked her what it was and she explained that it was a sign used by the early Christians as a code to show their secret beliefs to fellow Christians. Dick was stunned. He later reported that this was the first time he ever experienced the pink light, the same light so central to the Beatles incident. He stated that a beam of this light shot out of the pendant and entered his brain. This light opened up a part of his brain that had long been asleep. He described it in this way:

> *I suddenly experienced what I later learned is called* anamnesis
> *– a Greek word meaning, literally, 'loss of forgetfulness'.*
> *I remembered who I was and where I was. In an instant, in the twinkling of an eye, it all came back to me.*[21]

He suddenly 'recalled' that not only was reality really the illusion he had so many times described in his novels, but also that he was not a single being but the lower member of a Dyad.

Up until March 1974 this other part of him had manifested itself on rare occasions such as the incident during the school exam. However after Dick's anamnesis his Daemon was to become very active in his life.

Dick was naturally amazed at what took place in early 1974. He was later to describe the events in the following graphic terms:

> *March 16, 1974: It appeared – in vivid fire, with shining colors and balanced patterns – and released me from every thrall, inner and outer.*
> *March 18, 1974: It, from inside me, looked out and saw the world did not compute, that I – and it – had been lied to.*
> *It denied the reality, and power, and authenticity, of the world, saying, 'This cannot exist, this cannot exist.'*

March 20, 1974: It seized me entirely, lifting me from the limitations of the space-time matrix: it mastered me as, at the same instant, I knew that the world around me was cardboard, a fake. Through its power I saw suddenly the universe as it was; through its power of perception I saw what really existed, and through its power of no-thought decision. I acted to free myself. It took on in battle, as a champion of all human spirits in thrall, every evil, every Iron Imprisoned Thing.[22]

However, his Daemon also showed some very prosaic traits. It decided that Dick had become far too slovenly in his personal appearance. He was made to go out and buy a pair of nasal hair-clippers and it suggested that he trimmed his beard. The Daemon even had him go shopping for new, more fashionable clothes. It was as if this sartorial Daemon had been too long trapped in the body of a particularly slovenly Eidolon and now was its chance to put things right.

But it was also concerned about the health of the shared body. It had Dick go through his drugs cabinet and forced him to throw out those medications that were proving inimical to his health. It discovered that wine was too acidic for Dick's sensitive stomach and suggested that he change to drinking beer. This being had many skills that its Eidolon sadly lacked, such as business acumen. It realized that Dick had made quite a mess of his tax matters and within weeks the Daemon had sorted this out. It also had Dick sack his agent after it had read over the royalty statements and discovered massive irregularities. Of course all these were minor interventions compared to its apogee, the saving of Dick's son's life.

The effect of this intervention was to convince Dick that he was not one but two separate beings. The writer began to argue that his Daemon was not only considerably more knowledgeable than he was but also that this being was immortal.

He called the immortal element of our being the 'Plasmate'. This is yet another of the many names he was to give the entity that we know as the 'Daemon'. This essence was, for Dick, a form of energy, of living information. The Plasmate can cross-bond with a consciousness to become what Dick termed a 'Homoplasmate'. For me this is a perfect description of my 'Daemon-Eidolon Dyad'. He went on to describe the whole human condition as follows:

One mind there is; but under two principles contend.[23]

and

Two realms there are, upper and lower. The upper, derived from hyperverse I or Yang, Form I of Parmenides, is sentient and volitional. The lower real, or Yin, Form II of Parmenides, is mechanical, driven by blind, efficient cause, deterministic and without intelligence, since it emanates from a dead source. In ancient times it was termed 'astral determinism'. We are trapped, by and large, in the lower realm, but are through the sacraments, by means of the plasmate, extricated. Until astral determinism is broken, we are not even aware of it, so occluded are we.[24]

And from the moment that the pink light first appeared, the entities that we have come to know as the Daemon and the Eidolon seemed to cohabit on an equal footing in Dick's everyday consciousness. He said that he had experienced 'an invasion of my mind of a transcendentally rational mind, as if I had been insane all my life and had suddenly become sane'. He further explained:

. . . mental anguish was simply removed from me as if by divine fiat . . . some transcendental divine power which was not evil, but benign intervened to restore my mind and heal

my body and give me a sense of the beauty, the joy,
the sanity of the world.[25]

He went on to describe this being's skills:

This mind, whose identity was totally obscure to me, was
equipped with tremendous technical knowledge – engineering,
medical, cosmological, philosophical knowledge. It had
memories dating back over two thousand years, it spoke
Greek, Hebrew, Sanskrit. There wasn't anything it
didn't know.

His wife Tessa was, quite naturally, amazed – and a little concerned
– about her radically transformed husband. She was also
fascinated by his newfound skills of precognition and linguistics.
Dick explained to her that the fish symbol had been a form of
password that installed a new programme in his brain. This
programme opened up the neural pathways to allow him access
to a totally new part of his brain, the place inhabited by a being
he initially called AI and then later Valis. We know this being to
be the Daemon.

We also know the communication channels the Daemon uses
to communicate with its Eidolon – hunches, dreams, aural
hallucinations and synchronicities. All these were to be
experienced by Dick in the months to come.

Dick was particularly fascinated by what he termed his
'Big Dreams'. He had picked this term up from his readings of
the works of Swiss psychoanalyst Karl Gustav Jung.[26] One
particularly curious dream-precognition took place over a series
of nights in the spring of 1974. Dick dreamed that a book was
presented to him night after night. This dream book had a blue
jacket and contained over 700 pages. He sensed that the
publication date was between 1966 and 1968 and that the title

ended with the word 'Grove', with another word similar to 'Budding' also featuring in the title.

This book became a massive preoccupation and he spent many waking hours scouring bookshops for it: and one day he found it. It had a blue cover, as predicted in his dream. It had the required number of pages and it was entitled *The Shadow of the Blooming Grove*. This was clear evidence of Daemon-inspired precognition. What is very curious is that the book proved to be of no significance. It was a biography of the American President Warren G. Harding.

This ability to see the future clearly worried him. In early 1974 he began a pen-pal relationship with an Alaskan graduate student called Claudia Krenz. On 9 May 1974 he wrote a typewritten letter to Claudia stating that he felt 'scared'. He didn't elaborate on this comment but at the bottom of the letter is a handwritten note that states the following:

> p.s. *What scares me most, Claudia, is that I can often recall the future.*

This is a fascinating statement. Note that he does not say 'I predict' or 'I see' the future but that 'I recall the future' as if it were a memory of an already lived time.

Indeed, Dick was so fascinated by the Harding biography incident that he became convinced that his 'Daemon' was trying to send him a message by sending him on what seemed, at first glance, a spurious quest. He then made the link. He thought back to his 1969 book *Ubik*. In this novel there is a character called Glen Runciter. Runciter exists in a curious near-death state termed 'half-life'. In this state he communicates with his employees by leaving cryptic messages in odd places. For example, he leaves messages such as 'you are all dead and I am alive' scrawled, graffiti-like, across a bathroom wall. He swiftly came to the conclusion that the Daemon was just like Runciter. It existed in another version of time and space that was between life and death and from this position it was sending him messages. Not only that but the message within the message was that his own book, *Ubik*, contained the answers. And, if the theory I propose in my first book is right, it really does.

You will recall earlier that I discussed my theory of the 'Bohmian IMAX'. This suggests that most of us exist within an inwardly generated facsimile similar in many ways to that proposed in the *Matrix* films. What I failed to explain was why and, indeed, where 'we' are located while observing this illusion. And this is where Philip K. Dick's 'take' on reality becomes so crucial to my theory. In my first book *Is There Life After Death?: The Extraordinary Science of What Happens When We Die* I suggest a solution to the location problem. I propose that most of us exist in our own personal, and ever-decreasing, segment of subjective time that is microseconds away from our physical death. Just like Runciter we are living a literal 'half-life' that never actually reaches the point of extinction.

In *Ubik* Dick presents the concept of half-life as being a slow winding-down of consciousness until death is reached. However, this is a misunderstanding of the concept as used in relation to radioactive material. The central point of half-life is that the material never reaches the point of zero activity. For example a half-life of 15 seconds would mean that 50 per cent of its radioactivity decays in 15 seconds, 50 per cent of that remaining 50 per cent (25 per cent) decays in the next 15 seconds and 50 per cent of what is left decays again in the succeeding 15 seconds. So in 45 seconds the amount of radioactive material has decreased by 87.5 per cent. However, as in Zeno's Paradox where the hare never reaches the tortoise's position so it is that the radioactive material never gets to the point of zero. It just continues halving for all eternity.

And so it is with my theory. Unlike Dick's half-lifers who, incorrectly as it happens, cease to exist, I contend that we all exist forever in ever-decreasing 'bits' of time. During this time we live our lives over and over again because each life we live will have its own last moment that will, in turn, divide in two. It seems that something inside Philip K. Dick was trying to explain my 'Ferryman Thesis', but the writer himself misunderstood the message. He applied some of his own beliefs and in doing so slightly confused what his Daemon was trying to say.

Dick had long considered that *Ubik* had been written under some form of mental control. The ideas expounded in its pages were not his at all. It was a message from his Daemon in 1969 for his Eidolon to read in 1974 when, after its 'anamnesis', this lower self could understand the real message.

For Dick this anamnesis was brought about by the two hemispheres of his brain coming together as one. For the first time in his life he perceived the world as a unitary being. It was also at this time that Dick was to give his *Daemon* yet another name – the 'Vast Active Living and Intelligent System', otherwise known by the acronym VALIS.

Confessions of a cracked Arctor

For Dick the idea that the two hemispheres of the brain usually act independently was curiously beguiling. It explained in very simple terms what had been happening to him in early 1974. He believed that the pink light had somehow brought together the two sides of his brain to make him a united being.

He was keen to find supportive evidence in science. This he found in the work of the American neurosurgeon Roger Sperry. As we have seen, Sperry had rocked the foundations of neuroscience by discovering that when separated the hemispheres of the brain seemed, at least to some degree, independently conscious.

Motivated both by his personal experiences and the implications of Sperry's work with split-brain patients Dick wrote his 1977 novel *A Scanner Darkly*. In this he explores the themes of duality, mental illness and disassociation from reality. His central character, Bob Arctor, is a drug-user addicted to a narcotic known as Substance D. However Arctor lives a dual existence in that he is also an undercover government agent named S.A. Fred. Fred's job is to infiltrate the murky world of the drug-users in order to capture the dealers who peddle this dangerous substance.

In this Dickian dystopia the drug cartels have infiltrated the government itself. As such all agents have to keep their identities secret even from their own associates. They do this by wearing what Dick calls 'scramble suits'. These project an ever-changing image sourced from a vast database of identikit faces and bodies. In order to protect their identities agents also have to compile dossiers and reports on all those addicts that they are observing, including themselves. So, by the very nature of his job Fred is never quite sure if his 'real' personality is himself or his alter ego Bob Arctor. Indeed, this psychic disassociation is exacerbated by the fact that agents have to continually monitor their own actions after the event by watching holographic surveillance tapes of themselves.

All this leads Arctor/Fred into an existential detachment similar to that experienced by schizophrenics. This psychic anomie has been the focus of some interest recently, subsequent to the publication of a book entitled *Disembodied Spirits and Deanimated Bodies* authored by the Italian psychiatrist G. Stanghellini. This discusses the breakdown of self-consciousness in severe cases of psychosis. Stanghellini describes these as being:

> . . . *disorders of the demarcation between me and not-me ('It is not me who is seeing that object over there – I am that object'), anomalous experiences of unity in the present moment ('I feel like I am two persons at the same time') and*

*of one's continuing identity across time ('Time and especially
my own actions are fragmented'), and finally the loss of
myness of one's own experiences ('It is not me who is doing
this action or having this perception').*[27]

Note here the use of the term 'I feel like two persons'. This is
fascinating when we take into account our knowledge of Dick's
relationship with his 'Daemon'.

Here again we have links with a schizophrenic state of mind,
a psychological state that Dick diagnosed in himself on many
occasions. It is highly likely that Dick wove both schizophrenia
and the implications of Sperry's split-brain research into *Scanner*
in yet another attempt to fictionalize how he really experienced
the world. Indeed, it has been long recognized that schizophrenia
is brought about by the patient's inability to transfer information
between the two hemispheres of the brain.[28]

As we have seen for Dick this was a far more complex situation
than the two sides of his brain failing to communicate. In his
own conception he was two people. For him his 'Higher Self' was
a very real inhabitant of his fractured consciousness.

His ability to communicate with his Daemon had solidified
his belief in the Gnostic view of the universe. He was later to
explain the role of this higher being within Gnostic theology:

*Each of us has a divine counterpart unfallen who can reach a
hand down to us to awaken us. This other personality is the
authentic waking self; the one we have now is asleep and
minor. We are in fact asleep, and in the hands of a
dangerous magician disguised as a good god, the deranged
creator deity. The bleakness, the evil and pain in this world,
the fact that it is a deterministic prison controlled by the
demented creator causes us willingly to split with the reality
principle early in life, and so to speak willingly fall asleep
in delusion.*[29]

This ability to 'fall asleep in delusion' has, according to Dick, been manipulated by the Gnostic Demiurge, the false creator, in such a way that we never perceive the real universe, the universe of the real god. He was convinced that the universe presented to us by our senses is a fake, an inferior copy of reality and one that is unique to each of us.

As we have seen there are strong elements of my theory in the three films in the *Matrix* trilogy. It is therefore not at all surprising to discover that Dick's philosophy was the basis of the underlying concept. Indeed, in an interesting reversal of the plot, for Dick the word 'matrix' is the one he uses to describe the reality that we are denied whereas in the film the 'matrix' is the illusory reality. As we have already seen Dick had a term for this false universe, he called it the 'Black Iron Prison' or BIP.

Dick considered that the process by which the BIP itself is created is by an application of holographic principles. In this way the Demiurge keeps human conscious awareness literally in the dark as regards their existence in the BIP. Outside this holographic illusion exists the real world; termed, as we have seen, the Pleorama by Gnostics, and called the 'Palm Tree Garden' (PTG) by Dick.

In the 'Tractates Cryptica Scriptura' that closes the novel *VALIS*, Dick argues that the world we perceive as real is, in fact, 'a hypostasis of information' that we, as nodes in the true Mind, process.

> We hypostasize information into objects. Rearrangement of
> objects is change in the content of information. This is the
> language we have lost the ability to read.

It is to this semi-autobiographical work that we finally turn.

The man in the high cranium

As we have seen, Dick was to call his 'Daemon' many names, but the one that he settled on was the 'Vast Active Living and

Intelligent System' or VALIS. However, it was not until 1981 that he was to write a novel by that name. Driven by the fact that his precognitive skills were telling him that he did not have long to live – again a precognition that was to prove correct as he was to die a year later of a stroke – Dick was keen to get his theories down on paper. For years he had been writing a narrative of his philosophy that he was to call *Exegesis*. However, this was virtually unpublishable so Dick decided that he would write a fiction around the facts of his life.

For those who have read my book *Is There Life After Death?*, *VALIS* makes a simply fascinating read. Yet again we have Dick embroidering a state of consciousness that I argue is more real than reality itself into a barely disguised biography.

Right from the start Dick wants it made clear that he is two personalities. The main character is the curiously named Horselover Fat. Curious only if you don't understand basic Greek and basic German in which case the pun is fairly clear. 'Horse lover' in Greek is translated as *Philos Hippus* and Fat is English for the German word *Dick*. So there you have it. Clearly, Horselover Fat is Phil himself. However, we soon discover that the narrator of this tale is a sober science fiction writer by the name of Philip K. Dick. We are already in the land of duality twins and *doppelgängers* that Dick was so fascinated with post March 1974. However, the writer Dick expands on many of the other themes that had filled his life for seven years.

Horselover Fat is convinced that reality is an illusion. He has come to this conclusion after years of reading Gnostic texts. Narrator Phil is not convinced of this belief but agrees to join Fat on a journey to northern California to find a band called Mother Goose. While there they meet a young girl by the name of Sophia. Clearly, the name was picked by Dick to show that this girl is some form of Gnostic deity. Indeed, this proves to be the case when she brings about the fusing of Fat and Dick into a single being. This is a clear reference to Dick's belief that his personal anamnesis fused his Daemon and Eidolon in March 1974.

This fusing of his two personalities allows the narrator to perceive reality as having two versions; Fat perceives the 'matrix' whereas Phil has always existed within the confines of the 'Black Iron Prison' of the Demiurge.

Sophia brings about the joining together of the two aspects of Dick's personality because she is the embodiment of a 'VALIS'. As we have already seen this is an acronym for Vast Acting Living Intelligence System. This is a form of metaphysical DNA that can replicate itself inside the brain. Like a virus it can spread through the cortex and in doing so open up that person's consciousness to perceive the reality of the 'matrix'. Once this takes place the person becomes a 'Homoplasmate' or a unified being that perceives the matrix as true reality.

In this way the real Philip K. Dick explained to his readers what had happened to him in 1974. For Sophia/Valis read my 'Daemon'. I contend that although involved in Dick's life from a very early age the 'Daemon' could only communicate with its 'Eidolon' in a more direct way when Dick's brain structures became open to the communication. This may have been brought about by the onset of temporal lobe epilepsy in his later years. Dick contended that he was diagnosed with schizophrenia as a young man. Perhaps this was why the messages were garbled and unclear until 1974.

If my theory is right then Dick's 'Daemon', under the pseudonym VALIS, made a concerted attempt to have its famous writer 'Eidolon' set out in fictional format the philosophy of reality that I was later to describe in my book *Is There Life After Death?* Literally everything is there. Dick was to misunderstand the message and confuse some of the elements. However, a careful reading of his work in the light of mine may bring you to some startling conclusions.

But there is one really fascinating proof of Dick's 'Daemon' and its precognitive abilities. I believe that I have discovered evidence that his 'Daemon' gave Dick an image of his own final moments.

As you may recall I have discovered a thus-far-unpublished treasure trove of letters sent by Dick to a penpal in the early 1970s. As I was looking for a suitable ending to this chapter I came across one written on 25 February 1975. This letter carried the following fascinating postscript:

> *I was up to 5 a.m. on this last night. I did something I never did before; I commanded the entity to show itself to me – the entity which has been guiding me internally since March. A sort of dream-like period passed, then, of hypnogogic images of underwater cities, very nice, and then a stark single horrifying scene, inert but not still; a man lay dead, on his face, in a living room between the coffee table and the couch.*[30]

On 18 February 1982 Dick's neighbours became concerned that they had not seen him that day. They knocked on his door then forced their way into the apartment. They found Dick lying unconscious in the living room. This was a place that Dick in 1975 would not have recognized. It is likely that he would have been found in exactly the position and location described so clearly in his Daemon-evoked hypnogogic vision, almost exactly seven years earlier. Dick was not dead at this time but clearly in his dream-vision he could not have known if the man was actually dead or unconscious. He was to die a few weeks later without really regaining consciousness.

Now please note that Dick was quite precise in his command to his Daemon – he requested that it show itself. I believe that is exactly what the Daemon did. It showed a future Dick in the last few moments of his conscious awareness before the stroke severed his links with 'reality' as he perceived it. In doing so the

Daemon implied that it was Dick himself in the final moments of his life – existing in the half-life described in *Ubik* and explained in my first book.

Could this be another Daemonic clue that we do, indeed, 'Cheat The Ferryman'?

[1] Lupoff, Richard A, 'A Conversation With Philip K. Dick', *Science Fiction Eye*, vol.1, no. 2 (1984)

[2] Erickson, M.H, 'A special enquiry with Aldous Huxley into the nature and character of various states of consciousness', *Amer. J. Clin. Hypn.*, 8, 14–33

[3] Dick, Philip K., excerpt from *Exegesis*

[4] Jung, C.G., *Memories, Dreams, Reflections*, ed. A. Jaffe, trans. R. & C. Winston, Pantheon, p.183 (1963)

[5] Sutin, L., *Divine Invasions – A Life Of Philip K. Dick*, Orion, p.107 (2006)

[6] Dick, Philip K., *Electric Shepherd*, Norstrilia, Melbourne, pp.31–2 (1975)

[7] Ferguson, M., *The Brain Revolution*, Taplinger, New York, p.226 (1973)

[8] Huxley, A., *The Doors of Perception*, Flamingo, p.11 (1994)

[9] Sèchehaye, M.A., *Journal d'une Schizophrène*, Presses Universitaires de France-PUF (2003)

[10] Huxley, A., *The Doors of Perception*, Flamingo (1994)

[11] Bleuler, E., *Dementia Praecox or The Group of Schizophrenias*, IUP, New York, p.98 (1950)

[12] Dick, Philip K., 'Man, Android & Machine' in Peter Nicholls (ed.), *Science Fiction At Large*, Gollancz, p.207 (1976)

[13] Exodus 20:5

[14] Pagels, E., *The Gnostic Gospels*, Trinity, p.62 (1979)

[15] Freke, T. & Gandy, P., *Wisdom of the Pagan Philosophers*, Journey Editions, p.40 (1998)

[16] Segal, R.A., *The Gnostic Jung*, Routledge (1992)

[17] Lane-Fox, R., *Pagans And Christians*, Penguin, p.565 (1986)

[18] Ibid.

[19] http://www.alphane.com/moon/PalmTree/portrait.htm

[20] Ibid.

[21] 'How to Build a Universe that Doesn't Fall Apart Two Days Later', published as an introduction to Philip K. Dick, *I Hope I Shall Arrive Soon*, Doubleday, New York (1985)

[22] Dick, Philip K., excerpt from *Exegesis*

[23] Dick, Philip K., *VALIS*, Vintage, p.229 (1991)

[24] Ibid.

[25] Platt, Charles, *Dream Makers*, Berkley, p.155 (1980)

[26] Dick, Philip K., 'Letter to Claudia Krenz', 13 July 1974

[27] Stanghellini, G., *Disembodied Spirits and Deanimated Bodies*, OUP (2004)

[28] Dimond, S.J., 'Disconnection and psychopathology', in J. Gruzelier & P. Flor-Henry (eds), *Hemisphere Asymmetries of Function in Psychopathology*, Elsevier, Oxford (1979)

[29] Dick, Philip K., excerpt from *Exegesis*

[30] Dick, Philip K., 'Letter to Claudia Krenz', 25 February 1975

EPILOGUE
Is The Case Proven?

For in and out, above, about, below,
'Tis nothing but a Magic Shadow-show,
Play'd in a box whose candle is the sun,
Round which we Phantom figures come and go.

Rubaiyat of Omar Khayyam

The inner ET

If they were asked to name the single most influential scientist of the 20th century the average layperson would probably suggest Albert Einstein. This would be a very reasonable choice. Einstein's genius was to think in a way that most people do not. As a child he wondered what it would be like to travel at the same speed as light. This simple question was to lead him to one of the greatest advances in science – his theory of relativity. However, Einstein could not accept the implications of his discovery. He opened up a Pandora's Box of quantum physics and once the new ideas were out they presented a totally counterintuitive scenario in which the very building blocks of the universe we see around us are mere shadows. He always hoped that by underpinning the chaos of the quantum world he could find another order that fitted in with logic and common sense. However, there was one area of experience of which he was sure – that he had been guided by something other than his everyday conscious awareness. He made this quite clear when he wrote:

My career has been determined by various forces over which I have no control, primarily those mysterious glands in which nature prepares the very essence of life. Henry Ford may call it his Inner Voice, Socrates referred to it as his daemon: each man explains in his own way the fact that the human will is not free . . . everything is determined . . . by forces over which we have no control . . . for the insect as well as the star. Human beings, vegetables, or cosmic dust, we all dance to a mysterious tune, intoned in the distance by an invisible player.[1]

Many have not unreasonably interpreted this to mean that Einstein was religious in some way or other, that his 'invisible presence' was God. This may or may not be the case, but for me he is clearly saying that he felt that his fate was not his own and that there is something inside him that guides him on. Indeed, it is fascinating that he uses Socrates' Daemon as one of his examples of this inner power.

In this book I have attempted to show that the existence of the being termed the Higher Self, Subliminal Self, Hidden Observer and many other names, is a very real possibility. I have presented evidence from science, theology, literature and subjective experiences. As far as I am concerned what is particularly noticeable is the fact that this evidence is consistent. Time after time I have shown how all the evidence can be related to any of these areas but can also be interpreted using whichever tools each specialism gives us. In other words there is an underlying truth to it all.

Since its publication in June 2006 my first book, *Is There Life After Death?: The Extraordinary Science of What Happens When We Die*, has sold thousands of copies across the world. Hundreds of people have felt the need to contact me with their experiences. Without exception every single response has supported the overall theory. I really feel that there is a sense of recognition out there. This is something that we have all been subliminally aware of all our lives. Could it be that by writing and reading these books we are, at last, opening up the channels of communication with our Daemon?

During 2007 I decided to take 'Cheating The Ferryman' on tour. I did a series of talks across the UK and Europe. After a time I started to notice that 'synchrondipity' was still active in my life. You will recall from my explanation in the prologue that synchrondipity is the way in which synchronicity and serendipity seem to conspire together to give the subject exactly what they need at exactly the right time. For example, at one library talk I needed a book to balance my projector on. I asked one of the librarians to find a book of the right size. She disappeared for a few seconds and came back with a copy of *In The Light of Death* by Timothy Freke. I looked at her in amazement. I had received an email from Tim that very day. However, there was more: this was a book of his of which I was totally unaware – a book that contained some interesting material that I needed for the book you now have in your hand.

However, the synchrondipity seemed to spread itself across the audience themselves. Time after time I was informed by the attendees that they had no idea why they had turned up to see me talk. One lady explained that a 'voice in her head' had called her attention to the poster that very afternoon. Another, during a literary festival, said that she had sat down expecting another talk by another writer. Both these ladies had one thing in common – they were temporal lobe epileptics!

Time and time again, people would come to me at the end of the talk and tell me the most amazing things that had happened to them and the way in which my talk had made sense of those events. Indeed, it was a regular occurrence that the audience and I would sit swapping empirical evidence for the existence of the 'Daemon-Eidolon Dyad'.

Some people would say to me that they had turned up at my talk quite by chance and others felt that they had been guided to attend. The latter group were particularly fascinating because many were temporal lobe epileptics. A number of these people then supplied me with simply amazing personal experiences that regularly supported my theory.

However, proving the existence of the 'Daemon-Eidolon Dyad' does not prove 'Cheating the Ferryman'. This I accept. But CTF does present an explanation for all the perceived elements of the Dyad. For example, it is fine to demonstrate that our Higher Self can predict the future – and we have seen lots of evidence for this – but this fails to explain how it is done. If the future is yet to happen, how then can part of our subconscious know what is yet to happen? The only explanation for me is that this intelligence has experienced this life before. For the Daemon the future is the past, therefore. It is a memory.

As I said in the prologue I really had no idea where my research was going to lead me. I felt as if I was being guided by something other than myself. Six years later I now find myself writing the last few words of my second book and I think to myself; 'How did this all happen, and where is it going to end?'

Indeed, even now I do not know where I will go next with this. My Eidolon would like to write a series of books that would examine each element of the theory in detail. For example, I feel that a lot of empirical work can be done with regard to the 'Scale of Transcendence'. I am also of the opinion that the 'Bohmian IMAX' needs a good deal more refining. However, who knows what my Daemon wishes to do? It is my intention to follow the advice of James Redfield in his book *The Celestine Prophecy*, when he suggests that we should just watch out for the coincidences.

And as if to prove his existence and deep involvement in my writing my Daemon kept one event back until literally the last line of this book.

It was my intention to send the manuscript to my publisher today, 18 March 2007. I finished the book last night and burned the document on to a CD Rom and placed it in an envelope with the intention of taking it to the post office this morning. However, I was not really happy with this final chapter. I felt that a book of this nature should end on an interesting and intriguing note and in my opinion it was slightly flat. Unfortunately, I had no original material that would fit the bill.

This morning my Daemon seemed to be actively trying to delay my trip to the post office. It kept making my attention focus on anything rather than the task in hand. At one stage I found myself watching a DVD of the BBC television series *Atom* (well worth watching by the way, particularly the last 20 minutes of the final programme) when I really should have been out and about. At around 2:00 pm I decided I would have to make a move. I had my keys in my hand and I was walking to the front door when I had an overwhelming urge to check my emails. Why then I have no idea because I had checked them five minutes earlier. At the very moment I looked at the screen an email dropped into my inbox. It was headed 'Amazing Experience'. I couldn't resist so I opened it. This is what it said:

> *I am a 28-year-old Yoga Instructor who also holds degrees in both Psychology and Social Work. On occasion I have experiences when I feel as though I 'fall into the place of the witness' or 'Daemon' as you refer to it in your book. These moments are brief. However, I feel as though I'm watching life pass by like I'm watching a movie.*

But wait, it gets even better.

> *My mother was diagnosed with Paranoid Schizophrenia when I was about 10 years old. To this day, she is heavily medicated, unemployed and leading a life that is less than fulfilling. I assist her on a weekly basis with medications, doctor's appointments and groceries. Two weeks ago on the back of her grocery list she had written, 'Don't throw her*

out.' I dismissed this statement as being another one of her 'crazy' thoughts or stories. I thought to myself, 'What? Throw her out in the garbage?' I didn't even ask her what it was supposed to mean.

The next day I was teaching a Latin dance class at a seniors home as I do every other week. In the process of teaching one of my male students how to lead the lady he was dancing with, I tried to explain how to lead her away from his body. I said to him, 'Just throw her out.' The couple looked at me in a strange way and I laughed and replied, 'Don't throw her out! I meant to say lead her away from your body.' And then I stopped completely. It was like I ran into a wall or something. It was one of those moments when I fall into the place of the 'witness'. I couldn't believe it. It was like my mom had seen it happening the day before it happened. I had a sense of just 'knowing' that the message my mom had received or heard was exactly what was to happen in the future for me. I have read that those who are schizophrenic in other cultures can be well respected because of their intuition and messages that they receive. It makes me wonder how many other 'crazy' things she has told me since I was 10 years old actually had some sort of meaning or were precognitions?

As soon as I read it I knew why my Daemon had made me act in the way I had. It knew that this email was due to arrive, indeed knew the exact time. It had to get its recalcitrant Eidolon in front of the screen at the right moment. I suspect that in my last time round the Bohmian IMAX I sent the manuscript off without this spontaneous proof of the theory, a perfect coda that neatly tops and tails the book.

Incidents such as this convince me that we are on the edge of something very significant. I use the term 'we' because I do not own this theory any more. Already I am in contact with individuals who wish to follow up certain aspects of the theory that are personal to them. For example, one contact wishes to apply the Dyad to biorhythms. Another sees similarities between the Dyad and Neuro-Linguistic Programming (NLP).

I am keen to involve as many people as possible. I want debate on the subject. After all CTF is only a theory. I am also very keen to know about your experiences. Do they prove elements of CTF – or indeed disprove them? Please let me know.

As of October 2007 I have a Blogsite at http://cheatingthe ferryman.blogspot.com and a very active Group on the website 'Library Thing' – http://www.librarything.com/groups.php?group= cheatingtheferryman&sent=1. In addition there is my personal website (http://www.anthonypeake.com) which I regularly update with news items.

I would now like to finish by returning to the mantra taken from the *Mundaka Upanishad*. In an interesting etymological coincidence the Sanskrit term *Upanishad* literally means 'sitting down beside'. How apposite that this book dealing with human duality should end with a poem dealing with man's dual nature.

> *Like two golden birds perched on the selfsame tree:*
> *Intimate friends, the ego and the Self*
> *Dwell in the same body. The former eats*
> *The sweet and sour fruits of the tree of life*
> *While the latter looks on in detachment.*
> *As long as we think we are the ego,*
> *We feel attached and fall into sorrow.*
> *But realize that you your Self are a Lord*
> *Of life, and you will be freed from sorrow.*
> *When you realize that you are the Self,*
> *Supreme source of light, supreme source of love,*
> *You transcend the duality of life*
> *And enter into the unitive state.*

For the 'Self' read the Daemon, and for 'the ego' read 'the Eidolon'. If we follow this advice maybe we can all 'transcend the duality of life' and finally break through the Bohmian IMAX and enter the glories of the Pleorama.

Just listen to your Daemon.

[1] Kaku, Michio, *Parallel Worlds*, Penguin, pp.154–5 (2006)

Index

Peer reviews of Anthony Peake's previous book *Is There Life After Death?: The Extraordinary Science of What Happens When We Die*

'This book is a remarkable intellectual adventure that has the qualities of a thriller – at times reading it is like a ride on the big dipper. *Is There Life After Death?: The Extraordinary Science of What Happens When We Die* reminds me of one of my favourite films, *Groundhog Day*. I found Anthony Peake's theory to be as thought-provoking and as exhilarating as this great film.'
Colin Wilson, author of *The Outsider*

'In *Is There Life After Death?: The Extraordinary Science of What Happens When We Die* the author, Anthony Peake, has managed to bring together in one tome an enormous amount of cutting-edge research from many different fields. This book will certainly get you thinking and make you re-examine a lot you took for granted up till now.'
Dr Art Funkhouser, author of *The Dream Theory of Déjà Vu*

'This book is beautifully written and organized and one learns something on every page, even for an old fellow like me who is familiar with much of the neuropsychology. It is rare that I get a book I can't put down, cover to cover.'
Dr Jason W Brown, Clinical Professor of Neurology, New York University and author of *The Self-Embodying Mind*

'Peake's explanation of your immortality is the most innovative and provocative argument I have ever seen.'
Bruce Greyson, Carlson Professor of Psychiatry, University of Virginia and editor of *The Journal of Near Death Studies*

'*Is There Life after Death?* is a magnificent achievement. Peake has the gift to explain complex theories in simple words. This book is an important contribution to the debates about a new understanding of reality.'
Evelyn Elsaesser-Valarino, author of *Lessons From The Light and Talking With Angel*

Printed in the United States
By Bookmasters